The Canon Of The Old Testament: An Essay On The Gradual Growth And Formation Of The Hebrew Canon Of Scripture...

Herbert Edward Ryle

THE CANON

OF THE

OLD TESTAMENT

MACMILLAN AND CO., Limited
LONDON · BOMBAY · CALCUTTA
MELBOURNE

THE MACMILLAN COMPANY
NEW YORK · BOSTON · CHICAGO
ATLANTA · SAN FRANCISCO

THE MACMILLAN CO. OF CANÁDA, Ltd.
TORONTO

THE CANON

OF THE

OLD TESTAMENT

AN ESSAY ON
THE GRADUAL GROWTH AND FORMATION OF
THE HEBREW CANON OF SCRIPTURE

BY

HERBERT EDWARD RYLE, D.D.

BISHOP OF WINCHESTER

Second Edition

MACMILLAN AND CO., LIMITED
ST. MARTIN'S STREET, LONDON
1909

Χρη μέν τοι γε τὸν ἅπαξ παραδεξάμενον τοῦ κτίσαντος τὸν κόσμον εἶναι ταύτας τὰς ϳραφὰς πεπεῖσθαι, ὅτι ὅσα περὶ τῆς κτίσεως ἀπαντᾷ τοῖς ζητοῦσι τὸν περὶ αὐτῆς λόϳον, ταῦτα καὶ περὶ τῶν ϳραφῶν.   Origen.

First Edition, 1892; *Second*, 1895; *Reprinted*, 1899, 1904, 1909

TO THE

RIGHT REVEREND WILLIAM BOYD CARPENTER
D.D.

LORD BISHOP OF RIPON

THIS BOOK IS DEDICATED

IN GRATEFUL ACKNOWLEDGMENT OF MUCH

PERSONAL KINDNESS AND SYMPATHY

BY ONE OF HIS CHAPLAINS

Nec temere nec timide

'*Canon non uno, quod dicunt, actu ab hominibus, sed paulatim a Deo, animorum temporumque rectore, productus est*'
LOESCHER

PREFACE

MOST students of the Bible know something about the history of the Canon of the New Testament, and about the process by which its limits were gradually determined. Few, by comparison, are aware that the Canon of the Old Testament passed through a very similar course of development. In the present essay the attempt is made to sketch the history of this gradual growth. It is but a slight contribution to the study of a large and difficult subject. But, inadequate though it is, I venture to hope its appearance may be welcome to some students, who have wished to obtain a more connected view of the historical process to which we owe the formation of the Hebrew Canon of Scripture.

That the view which is here presented should differ widely in certain respects from that of traditional opinion, will be no sort of a surprise to those who have made themselves acquainted with modern Biblical research. Restricting myself to the limits which appear now to be generally recognised by the best scholars, I have sought to reap the full advantage of the additional evidence which the results of modern criticism have placed at our disposal. But it will be understood that the enquiry treats of the Sacred Collection as a whole, and that questions dealing with details of authorship, date, and structure are only touched upon so far as they help to throw light upon the admission of the individual books, or groups of books, into the Canon of Holy Scripture.

There is no need, in the present day, to 'apologize' for such use of Biblical criticism. There are, no doubt, some who would still include all Biblical critics under the same sweeping charge of repudiating Revelation and denying the Inspiration of Scripture. But they thus show so plainly either their want of acquaintance with the literature of Christian criticism or their disinclination to distinguish between the work of Christian scholars and that of avowed antagonists to religion, that the complete misapprehension under which they labour is not likely to be widely shared, and only calls for the sincere expression of a charitable regret.

The Church is demanding a courageous restatement of those facts upon which modern historical criticism has thrown new light. If, in the attempt to meet this demand, the Christian scholarship of the present generation should err through rashness, love of change, or inaccuracy of observation, the Christian scholarship of another generation will repair the error. Progress towards the truth must be made. But it will not be made without many a stumble. Still, if it is progress, it is not stagnation nor self-satisfied repose. Those who have gone before us have made their mistakes (see Excursus A), and we shall not enjoy an immunity from error. But we shall at least, I trust, endeavour to make use of the gift with which God has enriched our age, the gift of historical criticism, to the very utmost of our power, so that the Church may be found worthy of the responsibility which the possession of such a gift entails. If we are true to our belief in the presence and operation of the Holy Spirit in our midst, we need never doubt that the Church of Christ is being guided—even through frequent failure—into a fuller knowledge of the truth.

So far as the present essay is concerned, criticism, it may gratefully be acknowledged, enables us to recognise the operation of the Divine Love in the traces of that gradual growth, by which the limits of the inspired collection were expanded to meet the actual needs of the Chosen People. It is the history of no sudden creation or instantaneous acquisition, but of a slow development in the human recognition of the Divine message which was conveyed through the varied writings of the Old Covenant. The measure of the completeness of the Canon had scarcely been reached, when 'the fulness of the time came.' The close of the Hebrew Canon brings us to the threshold of the Christian Church. The history of the Canon, like the teaching of its inspired contents, leads us into the very presence of Him in Whom alone we have the fulfilment and the interpretation of the Old Testament, and the one perfect sanction of its use.

In order to record my obligations to other writers, I have drawn up a list of the books which I have most frequently used. I ought perhaps to state that Prof. Wildeboer's book came into my hands after I had already completed the main outline of the work; but I gratefully acknowledge the help which his treatise has rendered me. Prof. Buhl's important work did not appear until I had almost completed the present volume. In the case of both these works, the student will find them very valuable for purposes of reference, but scarcely so well adapted for purposes of continuous reading.

To Canon Driver's *Introduction to the Literature of the Old Testament,* the importance of which can hardly be over-estimated, I have been able to make occasional references, while correcting the sheets for the press. It is a pleasure to feel that the results of Biblical criticism, a knowledge of which I have often been obliged to presuppose, have thus been rendered accessible to English students in so admirable a form.

Prof. Kirkpatrick's *Divine Library of the Old Testament* appeared too late for me to make use of it. But I have added these useful lectures to the list of books which is placed after the 'Contents.'

To Dr. Hort, who read these pages in proof, I am most grateful for numerous suggestions and friendly criticisms, of which I have been glad to avail myself, as far as has been possible.

In conclusion, I would humbly express the hope that the present work, with all its shortcomings, may enable the reader to realize, in however slight a degree, that the growth of the Canon of the Old Testament was bound up with the life of the Jewish Church, and with the discipline of preparation for the coming of Christ.

HERBERT E. RYLE.

MEADOWCROFT,
    CAMBRIDGE.
The Festival of the Epiphany, 1892.

PREFACE TO THE SECOND EDITION

IN issuing a Second Edition of *The Canon of the Old Testament*, I desire very gratefully to acknowledge the kind reception that has been accorded to it, in spite of its many defects, by scholars and critics as well as by the public generally.

There are only two substantial changes made in the present edition. An Appendix has been added to Chap. IV, dealing with the subject of the Samaritan Version of the Pentateuch; and Excursus C has been completely rewritten on the strength of a most generous loan of valuable material from the renowned Hebrew scholar, Dr. Ginsburg, who with great kindness caused to be forwarded to me the first sheets of his learned and exhaustive *Introduction* to the Massoretico-critical edition of the Hebrew Bible.

My thanks are due to kind friends, and in particular to Mr. G. von U. Searle, for calling my attention to numerous points that needed correction, and for various useful suggestions.

I have been reproached by some of my critics for so often presenting the results of literary enquiry in the light of probability rather than of certainty. I have done so from the simple desire of telling what seems to me to be the truth. I may be convinced of a thing in my own mind; but if the evidence be insufficient for absolute proof, it is right that it should be stated to the reader, not in terms of certainty, but in those of a greater or less degree of probability.

In a little treatise, *Essai sur la Formation du Canon de l'Ancien Testament* (Paris, 1894), the learned writer, Mons. X. Kœnig, who is, I am glad to find, in general agreement with the present work, has thus expressed the position of the student of the Old Testament Canon: 'Mais ce qui nous console de l'apparente incertitude planant sur notre essai, c'est que, s'il fallait se résigner à ignorer tout ce qui n'est pas prouvé mathématiquement, nos connaisances se réduiraient à peu près à rien. Il est possible que l'histoire du canon ne se soit point passée comme nous le croyons. A tout le moins notre récit paraîtra vraisemblable. Cela suffit-il en histoire? Peut-être. Pour nous, si nous ne le savons pas, nous le croyons non seulement vraisemblable mais vrai.'

The absolute caution and reverence with which Professor Sanday has handled the whole subject of the Canons of the Old and New Testament in his Bampton Lectures on *Inspiration* (1893), deserve the thankful recognition of every one who is interested in this branch of Christian literature.

That the present work should have received in some quarters very severe condemnation for accepting the main outline of modern critical studies as the basis for historical investigation, is only what was to be expected. The interval of three years has increased my conviction that English readers wish to have the new positions stated, without any spirit of controversy, by men whose faith and hope, for this life and the life to come, rest unshaken in the Lord Jesus Christ.

Those who are still under the impression that the character of a spiritual Revelation is imperilled by the processes of literary analysis, cannot be expected to preserve a very tolerant attitude towards Critical Studies. That criticism, however, is concerned simply with literary facts, and that the spiritual force of the Old Testament cannot therefore be impaired by it, are principles by which we may securely abide. The position of the Bible in the Church of Christ is strengthened by every honest endeavour to set forth the human elements in its growth and history. The more clearly we discern the human structure, the more readily shall we recognise the presence and power of the Divine Spirit, through Whom alone it is that the Bible is the Word of God to us.

H. E. R.

Meadowcroft, Cambridge.
    Jan. 14, 1895.

CONTENTS

CHAPTER II.

THE BEGINNINGS OF THE CANON.

CHAPTER III.

THE BEGINNINGS OF THE CANON (continued).

CHAPTER IV.

THE COMPLETION OF THE FIRST CANON: THE LAW.

CHAPTER V.

The Second Canon, or the Law and the Prophets.

CHAPTER VI.

The Third Canon, or The Law, the Prophets, and the Writings.

CHAPTER VII.

The Third Canon (continued).

CHAPTER VIII.

THE THIRD CANON (*concluded*).

CHAPTER IX.

AFTER THE CONCLUSION OF THE CANON.

CHAPTER X.

LATER JEWISH TESTIMONY.

CHAPTER XI.

THE HEBREW CANON IN THE CHRISTIAN CHURCH.

CHAPTER XII.

THE ARRANGEMENT OF THE BOOKS.

EXCURSUS A.

EXCURSUS B.

EXCURSUS C.

EXCURSUS D.

EXCURSUS E.

A List of some of the more Important Books consulted in the present Work.

––◆◆––

BLOCH, J. S., *Studien zur Geschichte der Sammlung der althebräischen Literatur* (Breslau, 1876).

BUHL, FR., *Kanon u. Text des Alten Testamentes* (Leipzig, 1891): Eng. Trans. (Edinburgh, 1892).

BUXTORF, JOH., *Tiberias sive Commentarius Massorethicus Triplex* (Basle, 1665).

CHEYNE, T. K., *Job and Solomon* (London, 1887); *The Origin of the Psalter* (London, 1891).

DAVIDSON, SAM., *The Canon of the Bible* (London, 1877).

DERENBOURG, J., *Essai sur l'Histoire et la Géographie de la Palestine* (Paris, 1867).

DE WETTE-SCHRADER, *Lehrbuch der histor.-krit. Einleitung* (Berlin, 1869).

DILLMANN, AUG., *Ueber die Bildung u. Sammlung heiliger Schriften des A. T.* (*Jahrb. f. Deutsche Theol.* 1858, pp. 419-491); *Ueber die Composition des Hexateuch* (*Kurzgefasstes Exeg. Handbuch zum A. T.*, 2te Auflage, Leipzig, 1886).

DRIVER, S. R., *Critical Study of the Old Testament* (*Contemp. Review*, Feb. 1890); *An Introduction to the Literature of the Old Testament* (Edinburgh, 1st ed. 1891, 6th ed. 1897).

ETHERIDGE, J. W., *Introduction to Hebrew Literature* (London, 1856).

FÜRST, JUL., *Der Kanon des Alten Testamentes* (Leipzig, 1868).

GEIGER, ABR., *Urschrift u. Uebersetzungen der Bibel* (Breslau, 1857).

GINSBURG, CH. D., *The Massoreth Ha-Massoreth of Elias Levita* (London, 1867).

KEIL, C. F., *Lehrbuch der histor.-krit. Einleitung in das A. T.* (Frankfurt a. M. 1873).

KIRKPATRICK, A. F., *The Divine Library* (London, 1891).

KÖNIG, ED., *Einleitung in das Alte Testament* (Bonn, 1893).

KŒNIG, XAVIER, *Essai sur la Formation du Canon de l'Ancien Testament* (Paris, 1894).

LEUSDEN, JOH., *Philologus Hebraeus* (Utrecht, 1672, *edit. sec.*).

MARX, GUST. ARM., *Traditio Rabbinorum Veterrima* (Leipzig, 1884).

RIEHM, ED., *Einleitung in das Alte Testament* (Halle, 1ter Teil, 1889; 2ter, 1890).

SANDAY, W., *Inspiration* (London, 1893).

SCHÜRER, EMIL, *Geschichte des Jüdischen Volkes*, 2ter Theil (Leipzig, 1886).

SMITH, W. ROBERTSON, *The Old Testament in the Jewish Church* (Edinburgh, 1881, 2nd ed. revised and enlarged 1892).

SPEAKER'S COMMENTARY, *Apocrypha* (2 vols. London, 1888).

STRACK, HERM. L., Article, *Kanon des Alten Testaments* (Herzog-Plitt. R. E.² vol. vii. 1880) ; *Talmud* (Herzog-Plitt. R. E.² vol. xviii. 1888).

STUART, MOSES, *Critical History and Defence of the O. T. Canon* (London, 1849).

TAYLOR, C., *Sayings of the Jewish Fathers* (Cambridge, 1877).

WEBER, FERD., *Die Lehren des Talmud* (Leipzig, 1886).

WELLHAUSEN-BLEEK, *Einleitung in das Alte Testament* (Berlin, 1886).

WESTCOTT, B. F., Article, '*Canon*' in *Smith's Bible Dict.* (London, 1863) ; *The Bible in the Church* (London, 1863–1885); *On the Canon of the New Testament* (London, 1855–1881).

WILDEBOER, G., *Het Onstaan van den Kanon des Ouden Verbonds* (Groningen, 1889).

(N. B.—Z. A. T. W. = *Zeitschrift für die Alttestamentliche Wissenschaft ; Z. D. M. G. = Zeitschrift der Deutschen Morgenländischen Gesellschaft ; M. G. W. J. = Monatsschrift für Geschichte und Wissenschaft des Judenthums.*)

Scriptural Quotations are uniformly taken from the Revised Version. Isaiah i–xxxix is sometimes, for brevity's sake, referred to as Isaiah I, and xl–lxvi as Isaiah II.

The clauses of verses are sometimes distinguished by the letters 'a' and 'b,' e. g. Gen. ii. 4 b.

CHRONOLOGY.

B.C.

621. Discovery of 'the Book of the Law.'

586. Destruction of Jerusalem by the Chaldeans.

536. Return from the Exile.

444. Nehemiah, Governor of Jerusalem; Ezra reads 'the Law' to the people.

432. Nehemiah expels grandson of Eliashib.

332. Conquest of Persian Empire by Alexander the Great.

219. Simon II, High Priest.

180 (?). Jesus, the son of Sirach, wrote Ecclesiasticus.

168. Persecution of Antiochus Epiphanes.

132. Prologue to Ecclesiasticus.

105. Death of John Hyrcanus.

A.D.

70. Destruction of Jerusalem by the Romans.

90 (?). Synod of Jamnia; and, possibly, composition of 2 (4) Esdras.

100 circ. Josephus, *Contra Apionem.*

THE CANON OF THE OLD TESTAMENT.

INTRODUCTION.

RECENT Biblical discussion has familiarised English readers with many of the chief problems raised by modern phases of Old Testament Criticism. But the interest, which is naturally felt in the investigation of the structure of the Sacred Books, has tended to throw into the background that other group of problems, which concerns their admission into the Canon. To the Christian student the latter, though a less attractive, or, at least, a less promising field of investigation, must always be one of first-rate importance. For, after all, whether a book has had a simple or a complex history, whether or no the analysis of its structure reveals the existence of successive compilation, adaptation and revision, are only secondary questions, of great literary interest indeed, but yet of subordinate importance, if they do not affect the relation of Scripture to the Church. They are literary problems. They need not necessarily invite the interest of the Christian student. Whether they do so or not, will depend upon his habits of mind. A better knowledge of the structure of a book will not, as a rule, affect his view of its authority. His conviction, that a book is rightly regarded as Holy Scripture, will not be shaken, because it proves to consist of elements whose very existence had been scarcely imagined before the present century.

Other problems, however, arise before the Biblical student. He never ceases to wish to learn more accurately, nay, he is compelled, against his will, to reflect more seriously upon, the process, by which the books of Holy Scripture have obtained recognition as a sacred and authoritative Canon.

The process, by which the various books of the Old *The O. T.* Testament came to be recognised as sacred and author-
Canon: How itative, would, if we could discover it, supply us with the
formed? complete history of the formation of the Old Testament Canon. By that process, we know, books, believed to be divine, were separated from all other books. By that process, we know, writings, containing the Word of God, became recognised as the standard of life and doctrine. These are only the results which lie at our feet. We instinctively inquire for the causes which led to them. How were these writings separated from all other Hebrew literature? When did the separation take place? What was the test of Canonicity, which determined, in one case, admission into, in another, exclusion from, the sacred collection? Questions such as these, cannot fail to suggest themselves to every thoughtful Christian mind. Indeed, the literature of the Old Testament is itself so varied in character, that an inquiry into the formation of a Canon, which includes writings so different as Genesis and the Song of Songs, Esther and Isaiah, Judges and the Psalter, needs no justification. It is demanded by the spirit of the age. It is even demanded, as just and

necessary, by the requirements of reverent and devout *Introduct.*
study.

The inquiry, however, is no simple one. The subject *External*
is involved in great obscurity. At the outset, we are *wanting.* *evidence*
confronted by the fact, that no historical account of the
formation of the Canon has been preserved. Neither in
Scripture, nor in Josephus, is any narrative given of the
process of its formation. A couple of legendary allusions, to be found in the Second Book of Maccabees (ch.
ii. 13-15) and in the so-called Fourth Book of Esdras
(ch. xiv. 19-48), supply all the light which direct external
evidence throws upon the subject[1]. The path is thus left
open ; and, in consequence, the investigation is beset by
all the usual obstacles that can be thrown in the way,
untrustworthy legend, popular assumption, clever, but
baseless, speculations.

The necessity of offering some account of the origin of *Legend:*
their Sacred Scriptures occasioned the rise of certain *Christian.* *Jewish and*
legends amongst the Jews, which, as is well known,
associated, now with Ezra, now with the Men of the Great
Synagogue, the task of collecting, transcribing, revising,
and promulgating the Hebrew Canon. What may have
been the origin of these legends, and what their relation
to particular phases of Jewish history, we do not stop here
to inquire[2]. They rest on no historical support, so far
as they relate to the final formation of the Canon of the
Old Testament.

In unscientific times, plausible legend is readily accepted, in the absence of direct testimony, for trustworthy history. Having once been adopted and cir-

---

[1] N.B.—Talmudic legend (Baba bathra, 14 b) does not touch the subject of the *formation* of the Canon. See Excursus B.
[2] See Excursus A.

culated in the Jewish Church, such legends were only too naturally transferred to the soil of the Christian Church. Accordingly, we find the belief that Ezra was inspired to rewrite and reissue the Sacred Books, which had been burned by the Chaldeans at the destruction of Jerusalem, commonly accepted, and repeated by successive divines of the Christian Church until the era of the Reformation[1]. Thenceforward the authority of a learned Jew, Elias Levita, who published his Massoreth Hammasoreth in 1538, caused a more credible tale to be generally accepted, that the work of collecting and editing the Scriptures of the Old Testament was performed by the 'Men of the Great Synagogue.' Many varieties of the same story have since found favour in the Church—a circumstance which is certainly not due to the more trustworthy character of the evidence for the narrative, but, probably, merely to the greater inherent credibility of its statements[2].

Recent investigation, which has given to these legends their proper weight at particular stages of the historical inquiry, has also brought convincingly to light their wholly untrustworthy character. It is recognised that, while Ezra's work was rightly connected, in the memory of his countrymen, with the preservation of the Scriptures, only legend has transformed that connexion into the work of officially promulgating the Books of the Old Testament. Again, the very existence of 'the Great Synagogue,' save as a name for a blank space in the annals of the Jewish people, has failed to stand the scrutiny of a close historical inquiry. The further we recede into the past, the more meagre grows the evidence

[1] See Excursus A. I.   [2] See Excursus A. II.

for that tradition. Indeed, if such an institution ever existed, if it ever exerted an influence over the Jewish people and over Jewish literature, it is, to say the least, a surprising, an inexplicable fact, that it was reserved for mediaeval writers to supply the names of its members and to describe the details of their functions.

It may be doubted whether, with the mass of modern English readers, ecclesiastical legend carries much weight. Those, to whom the work of Ezra and of 'the Great Synagogue' upon the Old Testament has been known simply as a pleasing tale, are not likely to feel distressed at learning its worthlessness as history. Few, we may be sure, have ever seriously regarded their Old Testament Scriptures in the light of a collection whose limits and character had been determined by Ezra and his colleagues. By the mass of readers, if any thought has ever been expended upon the origin and formation of the Old Testament Canon, ecclesiastical tradition has probably been generally set aside in favour of a vague popular assumption.

Popular assumption is apt to follow the line of least *Popular as-* resistance. It is impatient of the slow, dull, processes *sumption.* and small results of historical research. Popular assumption accounts a general belief in the great fact of Inspiration sufficient for all practical purposes. Armed with that weapon, a man can afford, it is thought, to dispense with the necessity of forming any careful opinion upon the origin of the Canon. Popular assumption has sometimes even thought it the part of true piety to stifle inquiry with the fallacious maxim, that, where we are not told a thing, there we are not intended to know it. Popular assumption identifies the age of which a narrative treats with the age of its

INTRODUCT. composition. Popular assumption regards the most eminent personage in the narrative as the individual most likely to have been its author. Popular assumption pictures to itself the whole Canon of the Old Testament as an unbroken succession of sacred writing; as a continuous stream, fed, in each generation, by tributaries from the most holy men, from Moses and Joshua down to Ezra and Malachi; as a mighty deposit, to which each age, by the hand of its holiest representative, has contributed an additional layer, until, in the days of Ezra and Malachi, the whole orderly work was brought to a conclusion.

For the purpose of a true conception of the history of the Canon, such unsupported assumptions, it is needless to say, are alike inadequate and misleading. We need not waste time with their refutation. They are contradicted by what we know both of the history of the people and of the analysis of the individual books.

Speculation. Hardly more satisfactory, however, are the conjectures which, in the absence of more direct evidence, have been put forward by men of learning and ability with the view of explaining the origin of the Canon. Thus, it has been suggested that the Canon contains merely the relics of Hebrew literature, which, having survived, in the language of ancient Israel, the ravages of time, were regarded by the Jews as sacred and authoritative; and that, hence, the sacred authority with which they were invested was only the recognition of their literary antiquity and rarity [1]. Recent criticism, however, if only by

---

[1] Hitzig, *Ps., histor. krit. Comm.* ii. p. 118, ' alle aus Christi Vorzeit stammenden hebr. Bücher sind kanonisch ; alle kanonischen hebräisch, während zu den Apocryphen alle griechisch geschriebenen gerechnet werden.' Bertholdt, *Einleit.* i. p. 13.

establishing the comparatively late date of the composition of such books as Chronicles, Ecclesiastes and Daniel,
will have sufficiently disposed of the assumption that
the Canon is a mere residue of archaic Hebrew writings; even if evidence were not abundantly at hand
to show, that Hebrew writing was very far from being
extinct in the days when the Canon was being brought
to a conclusion. To suppose that books were constituted a sacred Canon of Scripture, because of the
accident of their having survived in the Hebrew language, is completely to invert the actual order of events.
Nothing can be more clear than this, that the Books of
the Old Testament have come down to us in the
Hebrew, because, having been, at the first, written in
that language, they were also, in that language, received
and reverenced as the Canon of Scripture in the Jewish
Church.

Similarly, we need here only mention, for the sake of
at once dismissing from view, the supposition that the
Old Testament is merely an anthology of Hebrew literature, a choice collection, as it were, of the gems of
Jewish classics, such as might have been made, in later
days, from Greek or Roman literature. Such a conception ignores the most distinctive and fundamental
feature of the Old Testament Canon. This, we feel,
is, beyond all dispute, its religious character. All the
evidence, external and internal, combines to show, that
the collection was intended to serve a religious purpose;
and, in the perception of that purpose alone, can we hope
to recognise the principles that governed its formation.

We assume, therefore, that the collection of the
sacred writings of the Old Testament cannot be accounted for on the ground, either of its containing the

relics of a past literature, or of its being intended to serve, for literary purposes, as the standard of Hebrew composition. We assume, that the writings included in the Canon of the Old Testament were brought together for a special purpose, and that that purpose was a religious one.

Of course, if we were justified, at this point, in making use of the analogy to be drawn from the *Canon of N.T.: Analogy.* Canon of the New Testament, we might forthwith assume, that the Scriptures were gradually selected from among the literature of the Jews, on the ground of their being believed to make known the Word of God in a special degree and manner; and that, as the result of their selection and by virtue of this belief in their divine origin, they acquired undisputed authority over the people. Such an analogy, it is true, would supply us at once with a key to our inquiry. We should look for the essence of Canonicity in the gradual selection from a people's religious literature, and for the principle of that selection in the popular recognition of the spiritual power and sanctity possessed by certain writings.

We must, however, be on our guard against the anachronism of freely introducing into our inquiry ideas which have been borrowed from the experience of the Christian Church. The formation of the Hebrew Canon belongs to an earlier time than that of the New Testament Canon. It belongs to a very different community. The circumstances attending its growth were as widely different as possible from those which accompanied the formation of the New Testament Canon. Accordingly, while it may be interesting to remind ourselves, from time to time, that the Canon of the New Testament was formed by gradual accretion,

and that its limits were determined rather by popular Introduct.
usage than by personal or official authority, we must not
suffer the comparison to bias the freedom of our investigation. Analogy may illustrate, it must not anticipate our argument. Even the use of such terms as Canon
and Canonicity are, so far, apt to be misleading. No
other terms can well be employed in their place. But
we must remember that they and, in some measure, the
ideas connected with them, have been derived from an
exclusively Christian usage, which dates, at the earliest,
from the fourth century A.D.[1]

What now remains with which we can prosecute our *Internal*
investigation? We have seen that Jewish and Christian *Evidence.*
legends are rejected as untrustworthy, so far as they
claim to give an account of the formation of the Canon,
and that they can only be employed, and then but with
caution, to illustrate particular points. We are confident,
that mere assumptions, whether popular and ignorant or
ingenious and speculative, cannot, in the present day,
be accepted as supplying any satisfactory substitute
for the results, however small they may seem to be, of
historical criticism. We are left face to face with the
books themselves. When the external evidence fails us,
it is to the internal evidence that we must turn. Scripture must tell its own tale. No record of the circumstances which led to the formation of the Sacred deposit
having elsewhere been preserved to us, we must pierce
down and investigate the signs of the strata themselves.
We must see, whether their history has not there been
told, and, if so, whether we cannot decipher it. The
testimony of other Jewish writings will, of course, be

---

[1] On the origin and use of the word ' Canon,' see Westcott, *On the Canon of the New Testament.* Appendix A.

Introduct. employed, where possible, for the purpose of illustrating and confirming the results that may be obtained. But, strictly speaking, the observation of details in Scripture itself will supply the needed clue to the history of the Sacred Canon more fully than any hints to be derived from other sources.

Tripartite Division of Books. At the outset, attention has usually, and perhaps rightly, been called by scholars who have written upon the subject, to the tripartite division of the books in the Hebrew Canon, expressed in the threefold name 'Law, Prophets, and Writings' (*Torah, Nebiim, Kethubim*), by which the Jews have designated their Scriptures. This tripartite division, of which the first direct evidence dates from the second century B.C.[1], is obviously no arbitrary arrangement. As we hope to show, in the course of the present work, it can only be rightly understood, when viewed in the light of that history of the Canon which we endeavour to sketch here. Its full discussion, therefore, as evidence to the formation of the Canon, must be deferred to the stage when the first mention of the three-fold division comes under our notice. Regarded, however, merely as the embodiment of a very ancient Jewish tradition, it deserves mention at this point, on account of its being opposed to the legends which have been alluded to above. For, whereas the Jewish legends, assigning to Ezra or to 'the Great Synagogue' the forma-tion of the Old Testament Canon, reflect the belief that it was the work of one man or of a single generation, the triple division of the Hebrew Scriptures embodies a far more ancient tradition, that of a gradual development in the formation of the Canon through three successive

---

[1] See Greek Prologue to Ecclesiasticus (written about 132 B.C.), quoted *in extenso*, Appendix D.

stages. If this be the correct explanation of the Tripartite
Division of the Hebrew Canon, and we believe it is so,
we shall be able to appeal to it later on as evidence,
which favours the representation of history to be made
in the following chapters.

For the sake of readers who may not before have
given close attention to this subject, we here subjoin the
contents of the Hebrew Canon of Scripture in the order
and arrangement in which they appear in Hebrew
Bibles :—

I. 'The Law,' or Torah, which is equivalent to our
Pentateuch.

II. 'The Prophets,' or Nebiim, which are divided into
two groups—

> (*a*) The Former Prophets, or Nebiim rishonim ; four
> narrative books, Joshua, Judges, Samuel,
> Kings.
>
> (*b*) The Latter Prophets, or Nebiim akharonim ; four
> prophetical books, three 'great prophets,'
> Isaiah, Jeremiah, Ezekiel, and 'the Minor
> Prophets,' the twelve being united in a single
> book.

III. 'The Writings,' or Kethubim, which are divided
into three groups—

> (*a*) The Poetical Books ; Psalms, Proverbs, Job.
>
> (*b*) The Five Rolls (Megilloth); Song of Songs,
> Ruth, Lamentations, Ecclesiastes, Esther.
>
> (*c*) The remaining books; Daniel, Ezra and Nehe-
> miah, Chronicles.

Upon some of the details of this arrangement we shall
have occasion to speak at the close of the present work[1].

---

[1] See Chap. XII, and Excursus C.

CHAPTER I.

THE PREPARATION FOR A CANON.

The human limitations of the Divine Message to Mankind.

EVERYWHERE throughout the history of the literature, as well as in the actual pages, of God's Holy Word we recognise the invisible presence and the constant operation of His Holy Spirit. Save, however, where express mention is made of some external miraculous agency, it is neither the part of true faith nor of sound reason to presuppose in the case of Holy Scripture the occurrence of any interference with the laws that regulate the composition and operate in the transmission of human literature. In this respect, we may say, it is the same with the Books of Scripture as with the Prophets and Apostles, who were inspired revealers of the Divine Will. We acknowledge in both the overruling guidance of the Spirit. But the sacred Canon was subject to the external conditions of the composition and preservation of human literature, as were the messengers to the laws of human existence. The men, thus highly privileged to be sent on their sacred mission, had been moulded and influenced by education and surroundings, by the very limitations of their place and time; nor should we think of attributing to them the possession of any supernatural powers of which no mention has been recorded in Scripture. Similarly, in the case of the Sacred Writings, we are not justified in assuming that the external circumstances of their origin, composition, and transmission were subject to any supernatural privilege or exemption. In their colouring and tone, they will reflect the literary characteristics which distinguished the day of their composition. In their structure and formation, they will reproduce the common standard of artistic skill, they will be the product of the usual methods pursued by authors in that age and country. The Divine Spirit penetrates their message with life; it quickens their teaching with power; but it does not supersede, nor become a substitute for, the exercise of the powers of the human intellect, the reason, the imagination, the discernment, the industry, which have, we believe contributed with unimpaired freedom to the formation of the Sacred Books.

So much it was needful to say by way of preface. For, wherever, as in the case of Holy Scripture, we are possessed with a strong belief in the active operation of Divine Inspiration, there we are subject to a proportionately strong temptation to anticipate every difficulty by the supposition, that a special miracle may have been permitted, even though it be in the domain of strictly human effort. 'Voluntary humility' is linked so closely to the indolent desire for interposition within the laws of our nature, that rather than acknowledge in Scripture the presence of the limitations of the human intellect, or patiently unravel the gradual unfolding of the Divine Will by the instrumentality of human weakness, it prefers to assume, that human powers were made divine, and raised above the liability to error and imperfection.

Let us therefore, in all reverence endeavour to bear in mind throughout this discussion that, in the formation

CHAP. I. and transmission of the Old Testament Canon, as in that of the New, we must expect to find the continual operation of the same natural laws, through which the Divine purpose is unceasingly being fulfilled on earth. Nor, on the other hand, let it ever be absent from our minds, that those efforts of the human intelligence, the results of which we here endeavour to trace, were ever being overruled, ' according to the commandment of the eternal God,' to furnish and to perfect those Scriptures that revealed His Will, and thus to prepare the way for the final Revelation vouchsafed in the coming of our Lord and Saviour in the flesh.

A preparation for a Canon to be presupposed. We consider first, the preparatory steps which led to the formation of a Hebrew Canon. That there were such preparatory steps, and that the Canon did not start into existence fully formed, might, indeed, appear self-evident. The very idea of a Canon of Scripture implies some preliminary stage. We can hardly think of it, save as of a collection of writings regarded as sacred and authoritative by a community professing, outwardly at least, to conform to its teaching. We therefore presuppose, in the idea of a Canon of Scripture, the existence of a community prepared to accept its authority. Further, if no Divine Revelation is recorded as specifying the writings of which it should consist, we must also assume that the writings, to which such honour was paid, were selected by that community from out of its general literature. We have, accordingly, one conception of the formation of a Canon in the selection, or adoption, by a religious community, of a certain body of writings from its existing literature. Now a community would hardly accept the sanctity, or acknowledge the authority, of writings, which it did not regard as containing, in some way, the expression of the Divine Will. Conversely, if a community did not recognise the Will of God, it would not acknowledge that those writings, which claimed to reveal His Will, possessed either sacredness or authority. In other words, the formation of a Canon of Scripture presupposes the existence of a community of believers.

Accordingly, when we reflect on it, we see how this very conception of a Canon of Scripture may point us back to a yet earlier time, when the writings of which it is composed had their place among the ordinary literature of a believing people. The literature must first arise, before the process of selection begins that leads to the formation of a Sacred Collection. Again, so far as the community is concerned, we see that a community which selects a Canon of Scripture will not only be a believer in the God Who is recognised in that literature, but must also have reached that particular stage in its religious history, when the possibility of the revelation of the Divine Will through the agency of human literature has dawned upon the consciousness of the nation. This last point is of importance. For there is nothing at all improbable in a religious community existing for a long period without the adoption of any particular writings as the embodiment of belief, or as the inspired and authoritative standard of worship and conduct: least of all would this be improbable, if there were other, and, seemingly, no less authoritative, means of declaring the commands of God and of maintaining His worship unimpaired. Circumstances, however, might arise which would alter the case, and make it advisable, either to embody in writing the sacred teachings of the past, or to recognise the authority and sanctity of certain writings already existing, which contained this teaching in any specially suitable form. For instance, the peril of national disintegration and the break up of national worship might reveal, of a sudden, that in such writings the people had a divinely ordained means of preserving the sacred heritage of the past and a standard providentially afforded them for the maintenance of true religion in the future.

A Hebrew Literature before a Hebrew Canon.

But, to turn from so purely a speculative line of thought, we find that, as a matter of fact, the Hebrew Scriptures themselves carry with them their own testimony to a previous stage of literature. For, setting aside for the moment their frequent allusions to and quotations from earlier writings, the composite character of the structure, which, in the case of many books, has been placed beyond all doubt by the careful analysis applied by modern criticism, conveys clear evidence of such a previous stage. It is only necessary to refer to the undoubted instances of composite structure presented to us in the Pentateuch, the Historical Books, Isaiah, the Psalter, and the Book of Proverbs. The fact that their present form has been reached by compilation from earlier writings would, in itself, be sufficient to demonstrate the truth of the principle, of which we need so often to be reminded, that *the beginnings of the Hebrew Canon are not to be confounded with the beginnings of Hebrew literature.*

This principle, however, by itself, important as it is, is not enough. For when we have fully recognised that periods of literary activity are presupposed by the composition of our Books, as we know them in their present literary form, it is scarcely less necessary to recognise

also *the distinction that is to be drawn between the*
process of literary construction and the process of ad-
mission into the Canon; the one, by which the Books
reached their present literary form by composition and
compilation; the other, by which they were separated
from all other writings as the sacred and authoritative
expression of the Word of God. The realization of this
distinction opens up a very interesting, but a very
intricate, field of investigation. Were any books, that
are now included in the Old Testament, originally expressly composed for the purpose of forming, or of help-
ing to complete, the Hebrew Canon? Or, was there, in
every case, an interval of time, more or less considerable,
which elapsed between composition and final acceptance
in the Canon?

We must not however anticipate. Let it be enough
here to insist, that great misapprehensions will be removed, if we are careful to distinguish between the three *Three*
stages, under which we recognise the guidance of the *stages,*
1. forma-
Holy Spirit in preparing for us the Revelation of the *tion,*
2. redaction,
Word contained in the Old Testament. These are *3. selection.*
firstly, the 'elemental' stage, or, that of the formation
of the literary antecedents of the Books of the Old Testament: secondly, the 'medial,' or that of their compilation and redaction to their present literary form: thirdly,
the 'final,' or that of their selection for the position of
honour and sanctity in the national Canon of Holy
Scripture. The distinction between these three phases
is essential.

We are not here concerned with the investigation
into the rise of the earliest Hebrew literature, but only

C

CHAP. I.

with the processes which led directly to the formation and growth of the Canon. We need not therefore waste time over a preliminary discussion of any side issues. We need not examine, as has so often been done in other works upon this subject, all the earliest instances in which the practice of writing is recorded in Holy Scripture (e. g. Ex. xvii. 14, xxiv. 4, 7, xxxiv. 27, Num. xxxiii. 2, Deut. xxxi. 9, 22, Josh. xxiv. 26, 1 Sam. x. 25, 2 Sam. xx. 24, 25 [1]). We rather proceed at once to examine the assured instances of collections of writings made before the reign of Josiah [2] for purposes of national and religious instruction. The earliest collections of this kind may be classed under (1) Songs, (2) Laws, (3) Histories, (4) Prophecies.

Songs: early national collections;

(1) Songs. The literature of Israel forms no exception to the general rule that ballads, recounting and glorifying the brave deeds of old, are to be reckoned as the earliest fruit of a nation's literary genius. Under this head we should class such poetical pieces as 'The Song of Moses and the children of Israel,' sung after the crossing of the Red Sea (Ex. xv. 1), the songs commemorative of the occupation of the Amorite territory on the east bank of the Jordan, and of the overthrow of Heshbon (Num. xxi. 14–18 and 27–30), the triumph song of Deborah (Judg. v), and the dirge of David over Saul and Jonathan (2 Sam. i. 19–27). In some of these songs we may sometimes discern the outline of a narrative differing somewhat from the prose narrative of the

[1] To this list some would add Jud. viii. 14 (R. V. *marg.*). On early Israelite writing, see an article by Neubauer on ' The Introduction of the Square Characters in Biblical MSS.' (*Studia Biblica*, vol. iii. 1891).

[2] The reign of Josiah is here referred to because, before that era, there is no certainty that any writing ever ranked as Canonical Scripture in Israel. Cf. Smith's *Dictionary of the Bible*, Art. ' Canon ' by Westcott.

historian who incorporates them.   Thus, for instance, it has been pointed out that the story of Deborah, as recorded in the song (Judg. v), differs in certain particulars from the story as narrated by the historian of Judg. iv.[1]   In those songs from which extracts are made in Num. xxi, events are related of which the Pentateuch elsewhere tells us nothing, although it is clear that the recollection of them produced a deep impression upon the minds of the children of Israel.

National collections were undoubtedly made of such patriotic songs at an early time.   The names of two such collections have been preserved, unless, indeed, as has been suggested, they are only two titles of the same collection.   These are 'The Book of the Wars of the Lord' (Num. xxi. 14), and 'The Book of Jashar, or The Upright' (Josh. x. 13, 2 Sam. i. 18).   The titles convey to us the purpose with which such collections of national poetry were formed.   Songs contained in the Book of the Wars of the Lord will have described how the Lord fought for Israel, and how truly Israel belonged to a God who had done such great things for them.   The songs contained in the Book of Jashar will have contained a series of pictures of great and upright men, judges, warriors and princes, measured by the best judgment of their time, but above all by the standard of the fear of Jehovah.

Very possibly, too, songs that were of undoubted antiquity, but of doubtful authorship, came to be grouped under certain honoured names.   Thus, for instance, it is possible that some of the oldest songs were ascribed to

---

[1] See the article by Professor Davidson in *The Expositor*, Jan. 1887, and the valuable dissertation on *The History and Song of Deborah* (Oxford, 1892), by the Rev. G. A. Cooke, M.A.

Moses, just as we know that those of a later time were commonly ascribed to David. The authorship of the song in Deut. xxxii, the contents of which clearly show that its composition dates from a period, when Canaan was already in the possession of the Israelites, and when the writer could look back upon a past generation in which Moses lived[1], was popularly attributed to Moses, or, at least, had been so attributed in the national collection of songs from which it was· transferred to its present place. So, too, the Blessing of Moses (Deut. xxxiii), which, if we may judge from verses 4, 7, 27, 28[2], belongs to a later period than that of the Lawgiver, has been taken from a similar collection; and the title, ' A Prayer of Moses,' to Ps. xc, was possibly introduced into the Psalter from a national collection of early songs in which it had traditionally been ascribed to Moses.

Although the art of writing may have been known and practised by Israelites in the days of Moses[3], the number of those who could read was at that time, and for *transmitted* centuries afterwards, very small. The songs mentioned *orally;* above, if they were at first committed to writing, which is in itself an improbable supposition, must have owed their preservation chiefly to oral tradition. Composed originally to be sung at sacred festivals, around camp fires, and at public gatherings, they were intended both to instruct the people generally upon the facts of their previous history, and, especially, to quicken their faith and to confirm them in the service of Jehovah. The attainment of this purpose could only be secured by the

---

[1] Cf. vv. 7–12.

[2] See Revised Version.

[3] Certainly the cuneiform character may have been used by them. Cf. Sayce, *Transactions Vict. Inst.* 1889. No Phoenician writing earlier than the 10th cent. B.C. has yet been found.

freest oral circulation, that is to say, by trusting to the memories of the common people. We shall therefore do well to observe that the Song of Heshbon is not quoted from a book, but is referred to as preserved in the current utterance of those 'that speak in proverbs' (Num. xxi. 27), a phrase which suggests a comparison with the recitations of Ionian bards and mediaeval minstrels. Again, we gather from 2 Sam. i. 18, that David's Dirge over Jonathan and Saul was taught to the people orally, and repeated from one to another.. The reason is clear. The oral preceded the written tradition of national song. The compiler of the Books of Samuel himself quotes from the written Book of Jashar. In his time, at any rate, the song had been incorporated in a national collection which commemorated the glories of Israelite heroes. Now we know, that, while the Book of Jashar commemorated the victory of Joshua at. Bethhoron (Josh. x. 13), it also, according to the very probable explanation of a tradition preserved in the Septuagint translation of 1 Kings viii. 53, contained an ode commemorative of the founda-tion of Solomon's temple[1]. The process of forming such a national collection of songs, covering the history of many centuries, may of course have been a gradual one. But, with the evidence at our disposal, we can hardly suppose that 'Jashar' reached the literary stage, at which it could be quoted as a well-known book by the writer of 2 Sam. i. 18, until, at the earliest, the first half of the ninth century B.C.

One word remains to be said upon the religious inten- *their religious purpose.* tion which led to the formation of such national collec-

---

[1] οὐκ ἰδοὺ αὕτη γέγραπται ἐν βιβλίῳ τῆς ᾠδῆς; it has been ingeniously conjectured that the last four Greek words indicate an erroneous reading בְּסֵפֶר הַיָּשָׁר for בְּסֵפֶר הַשִּׁיר.

tions of songs. It may be illustrated from the language of the Deuteronomist. The song which is there put into the mouth of the great Lawgiver is regarded as an instrument of instruction in the true faith of Jehovah: ' Now, therefore, write ye this song for you, and teach thou it the children of Israel ; put it in their mouths that this song may be a witness for me against the children of Israel' (ch. xxxi. 19). The teaching of the people by means of this song (ver. 22) is kept quite distinct in the narrative from the priests' duty of guarding and transmitting the law which Moses had received (ver. 9).

National songs must therefore be regarded as having been, in early times, a recognised means of giving instruction to the people. The formation of collections of such songs marks a step, though it be but a slight one, in the direction of the selection of literature which should more fully and authoritatively reflect the teaching of the Spirit of the Lord.

We have purposely refrained from mentioning the collections of Psalms made in the name of David[1]. That he was a Psalm-writer, appears from 2 Sam. i. 17–27, iii. 33, 34, xxii, xxiii. 1–7. But it does not appear whether *collections* of Davidic Psalms existed before the Exile. By Amos his name is mentioned, but as a musician rather than as a poet (Amos vi. 5).

Laws :　(2) Laws. Analysis of the Pentateuch has shown conclusively that numerous collections of Israelite laws were made at different times, before any part of our present Pentateuch had received from the people generally the recognition which was afterwards given to the Canonical writings of Holy Scripture. Such a statement in no way

---

[1] The majority of the Psalms ascribed to David are to be found in Books I (i-xli) and II (xlii-lxxii).

calls in question what we may call the Mosaic basis of the legislation. But it suggests that the form in which the laws have come down to us does not reproduce them in the shape of their first promulgation. The laws, that is to say, are not transmitted to us, stamped with the mark of their first official codification. Rather, they contain the substance of the legislation, either as it was handed down by oral tradition, or as it was transcribed for the guidance and direction of rulers, by men who were eager that the government and worship of Israel should be carried out in the spirit of the great Lawgiver, and on the lines of the revelation that had been made to him. In either case they have been modified in expression and developed in detail, in order that they might be adapted to the requirements of later times. The importance of a servile verbal reproduction was not therefore taken into account in the degree which seems essential to us who have been accustomed for centuries past to the idea of an unalterable Canon of Scripture. The continual change of circumstances in every age demands either the change of old laws or the creation of new ones. One thing, however, would have been regarded as indispensable in the framing of new, no less than in the transmission and modification of old laws, namely, the duty of preserving the legislation upon the old lines and of attaching the requirements of new circumstances to the terms and phraseology, even to the external setting of the most ancient precepts.

Of the early collections of laws the earliest is undoubtedly to be seen in the Moral Code of the Decalogue, *The Decalogue.* which was inscribed upon the two tables of stone. Two versions of the Decalogue are found (Ex. xx. 1–17 and Deut. v. 6–21), which, as is well known, differ from one

CHAP. I. another in certain details of quite inconsiderable importance. But the fact of these differences, if the argument from style were not sufficient to show it, points to the Decalogue having originally existed in a still shorter form [1]. It argues also the freedom with which the compilers, the Elohist[2] and the Deuteronomist[2], the one in the eighth or ninth, the other in the seventh century B.C., considered themselves at liberty to vary the form in which the fundamental Moral Code was transmitted. Both writers have introduced some touches of individual style and colouring into the explanatory clauses of the longer commandments, e. g. fourth and fifth. They have not thereby impaired the substantial accuracy of their record; but, by leaving impressed upon the Decalogue itself the literary stamp of the age to which they respectively belonged, they showed as conclusively as it was possible for them to show, that, in their days, the most sacred laws of Israel were not yet fenced about with any scrupulous regard for the letter apart from the spirit.

The Book of the Covenant. Another collection of laws of the greatest antiquity is preserved in the so-called 'Book of the Covenant' (Ex. xx. 20–xxiii. 33). It is a disputed point whether it has been incorporated directly into the Pentateuch from the writings of the Jehovist[2], or whether it was introduced by the hand which combined the Jehovist

---

[1] E. g. 2nd Commandment, 'Thou shalt not make to thyself any graven image.'

4th	,,	'Remember the Sabbath day to keep it holy.'
5th	,,	'Honour thy father and thy mother.'
10th	,,	'Thou shalt not covet.'

In this short form they could easily be inscribed, in two groups of five, upon two tablets.

[2] For a description of the sources from which the Pentateuch and the Book of Joshua were compiled, see Driver's *Introd. to the Literature of the O. T.*

and the Elohist writings. In either case, it has been derived from an earlier, and doubtless a much earlier, literary source. As a body of laws, it is suited to the needs of a society in a very early stage of civilization. If, as may well be allowed, the main substance of its laws has descended from the Mosaic legislation, there is no reason to doubt, that it has also at different times been adapted by subsequent revision to the requirements of the people, when they were in the enjoyment of a settled agricultural life. Several stages must have intervened between the transcription of the laws by the Jehovist and their original promulgation. Their abrupt commencement (xxi. 2), the loose order in which subjects (e.g. xxi. 28–36, xxii. 18–20, xxiii. 19) follow one another, the frequent breaks in the thread of the legislation, indicate that the collection is not to be regarded in the light of an exhaustive official code of statutes, but rather as an agglomeration of laws, perhaps transcribed from memory or extracted fragmentarily, for some private purpose, from an official source.

With the Book of the Covenant agree very closely the laws contained in Exodus (xxxiv. 10–26), which in all probability were found in the writing of the Jehovist. Some scholars have detected another group of 'ten words,' a second Decalogue, embedded in them (cf. xxxiv. 27, 28). The identification remains a matter of uncertainty. But if the hypothesis should prove to be correct, it is possible that we should recognise, in these two instances, traces of an ancient custom of assisting the recollection of laws by *collecting* them in groups of ten.

Another ancient, and very distinct, collection of laws is *The Law of Holiness.* incorporated in the section which has been called by scholars 'The Law of Holiness' (Levit. xvii–xxvi). The form in which this collection of laws has come down to us, reflects in some degree, no doubt, the later style which characterizes the compilation of the priestly laws generally. But although this be admitted, it is a fact, which no scholars have ventured to dispute, that these chapters contain extensive excerpts from a collection of laws whose general character must have closely resembled the Book of the Covenant, differing only from it in subject-matter so far as it is occupied more generally with ceremonial than with civil regulations.

The Deuteronomic Laws. The Deuteronomic Laws (Deut. v–xxvi), contain many clear instances of parallelism with the Law of Holiness. But, apart from parallelisms, they are also clearly dependent, in a very direct manner, upon other earlier collections of laws. They embody the substance of existing legislation, and they expand it with freedom of purpose, in order to adapt its requirements to the circumstances of a later century. The writer does not create new laws. He accepts the form in which they were current in his own day. He employs them in the spirit of a true prophet of Israel. He makes them the text of his exhortation. He feels the religious needs of his generation may be met by the interpretation of the spirit of the laws which the people inherited from their forefathers. Scholars have pointed out that, while there are numerous points of contact with 'The Law of Holiness,' by far the most distinctive feature of the Deuteronomic Laws is the way in which they so evidently presuppose acquaintance with the Decalogue and the Book of the Covenant, and, so far as they differ, contain but a development of their teaching.

The use, which was thus made of collections of laws for purposes of religious instruction, was not probably an isolated instance. The custom, if custom it was, marks CHAP. I. a step in advance towards the adoption of an authoritative standard of teaching.

Modern criticism has probably shown incontrovertibly *The Priestly* that the period of the final literary codification of the *Laws.* Priestly legislation, by which is denoted the great mass of the Levitical Laws exclusive of 'the Book of the Covenant,' 'the Law of Holiness,' and 'the Deuteronomic Laws,' can hardly be placed before the era of the Exile[1]. It teaches, however, no less emphatically, that *the Priestly Laws themselves have been gradually developed from previously existing collections* of regulations affecting ritual and worship. Of this result of criticism we believe a clear confirmation can be obtained from any careful comparative study of their enactments. Such a comparison, candidly drawn, has forbidden us to regard the Priestly Laws as homogeneous, or as the product of one generation. We recognise in our Pentateuch different *strata* of priestly and ceremonial laws. They have come down to us from different periods of the history. When we once grasp this idea firmly, we see that it would be as much a mistake to affirm, that the Priestly Laws were created *en bloc* in the days of the Exile or of Ezra, as to maintain that they had been promulgated, in the form in which they have come down to us, in the days of Moses.

The importance that has been attached to the subject of the Ritual Law compels us to make here a brief explanatory digression. Much misconception has arisen, *Semitic In-* because it has not been sufficiently realized, that tne *stitutions.* merely ceremonial system of the Israelite religion had

[1] See Driver, *Introduction to the Literature of the Old Testament,* pp. 128 ff.

its roots in a quite prehistoric antiquity. It is clear that, in its general features, it resembled the ceremonial systems prevalent among the religions of other Semitic races (cf. Robertson Smith's *The Prophets of Israel*, p. 56). At the call of Abraham it received the quickening impulse of a new spiritual life. But we have no reason to suppose, that the rules of worship, the distinctions of cleanness, and the regulations of sacrifice, that were observed by the patriarchs, differed substantially from those which they had received by tradition from a period when their forefathers were polytheistic (Josh. xxiv. 2). Rules of Sacrifice (Gen. xv. 10), the Rite of Circumcision (Gen. xvii, Ex. iv. 24–26), the custom of Tithe payment (Gen. xiv. 20, xxviii. 22), the observance of the Sabbath (Gen. ii. 1–3, viii. 10, Ex. xvi. 23), Vows (Gen. xxviii. 20), all these, later tradition considered to be in force among the Israelites before the Sinaitic covenant was concluded, equally with the prohibition of moral offences, of murder (Gen. ix. 4–7), of theft (Gen. xxxi. 32, xliv. 9), of adultery (Gen. xxxviii, xlix. 4). In respect of their national customs and institutions, which were nothing if not part of their religion, we cannot detach the people of Israel from the great Semitic stock of which they were a branch. Nor indeed can we altogether leave out of view the possibility of a survival of such customs from an earlier stage of religion and a society yet more primitive.

The Sinaitic legislation, therefore, so far as it related to the priesthood, to sacrifice, to ritual, was intended not so much to create a new system as to give a new *The Spirit new rather than the system.* significance to that which had already long existed among Semitic races, and to lay the foundation of a higher symbolism leading to a more spiritual worship.

In a word, it was not the rites, but their spiritual signifi- CHAP. I.
cance; not the ceremonial acts, but their connexion with,
and interpretation of, the service of Him who made Himself known as the pure, the spiritual, the loving God of
Israel, that determined the true character of the revelation granted on Mount Sinai. Then, as in every other
epoch of religious creativeness, life was conveyed not by
the external imposition of a new ceremonial, but by the
infusion of a truer spiritual force into the customs of
popular worship, making them instinct with new meaning, and rescuing the souls of men from bondage to
a barren externalism.

Rules of sacrifice, of cleanness, and of worship would *Priestly tradition.*
generally be transmitted from one generation of priests
to another, in a very large degree, and especially in early
times, by oral tradition. But, as time went on, a written
tradition would, sooner or later, be formed. In either case,
whether committed to writing or entrusted to memory,
a stereotyped cast of language would arise from the
transmission of such regulations through a succession of
priestly families. It is this stereotyped cast of language
which is reproduced throughout the Priestly Laws, and
which itself witnesses to their derivation through long
periods anterior to their compilation.

What, however, is the verdict of modern criticism, so *Priestly rules known before codified.*
far as collections of these Priestly Laws are concerned?
We seem to be brought to the following conclusion. In
the pre-exilic writings of the Old Testament, ritual and
ceremonies, which are mentioned in the Priestly Laws of
the Pentateuch, are undoubtedly occasionally referred to:
the references do nothing more than testify to the
existence of such institutions at the time spoken of.
Unless clear traces of quotation accompany them, they

CHAP. I.   cannot be taken to prove the existence of one authoritative code of Priestly Laws.   Before the Exile, quotations from Priestly Laws are, it is universally admitted, exceedingly rare.   Their rarity and doubtfulness make it probable that no authoritative collection had been made, or, at any rate, officially formulated before the era of the Captivity.   On the other hand, the few certain quotations which are to be found, e. g. Deut. xiv. 4–20, 1 Sam. ii. 22, 1 Kings viii. 1 and 5, may indicate at the most, that collections of Priestly Laws, possibly of a private nature, existed for the use of priests[1].   A careful comparison of the detail of the Priestly Laws with that of the laws in Deuteronomy shows conclusively, that the codification of the former is later, and belongs to a more advanced period of worship, than the age of the Deuteronomist.   This, however, in no way invalidates the conclusion upon which all critics are agreed, that in the Priestly Laws are embedded groups of laws derived from much earlier usage.   Unmistakable instances of this mixture of earlier with more recent regulations are to be found in Lev. i–viii, xi–xv, Num. v, vi, ix, xv, xix.

Purpose of collections of laws.   Enough, and more than enough, has now been said upon the laws, to convince us that various collections of laws were made at different times during the history of the people.   Some have become lost to view.   Others the Hebrew scholar has little difficulty in distinguishing even now in the Pentateuch.   The clearly marked characteristics of language, which, speaking gene-

---

[1] The LXX text in 1 Sam. ii. 22, 1 Kings viii. 1, 5, omits the language agreeing with the usage of the Priestly Laws.

On the whole of this intricate question, see Driver's *Literature of the O. T.*

rally, distinguish the three legislative periods represented by the Book of the Covenant, the Deuteronomic Laws, and the Priestly Laws, force themselves upon our notice.

The purpose with which the more ancient collections, to which attention has been drawn, were made, must, doubtless, have differed in different cases. Sometimes, the object may have been to render assistance to a ruler or a judge in the discharge of his office; sometimes, merely to preserve an oral tradition, which threatened to become obsolete; sometimes, to keep intact from foreign or idolatrous taint the inherited institutions of the people. But in all cases, the originator of the collection, were he king, priest or prophet, would have promoted its formation for the benefit of his people, for the safeguarding of their society according to the law of Jehovah, and for the preservation of the pure Israelite Monotheism.

One point remains to be noticed, which arises naturally from the mention of collections of Israelite law. What is the sense to be ascribed to the words, 'The Law of Moses,' which frequently occur in the later portions of the Book of Joshua, and in the Books of Kings, Chronicles, Ezra, Nehemiah and Daniel? It is clear that they cannot be referred to any one particular code of laws that has escaped all modification from later times. The fact, now so clearly established, that the Laws of Israel, as of other nations, only reached their final literary form by development through gradual stages, must show conclusively, that Moses was not the writer of them in the form in which they have come down to us, and in which they were certainly known after the Exile. But just as, in Deut. xxxi. 9 and 24, Moses himself is said to have committed to writing the law, which formed the nucleus of the Deuteronomic legislation, so we understand the

'The Law of Moses.'

legislation which was initiated by Moses to have become expanded into the complex system of laws included in the Pentateuch. The great Lawgiver, who was the founder, became also the personification of Hebrew legislation, as David was of the poetry, and Solomon of the wisdom of Israel[1], and, it may be added, as Solon was of Athenian legislation.

'Torah.'   As has often been shown, the word, Torah, is only associated with the idea of the written Law after the Exile. Primarily, it means 'a pointing out,' an individual decision, it may be, on a moral question of right or wrong, or on a ceremonial question of clean or unclean. It is to be remembered that in early Semitic life government was largely administered by means of 'Torôth,' authoritative decisions, delivered by the chief or judge who gave his verdict upon the basis of custom and precedent. It was the reign of Themis, or of what we might call Consuetudinary Justice. A picture of such an administration, actually conducted by Moses on such lines, stands before us in the narrative of Ex. xviii. 13–27. Priests, as the repositories of sacred tradition, were required to give such decisions (cf. Deut. xvii. 9–12, xxiv. 8, Haggai ii. 11, 12); and in the Book of Micah we find the prophet rebuking the priests for taking bribes before pronouncing sentence (Micah iii. 11).

---

[1] Cf. Professor Driver: 'The laws even in their developed shape, may be supposed to have been attributed to Moses, because Hebrew legislation was regarded, and in a sense regarded truly, as derived ultimately from him' (*Contemporary Review*, Feb. 1890). 'The " law of Moses " is indeed frequently spoken of; and it is unquestioned that Israelitish law did originate with him: but this expression is not evidence that Moses was the *writer* of the Pentateuch, or even that the laws which the Pentateuch contains represent throughout his unmodified legislation' (*Introd. Lit. of O. T.* p. 118 n.).

In the rebukes which the prophets deliver against their countrymen, they make no appeal to the sacred authority of any written standard of law or doctrine. The prophet's utterance is derived directly from God. The prophet is a spokesman on God's behalf. He appeals to no authoritative writing which should regulate the life of Israel. Hosea enumerates the ways in which Jehovah had made himself known to his people, 'I have also spoken by the prophets, and I have multiplied visions and used similitudes by the ministry of the prophets' (xii. 10). But he makes no mention of the ministry of a written code of law or of anything corresponding to an authoritative Canon of Scripture. It is true that, in a much controverted passage (viii. 12), he uses the words 'Though I write for him my law in ten thousand precepts.' But considering the invariable usage of the word 'law,' or 'Torah,' before the Exile, we are not justified in supposing that it can refer here to any book of ritual. The allusion is probably to the 'Torah' or 'instruction' of the prophets embodying the true teaching of Jehovah. This is 'The Torah,' the Law of the Lord (Hosea iv. 6, Amos ii. 4), which differed so widely from the 'Torah' of priests; it was concerned with no mere lists of statutes touching ritual and cleanliness, but with the eternal principles of truth, justice and mercy. These the prophet may well have known in a written form, embodied, even in his time, in those written collections of moral law and prophetic teaching, of which the main substance may have been preserved to us.

(3) History. The composition of prose narrative *History.* among the Israelites doubtless belongs to a later stage of literature than the composition of ballads and primitive laws.

D

CHAP. I.

Official Records.

In the records of the Old Testament we have fairly clear evidence of different classes of prose narrative. There is, for instance, the narrative of the official memoir. In the court of David, and of his successors on the throne, we find the scribe, or recorder, occupying a prominent place among the officials (cf. 2 Sam. viii. 16, xx. 24, 1 Kings iv. 3, 2 Kings xviii. 18, &c., &c.). The short, dry, record of the official chronicle is probably to be recognised in the skeleton structure of our Books of Kings. Upon the mere outline of events, thus officially sketched, more complete histories would afterwards be built up by compilers, who made extracts from these among other written sources of information, but relied chiefly upon the abundant materials of oral tradition to furnish them with a narrative of living interest.

Compilation.

Most of the historical books of the Old Testament are unmistakably the result of compilation. It is not always easy to say where the compiler is simply transcribing his authorities, and where he is himself working up and redacting material derived from a hundred different sources. It is generally possible to analyse a compilatory work so as to reduce it to its main component literary elements. But it becomes a precarious task, one on which we cannot place much reliance, when the attempt is made to break up each of those component parts, in their turn, into their ultimate constituents. Some portions, however, in the historical narrative bear the stamp of having been transferred, in their entirety, directly from their original sources, e. g. the narratives in Judges xvii, xviii, xix, the older narrative of the life of Saul (1 Samuel ix. 1–10, xiii, xiv), and the narrative of the reign of David (2 Samuel ix–xx). For the most part, however, the compilation of a Hebrew narrative was a complex and artistic process. Previously written accounts were condensed or expanded, revised or re-written, before they could be inserted in the new history.

Full importance must be granted to the part played in Hebrew narrative by the direct transcription of oral tradition. We can hardly doubt that the brightness and vividness of much of Hebrew narrative is due to its having been derived from the lips of practised story-tellers. To this source we are probably indebted for those portions in the Books of Judges and Samuel which are regarded as presenting the best style of Hebrew prose. With them we must associate the two great collections of narrative, called by critics the Elohist and Jehovist writings, which form so large a portion of the compilation of the Pentateuch. They, too, had been compilations; they, too, incorporated early written records. But in their pure and simple style, resembling closely the best portion of Judges and Samuel, we trace the influence of oral tradition. It makes itself heard and felt in the simple conversational prose, in the vividness of the description of scenes, and in the naturalness and ease of the dialogue. Scholars have been divided in opinion as to the date to which these two great narrative collections should be assigned. Very probably their composition preceded the time when the prophets Amos and Hosea wrote. The fact, however, that those two prophets allude to incidents recorded in the patriarchal narrative of the Elohist and Jehovist (Hosea xii. 3, 4, 12, 13; cf. Amos ii. 9) must not be relied on too confidently as proof of their acquaintance with the precise materials that have come down to us. The prophets do not actually quote the words familiar to us in Genesis.

Chap. I.

Oral Tradition.

The narratives would be current in popular tradition. They may possibly have existed in other written forms, besides those which have been incorporated in the Pentateuch. The argument, however, whatever be its value, derives a certain degree of confirmation from the beauty and simplicity of the style, which point to a date at which Hebrew prose literature was neither in its infancy, nor yet had reached the beginning of its decadence. Such a date may well have been the century before the ministry of Hosea and Amos.

Prophetic purpose of Narrative.

Accordingly, we have, in the compilations of narrative, another instance of the tendency, in preexilic times, to make collections of literary materials, of which use could be made for the purpose of providing religious instruction for the people. It is interesting, therefore, to find that careful critical analysis of the Pentateuch shows that, in all probability, the Jehovist and Elohist writings were themselves welded into one historical work, dealing with the narrative from the Creation to the death of Joshua. The existence and influence of this compilation are presupposed in the writings of the Deuteronomist, so that the work of welding them together can hardly be later than the middle of the eighth century B.C. The object of the compilation was obviously a religious one. It was intended to give the history of the Israelite people from the beginning, to show their Divine selection, and to testify to the special providence which had delivered them from the bondage of Egypt, which had built up the constitution upon the foundation of the Covenant of Sinai, and which had brought the people, in fulfilment of the promises made to the patriarchs, into the possession of the land of Canaan. We fancy that the construction of this vivid retrospect of Israel's early history must have

been connected with the efforts of the prophets to encourage a more pure and spiritual religion. They foresaw the fall of the Northern kingdom ; the danger of
the sister kingdom could not be disguised. The hope
of averting this catastrophe lay in the spiritual reunion of
the people. Historical narrative played its part by re-
calling to memory the Covenants made of old with the
Patriarchs.

(4) Prophecy. What has just been said, leads us to *Prophecy.*
make a few references, at this point, to the functions of
the prophet, and to the commencement of the system of
collecting prophecies in writing.

Communities of prophets were not originally, as is so *The Pro-*
often erroneously supposed, banded together for purposes *fession of Prophet.*
of study, or of literature, or even of sedentary devotion.
From the earliest notices which we have of them in
Scripture (1 Samuel x), we gather that the 'Sons of the
Prophets' thronged together for the purpose of inspiring
the common people with religious enthusiasm by practices of ecstatic fervour. Their conduct and life may, in
some respects, be illustrated, as has often been pointed
out, by the dervishes of the East in modern times.
The institution of prophets was, we find in Holy
Scripture, connected, both in Palestine and in the ad-
joining countries, with the service of different deities. The
reader need only refer to the narrative in 1 Kings xviii
and 2 Kings x, to see how conspicuously the prophets of
Baal figured in one great crisis of the history of Israel.

Throughout the days of the Monarchy, the Exile and
even after the Return, the prophets of Jehovah appear
constantly. But many were false prophets, professional
deceivers (cf. 1 Kings xxii. 6-28, Neh. vi. 10-14, Ezek.
xiii, xiv) ; the majority of them were quite inconspicuous

(cf. 2 Kings vi. 1–7). Only a few attained to any great eminence. The leading men amongst them had their disciples, or, as they were called, their 'sons' (cf. 1 Samuel x. 12), who served them, imitated them, and perhaps aspired to fill their place (2 Kings ii. 15). The greater prophets were consulted on all occasions of difficulty and trouble. Their reputation frequently spread beyond their immediate neighbourhood (cf. 2 Kings v and vi). They seem to have had special days for teaching the people and for giving answers to applications made to them from different quarters (2 Kings iv. 23). The reply of a prophet was vouchsafed, sometimes upon matters of fact (cf. 1 Samuel ix, x, 1 Kings xi. 26–40, xiv. 1–16), sometimes upon questions of morality (cf. 1 Samuel xv, 2 Samuel xii. 1–14); but the most important part played by the prophet, in the time of the monarchy, was when he came forward to speak in the name of the Lord upon questions of national policy (e. g. 1 Kings xi. 26–40, xviii. 1 ff., 2 Kings vii–ix), to encourage (2 Kings xix. 20), or to warn (1 Kings xxi. 17–22, Isaiah vii. 3–17). Each prophetic utterance was a pointing out, a ' torah,' an instruction, based upon the principles of the Law of Jehovah.

The more important of such utterances would be preserved by the disciples of the great prophets. In earlier times they were probably only committed to memory. Afterwards, as the practice of writing became more common, they would be transcribed, sometimes by the prophet himself, sometimes by his followers, from the recollection of the utterance. The earliest specimens of prophetic utterance, committed to writing, that have come down to us, are to be found in the Books of Amos and Hosea. Whether these prophets themselves pre-

pared them for publication, we cannot say. Doubtless, CHAP. L
by comparison with the actual spoken word of which the
prophets delivered themselves, the books are mainly
condensations. In the Book of Amos the work of condensation has been done so dexterously as to present us
with a smooth and flowing style; but in the Book of
Hosea the process of condensation was not so skilfully
effected, and this will probably account for the enigmatical
abruptness and obscurity of the prophet's style. For
another extensive illustration of the way in which groups
of prophecies were collected and summarised, we need
only refer to the contents of the first portion of Isaiah
(i-xxxix) [1].

The necessity of committing their utterance to writing *Written.*
was often imposed upon the prophets by the refusal of
the people to listen to their warnings, or by the prohibition, on the part of the authorities, of liberty to speak in
the hearing of the people (Amos ii. 12, vii. 12, 13,
Micah ii. 6). It is for some such reason that Isaiah
solemnly commits to his disciples the charge of his testimony and his 'torah' (viii. 16-20).

The utterances of earlier prophets were cherished in
the memories, or in the tablets, of those who succeeded
them. We find that Micah and Isaiah quote from
the same utterance of some prophet, unknown to us,
who had testified before their day (cf. Isaiah ii. 2-4
and Micah iv. 1-3). Whether it was extant in writing,
we cannot say. But the preservation of prophecy for
the benefit of disciples was only a step in the direction
of continuous formal compositions such as we find in
Jeremiah and Ezekiel.

[1] See the Commentaries by Cheyne and Dillmann, and Driver's *Isaiah,
his Life and Times*, ed. 2, 1893 ('Men of the Bible' Series).

Thus was a commencement made of preserving, in writing, collections of prophetic utterances intended for the instruction of the people. In vain, it seemed, had the witness of the faithful prophet been borne by word of mouth in the face of a malignant court and a time-serving people. But the very rancour of princes, the very obstinacy of the people, their very refusal to listen, their very contempt of the prophet's speech, were overruled to be the means of preserving the memorial of the sacred message. The prophets wrote what they could not or might not utter. The true value of the written collections of prophecy was thus discerned. Yet not at once; only through the discipline of the exile were the lessons of prophecy, that had been preserved by the writings of the prophets and their disciples, fully taken to heart. For our purpose it is enough that, in the collections of prophetical utterances which were made, some by those who spake them, others by those who heard them, we may recognise another advance made in the direction of the formation of a Canon of Scripture.

As to the methods by which these collections of songs, laws, narratives, and prophecies were made and transmitted, we have, it must be confessed, practically no evidence. It is sufficient, however, to note their existence, and to observe in passing that, in the extant memorials of Israel, there is no appearance of such collections, with the possible exception of the Decalogue, having ever acquired authority, resembling that of Canonical Scripture, over the public life of the nation. We might, indeed, fairly infer from the religious thought which characterises the extant remnants of these collections, that their contents were scarcely likely to have

been in agreement with the forms of religion which CHAP. L
found favour with the people during the greater part of
the monarchy. In proportion as they approximated to
the pure spiritual tone and religious sincerity of the
faithful prophets of Jehovah, they must have come into
collision with the cruder externalism, which prevailed
even in Jerusalem. Their worth was proved in the
furnace of opposition. Those that survived the ordeal
were destined afterwards to receive enduring recognition.

The preservation of public documents in a place of *Tradition*
safety, and therefore, probably, in a place of sanctity, *of laws kept in Sanctu-*
was doubtless a practice observed by the Israelites as *ary.*
well as by other nations of antiquity. The evidence is
not sufficient to show that any of the collections which
we have described, save, possibly, of certain laws, came
under the category of documents that were preserved
with especial care. Out of the passages generally quoted
to show that we should attribute the preservation of the
Old Testament Scriptures to the practice of storing
archives in the sanctuary, one passage refers to the two
tables of stone (Exodus xl. 20), three passages, to the
substance of the law of Deuteronomy (Deut. xvii. 18,
xxxi. 24–26, 2 Kings xxii. 8) [1]; one, a very doubtful
case, to a writing of Joshua which has not survived
(Joshua xxiv. 26); one, to a law of the monarchy, of
which we are told nothing beyond the fact, that Samuel
committed it to writing and laid it up before the Lord
(1 Samuel x. 25). At the most, then, it may be said,
tradition, as represented by these passages, favours the
view that some portions of the earliest law were wont to
be preserved in sacred precincts. But, judging from the
history, it does not appear that, until the reign of Josiah,

[1] On 'the Book of the Law' in 2 Kings xxii, see Chap. III.

any such portions of the law received the veneration of the people to which they afterwards became entitled. It is only too evident from 2 Kings xxii, that the preservation of a book, even in the Temple, afforded no protection against forgetfulness and utter neglect.

The habit of preserving ancient portions of the law in a place of sanctity was not identical with investing them with Canonical authority. Let us take the case of the Decalogue. It is open to question, whether even this sacred nucleus of the law was, in all times, regarded by the people of Israel as authoritative. If it was, it is strange that its authority should not have been more generally recognised, that appeals to its prohibition of idolatry should not have been made by kings and prophets who were bent upon the purification of religion. Certainly, if its position had been that which later usage learned to ascribe to it, it is quite unaccountable that so little allusion is made to its claims.

Two Tables of Stone. Nevertheless, the account which is preserved of the two tables of stone, on which the Ten Words, or Commandments, were inscribed, shows plainly that in them we have the nearest approach to the Canonical Scriptures of a later stage in the people's history. It appears from a statement in the Books of Kings that, in the days of Solomon, the tables of stone were still preserved in the ark within the Holy of Holies (1 Kings viii. 9). But did they exert any practical influence over the religious life of the people? Our answer must be in the affirmative; they may have remained to all appearances a dead letter, their testimony may not have been directly appealed to by the prophets; but on them had rested the whole fabric of civil and religious order. They were known by writers, in the first stages of Israelite literature, to contain the foundation of the moral law, the first CHAP. L 'torah' of Jehovah (Ex. xx. 1–17, Deut. v. 6–21).

The sanctity of the two tables of stone is inseparable, in the priestly tradition, from the sanctity of the ark which was constructed to receive them ; and, as we know from Jeremiah (iii. 16), the sanctity of the ark was connected in the remembrance of the people with the earliest stages of their religious history[1]. The Laws of the Decalogue were the Testimony ; so the ark was called the Ark of the Testimony, and the two tables of stone the Tables of the Testimony. The Decalogue embodied the Covenant of Sinai ; so the ark was called the Ark of the Covenant.

That the Ten Commandments were considered to *The Testi-* contain the fundamental charter of the Israelite con- *mony at* stitution, is a view that has sometimes been thought to *of Joash.* receive an illustration from the narrative of the coronation of Joash (2 Kings xi. 12, 2 Chronicles xxiii. 11). We there read that the high priest Jehoiada 'put the crown upon him and gave him the testimony,' or, as the translation is more literally, 'put upon him the crown and the testimony.' The traditional interpretation of these words has always been, that the high priest either rested upon the head, or placed in the hand, of the young king the Tables of the Testimony, in order that the royal purpose of reigning in accordance with the Covenant of Sinai might thereby be symbolised. The reading of the passage, however, is not quite certain. The literal translation of the words sounds harsh and abrupt, to say the least of it. Is the text at fault ? Was it that *Text of 2* *Kings* xi.

---

[1] Outside the Hexateuch, cf. Jud. xx. 27 ; 1 Sam. iii–vi, xiv. 18 ; 2 Sam. vi, vii. 2, xi. 11, xv ; 1 Kings ii. 26, iii. 15, vi. 19, viii. 1–9, 21 ; Ps. cxxxii. 8, Chron. *pass.*

CHAP. I. Jewish scribes, in after times, left out the words ('the two tables of'), hesitating to record in writing what they understood in the mention of the sacred tables, i.e. the removal of them from out of the Ark of the Testimony and the obtaining of them from the Holy of Holies, which was inaccessible to all save to the high priest alone, and to him only once in the year? Or was it, as has been suggested by some recent scholars, that the word 'Testimony' is a wrong reading and that the

Proposed emendation. original word, in the place of which 'Testimony' has been inserted, meant 'the bracelets' which were the insignia of royalty (cf. 2 Samuel i. 10)? This latter suggestion is ingenious enough; for, in the Hebrew spelling, the two words, rendered 'Testimony' and 'bracelets,' very closely resemble one another. But it is an objection that the proposed word rendered 'bracelet' occurs in this sense only once elsewhere in the Bible, (Isaiah iii. 20)[1]. It is a much more serious objection, that the substitution of the word 'Testimony' for the word 'bracelets' was hardly likely to have been made. 'Testimony,' the commoner word, was the harder reading. There was nothing which would tempt a scribe to introduce into the narrative such an apparent profanation both of the Ark of the Testimony and of the Holy of Holies. The suggestion therefore of a false reading does not commend itself on the ground of inherent probability.

It is unfortunate, that critics should thus have attempted to alter the significant word of a passage, a word which happened also, apparently, to tell against the particular views which the critics upheld. 'Testimony' is the reading found in this passage in both

---

[1] צערות 'bracelets,' ערות 'testimony.'

accounts (Kings and Chronicles). It occurs both in the
Hebrew and in the Septuagint text. Now the word-
'Testimony' is applied, in the Priestly portion of the
Pentateuch, to the tables of the Law (e.g. Exodus xxv.
16, 21, xl. 20), and to the ark (e.g. Exodus xvi. 34, xxvii.
21, Leviticus xvi. 13, xxiv. 3, Numbers xvii. 4, 10). It is
obvious therefore that the occurrence of the word, in its
former technical sense, in this passage of the Book of
Kings, might be claimed as proof of acquaintance with
the phraseology of the priestly writings of the Pentateuch,
at least in the times of the exile, if not at a considerably
earlier date, since the history of the Jehoiada episode is
clearly based on contemporary records. On this account,
the proposal to remove so significant a word from the
text can hardly escape the charge of appearing either
arbitrary or disingenuous. It seems the more candid
course to accept the reading 'testimony,' while acknowledging that the text may not be free from suspicion.

We are thrown back, therefore, upon the former alternative, that the difficulty in the reading was due to an
omission, which is to be accounted for by the hesitation of scribes to record an apparent instance of the
profane handling of the tables of the Law and the viola-
tion of the rule respecting the sanctity of the Holy of
Holies.

The difficulty, however, admits of another solution. *Suggested*
Retaining the reading 'Testimony,' are we obliged to *explanation.*
restrict the meaning of the word to its special, and, according to the critics, later, technical sense of 'the tables
of stone'? If the two tables had survived the disasters
of Shiloh, is it probable that they would have been
brought out of the Ark, or fetched from the innermost
shrine? The 'Testimony' may surely refer to the

CHAP. I. substance of the fundamental laws of the Covenant, without necessarily conveying the idea of the two stone tables on which it was originally inscribed. The contents of the Testimony may well have been preserved on parchment or on tablets (cf. Isaiah viii. 1). The requirements both of the word in the original and of the context in which it occurs are satisfied to the full, if we suppose that Jehoiada handed to the young king a roll or tablets, on which was inscribed the fundamental charter of the constitution. Whether such a charter was limited to the Ten Commandments, or whether it contained other laws that are embodied in documents which have been incorporated in the Pentateuch, we cannot, of course, pretend to do more than conjecture. But it is a natural conjecture, that portions of the civil law, such as were, for instance, formulated in a prophetic form by the writer of Deuteronomy, may have received ratification from the king on the occasion of his enthronement (cf. Deut. xvii. 14–20).

But a Magna Charta is not a Bible, nor can the fundamental law of a constitution, ratified at a coronation, be the equivalent of a Canon of Scripture.

CHAPTER II.

THE BEGINNINGS OF THE CANON.

The Book of the Law.

IT is not till the year 621 B.C., the eighteenth year

of the reign of King Josiah, that the history of Israel presents us with the first instance of 'a book,' which was regarded by all, king, priests, prophets, and people alike, as invested not only with sanctity, but also with supreme authority in all matters of religion and conduct.

The book had been discovered in the house of God by the High Priest, Hilkiah. The discovery was quite accidental; for the book was apparently brought to light by workmen in the course of certain structural repairs in the Temple. It was at once recognised by the High Priest, who apprised Shaphan, the scribe, and gave it into his charge. The King was informed of the start-ling intelligence, and he, on having its contents read aloud to him, was thrown into sudden and vehement consternation. He despatched messengers to consult the prophetess Huldah. They returned with the dis-couraging reply, that the woes predicted in the book could not be averted. Nothing daunted, Josiah and his counsellors addressed themselves at once to energetic measures of religious reform. The worship at the high places which King Hezekiah, nearly a century before, had vainly attempted to put a stop to, was now sum-

CHAP. II.   marily suppressed.   All public worship of Jehovah was
Its influence. to be concentrated at the Temple of Jerusalem (2 Kings
xxiii. 1–20).   A great celebration of the Passover was
kept in conformity with the requirements of this book,
and, we are told, 'there had been none like it since the
days of the Judges' (*vv.* 21–23).   In order 'that he
might confirm the words of the law which were written
in the book that Hilkiah the priest found in the house
of the Lord,' Josiah put away 'them that had familiar
spirits and the wizards and the teraphim and the idols'
(*ver.* 24); and amongst the relics of false worship which
he destroyed we have particular mention of images used
for the worship of the heavenly bodies (*vv.* 4–11).   The
King's action had the support of the whole people.
When he 'made a covenant before the Lord . . . to
confirm the words of the covenant that were written
in the book,' it is added, 'and all the people stood to
the covenant' (*ver.* 3).

In this familiar scene, 'the Book of the Law' stands in
the position of Canonical Scripture.   It is recognised as
containing the words of the Lord (xxii. 18, 19).   Its
authority is undisputed and indisputable.   On the
strength of its words the most sweeping measures are
carried out by the King, and accepted by the people.
The whole narrative, so graphically told by one who
was possibly a contemporary of the events he describes,
breathes the conviction that the homage paid to 'the
book,' was nothing more than its just due.

Its contents.   When we enquire what this 'Book of the Law' comprised, the evidence at our disposal is quite sufficiently
explicit to direct us to a reply.   Even apart from the
knowledge which we now possess of the structure of the
Pentateuch, there was never much probability in the

supposition, that the book discovered by Hilkiah was
identical with the whole Jewish 'Torah,' our Pentateuch.
The narrative does not suggest so considerable a work.
Its contents were quickly perused and readily grasped [1].
Being read aloud, it at once left distinct impressions
upon questions of national duty. Its dimensions could
not have been very large, nor its precepts very technical.
The complex character of the Pentateuch fails to satisfy
the requirements of the picture. Perhaps, too (although
the argument is hardly one to be pressed), as it appears
that only a single roll of the Law was found, it may not
unfairly be remarked, that the whole Torah was never
likely to be contained in one roll; but that, if a single
roll contained any portion of the Pentateuch, it was most
probably the Deuteronomic portion of it; for the Book
of Deuteronomy, of all the component elements of the
Pentateuch, presents the most unmistakable appearance
of having once formed a compact independent work [2].

But, there is no need to have recourse to arguments of such a doubtful kind. For while the evidence shows that a completed Torah could not have
existed at this time, we seem to have convincing proof
that 'the Book of the Law' was either a portion of our
Deuteronomy or a collection of laws, Deuteronomic in
tone, and, in range of contents, having a close resemblance to our Book of Deuteronomy. The evidence is
twofold. (1) The description which is given of the
book found in the Temple shows, that, in its most
characteristic features, it approximated more closely
to portions of Deuteronomy than to any other section

Char. II.

Not the whole Pentateuch,

but collection of Deuteronomic Law.

---

[1] 2 Kings xxii. 11, xxiii. 2.

[2] Cf. Ps. xl. 7: 'In the *roll* of the book it is prescribed to me': with
Prof. Kirkpatrick's note (Psalms, vol. i. *Camb. Bible for Schools*).

E

CHAP. II. of the Pentateuch. (2) The historian, from whom we obtain the account, appears, when he speaks of 'the law,' to have in view the Deuteronomic section, and scarcely to be acquainted with any other. These arguments have been frequently and fully discussed in other works, so that we need not here do more than summarize them very briefly.

Evidence : (1) The description of the book shows that, in its
1.Similarity most conspicuous features, it was in close agreement
to Deut. with the contents of Deuteronomy.

(a) Presence (a) The book contained denunciations against the
of Denun- neglect of the covenant with Jehovah (2 Kings xxii. 11–
ciation. 13, 16, 17).

Now the Pentateuch contains two extensive passages describing the fearful visitations that should befall the people of Israel for following after other gods (Lev. xxvi; Deut. xxviii–xxxi). Of these, the passage in Deuteronomy is the longest, and while the passage in Leviticus would be calculated to produce a very similar impression, it may be noticed that the words of Huldah, in referring to the curses contained in 'the Book of the Law,' possibly contain a reference to Deut. xxviii. 37, xxix. 24 (cf. 2 Kings xxii. 19). It cannot be doubted that one or other, or both of these denunciations, must have been included in Josiah's 'Book of the Law.'

(b) Reforms (b) The reforms carried out by the king and his
produced by advisers, in order to obey the commands of 'the Book
book. of the Law,' deal with matters all of which are mentioned, with more or less emphasis, in the Deuteronomic legis- . lation. (i) The principal religious reform carried out by Josiah was the suppression of the worship at the high places, and the concentration of worship at the Temple. No point is insisted on so frequently and so emphatically

in the Deuteronomic laws as that all public worship is to be centralised at the one place which Jehovah himself should choose (Deut. xii. 5 and *passim*). (ii) Josiah took measures to abolish the worship of the heavenly bodies, a form of idolatry distinct from the worship of Baal and Ashtoreth. His action is in obedience to the commands of Deuteronomic laws (Deut. iv. 19, xvii. 3). There alone in the Pentateuch is this particular form of idolatry combated. For, although it had existed in an earlier time, it does not seem to have infected the religion of Israel until late in the monarchical period (cf. 2 Kings xxi. 3, 5, xxiii. 4, 5, 12). (iii) Josiah celebrated the Feast of the Passover (2 Kings xxiii. 21–23) in accordance with 'the Book of the Law'—we find the Law of the Passover laid down in Deut. xvi. 1–8. (iv) Josiah expelled the wizards and diviners from the land in express fulfilment of 'the Book of the Law' (2 Kings xxiii. 24): we find the prohibition of this common class of impostor in Oriental countries expressed in strong language in Deut. xviii. 9–14.

It is not, of course, for a moment denied that laws, dealing with these two last subjects, are to be found elsewhere in the Pentateuch. But as in all four cases Josiah's action was based upon 'the law,' whatever 'the law' was, it must have dealt with 'feasts' and with 'wizards' as well as with 'concentration of worship' and 'star-worship.' In the Deuteronomic laws all four points are touched upon.

(c) The book found in the Temple is designated 'the *(c) Called a* Book of the Covenant' (2 Kings xxiii. 2, 21), and it *'Book of the Covenant.'* appears that it contained a covenant, to the observance of which the king solemnly pledged himself (id. 3). In the Pentateuch we find, it is true, a mention of 'the Book of the Covenant' (Ex. xxiv. 7), by which the

substance of the Sinaitic legislation (Ex. xx–xxiii)
seems to be denoted.   But it is clear, from the fact that
the section, Ex. xx–xxiii, contains no denunciation;
from the fact that it contains only the very briefest
notice of the Feast of the Passover, and then under
another name, 'the Feast of Unleavened Bread' (Ex.
xxiii. 15); from the fact that it makes no mention of
either wizards or star-worship;—that this portion of
the Israelite law cannot be 'the covenant' referred to in
2 Kings xxiii.   On the other hand, an important section
at the close of our Book of Deuteronomy is occupied
with a 'Covenant'; and it can hardly be doubted, that
a 'Book of the Law,' which was also 'the Book of the
Covenant,' must have included such passages as Deut.
xxix. 1, 'These are the words of the covenant which
the Lord commanded Moses to make with the children
of Israel'; ver. 9, 'Keep therefore the words of this
covenant'; ver. 14, 'Neither with you only do I make
this covenant and this oath"; ver. 21, 'According to all
the curses of the covenant that is written in the book of
the law'; vers. 24, 25, 'Even all the nations shall say,
Wherefore hath the Lord done thus unto this land? . . .
Then men shall say, Because they forsook the covenant
of the Lord.'

2. Evidence of writer of Books of Kings.   (2) The historian who has preserved to us the narrative of the finding of 'the Book of the Law' himself
quotes directly from 'the law' in two passages, and in
both instances from Deuteronomic writing.   In 1 Kings
ii. 3, 'And keep the charge of the Lord thy God to walk
in His ways, to keep His statutes, and His commandments, and His judgements, and His testimonies, according to that which is written in the law of Moses,
that thou mayest prosper in all that thou doest and

whithersoever thou turnest thyself,' the words used
are characteristically Deuteronomic, and the thought is
possibly based on Deut. xvii. 18–20 (cf. Josh. i. 8). In
2 Kings xiv. 6, 'But the children of the murderers he
put not to death ; according to that which is written in
the book of the law of Moses, as the Lord commanded,
saying, The fathers shall not be put to death for the
children, nor the children be put to death for the fathers ;
but every man shall die for his own sin,' the citation is
taken almost word for word from Deut. xxiv. 16. In
numerous characteristic expressions and phrases the compiler of the Books of Kings shows a close acquaintance
with the Deuteronomic portion of the Pentateuch, though
nowhere, perhaps, so frequently as in 1 Kings viii, ix, e.g.
viii. 51 (cf. Deut. iv. 20), ix. 3 (cf. Deut. xii. 5), ix.
7, 8 (cf. Deut. xxviii. 37, xxix. 24). Generally speaking, where reference is made to 'the law' in the Books of
Kings, the allusion can only be satisfied by a reminiscence of a Deuteronomic passage. Thus, exclusive of
the two passages already quoted, may be noted 1 Kings
viii. 9 (cf. Deut. x. 5, xxix. 1), 53 (cf. Deut. iv. 20), 56
(cf. Deut. xii. 9, 10, xxv. 19), 2 Kings x. 31, xviii. 12,
xxi. 8, xxii. 8, xxiii. 25.

If, therefore, the compiler of the Books of Kings identified 'the law of Moses' and 'the book of the law'
with Deuteronomy, or, at least, with a Deuteronomic
version of the law, we may nearly take it for granted,
that, in his narrative of the reign of Josiah, when he mentioned 'the Book of the Law' without further description,
he must have had in his mind the same Deuteronomic
writings with which he was so familiar.

The language of the compiler of the Books of Kings *Conclusion.*
tends therefore to strengthen the argument from the

effect produced by the perusal of 'the Book of the Law,' and from the nature of the reforms based upon its authority. We see no reason to question the accuracy of the conclusion, that 'the Book of the Law' found in the house of God, in the eighteenth year of King Josiah's reign, was substantially identical with the Deuteronomic portion of our Old Testament.

Previous history of book.

If this be granted, we have next to inquire into the previous history of this book. Had it ever before received the recognition which it received in Josiah's reign? Had it ever before been known as a sacred writing whose authority could be recognised as paramount over the kingdom of Judah? In other words, was its position of canonical authority in Josiah's reign a restoration to prestige previously enjoyed? or was it due to a combination of especially favourable circumstances, that a writing, never before so recognised, was now, for the first time, promoted to a position of religious pre-eminence in the nation?

A theory: forgery by Hilkiah.

To these questions, the scholars who suppose the composition of the book to have been the work of Hilkiah himself and of his friends, and who ascribe its discovery, not to chance, but to collusion, have no difficulty in making reply. Viewed from such a point of view, the book played a part in a clever intrigue conducted by the priests at Jerusalem, who aimed at dealing a finishing stroke to the rival worship at the high places.

But we have no reason to impugn either the accuracy or the sincerity of the historian, who describes an incident of which he was possibly a witness [1]. An unpre-

---

[1] For according to some scholars (e. g. Wellhausen and Kuenen) the compilation of the Books of Kings took place *before* the exile and only received a few additions at a later revision.

judiced perusal of his narrative leaves the impression, that
he has no shadow of a suspicion of the discovery having
been anything else but a fortunate accident, and that, in
the opinion of those living at the time, the book was supposed to have existed long before and to have been lost.

Assuming then that this Deuteronomic 'book of the *Unknown*
law' was honestly regarded as an ancient book in the *before 7th*
eighteenth year of Josiah, we must take into considera- *Cent. B.C.*
tion the following facts :—

(1) That never before, on the occasion of a religious
reform, do we find, in the books of Samuel and Kings, any
appeal made to the authority of a book; (2) that, even in
Hezekiah's reign, the attempt to suppress the high places
was not, so far as the history tells us, supported by any
such appeal; (3) that the earlier prophets, Amos, Hosea,
Micah, and Isaiah (I), give no certain sign of having been
influenced by the Deuteronomic law. Of course, as has
been already pointed out, ancient laws are copiously
incorporated in Deuteronomy, and the mere mention of
institutions and customs, which are spoken of in Deuteronomy, does not prove the existence of the book itself.
The force of the argument from silence, however, will at
once be appreciated when the pronounced influence of the
Deuteronomic writings upon the style of authors, to whom
the Book of Deuteronomy was well known, e. g. Books
of Kings, Jeremiah, and Zephaniah, is fully taken account
of. There is nothing parallel to it in the undoubtedly
earlier Hebrew literature. The inference is obvious: the
Book of Deuteronomy, in the earlier period, was either
not yet composed or not yet known. But if written,
could it have escaped the notice of Amos, Hosea, and
Isaiah? could it have failed to leave on them something
of the mark it made on later literature?

One well-known passage (Isaiah xix. 19) should .be sufficient to disprove the possibility of that prophet's acquaintance with the Deuteronomic law. ' In that day there shall be an altar to the Lord in the midst of the land of Egypt, and a pillar (*mazzébah*) at the border thereof to the Lord.' Isaiah could hardly have said this, if he had been acquainted with the prohibition of Deut. xvi. 22, 'Thou shalt not set thee up a pillar (*mazzébah*) which the Lord thy God hateth.' Nor is the reply satisfactory that Isaiah refers to the soil, not of Palestine, but of Egypt; for the prophet is contemplating a time when all the world should be subject to the 'law' of Israel's God[1]. It would appear, therefore, that the Deuteronomic 'book of the law' was not known to Isaiah or his prophetic predecessors, and could hardly have been written before the reign of Hezekiah. Seeing that, in addition to this, the marked characteristics of its style correspond to those which are found in the Hebrew writing of the 6th and latter part of the 7th cent. B.C., it is the most natural conclusion, that the literary framework of the book is not to be placed earlier than the close of Isaiah's ministry (circ. 690 B.C.).

Possible date of composition.

The conclusion to which we incline is that the book was compiled in the latter part of Hezekiah's, or in the early part of Manasseh's, reign. Under the idolatrous reaction that took place in the reigns of Manasseh and Amon, such a work, breathing the fervent spirit of the purest worship of Jehovah, may well have disappeared from view, whether forcibly suppressed or silently with-

[1] Cf. Is. xix. 21, 'And the LORD shall be known to Egypt, and the Egyptians shall know the LORD in that day; yea, they shall worship with sacrifice and oblation, and shall vow a vow unto the LORD, and shall perform it.'

drawn.   Its recognition by Hilkiah shows that a recollec- Chap. II.
tion of the laws was retained among the priests.   The
narrative shows also that an accurate knowledge of the
laws was not to be found outside the priesthood and the
prophets.

Even by those who do not share the view here put
forward with respect to the date of its composition, the
admission is generally made, that, at no time previous
to Josiah's reign, is there any evidence of such a book
having exerted what we should call canonical authority
over the people.

In order to account for the extraordinary regard thus
manifested for 'the book of the law,' we must understand the nature of its contents.   Two mistakes have
commonly been made with respect to the Deuteronomic *Deutero-*
laws.   On the one hand, it has been assumed, and the *nomic Laws.*
name 'Deuteronomy' is partly accountable for it, that *Not all repe-*
tition of old,
the book consists solely of a reiteration of the laws con- *nor all new.*
tained in previous codes.   On the other hand, it has been
supposed—and the theory that it was composed to aid a
priestly intrigue would support the idea—that the book
consists of a new, a second, code of laws.   A closer inspec-
tion of its contents, and a comparison with the other
laws, show the erroneousness of both suppositions.   It is
not a reiteration of the Sinaitic laws.   For, while it
doubtless repeats some unchanged, it reproduces others
so far altered and modified, that their identity is only
faintly discernible.   Such alterations and modifications
illustrate the interval of time which separates the later
legislation from that of 'the Book of the Covenant' (Ex.
xx–xxiii).   Again, it is not a new legislative creation;
for even where its precepts differ from the older laws,
it is the difference which arises from expansion and

development rather than from contradiction. The fact that its legislation rests upon earlier laws is admitted on all hands.

Chief char-acteristic. But the characteristic feature of the Deuteronomic 'book of the law' is its homiletic setting. Its oratorical style, so smooth, so copious and redundant, and yet so impassioned, distinguishes its literary form from that of any formal official code. It forbids us to assign Deuteronomic literature to any early date. It marks at once the age from which its composition springs. It conveys no less clearly the purpose of popular exhortation, with which some ardent prophet moulded into its present shape a collection of his people's laws.

Collections of laws, as we have seen in the previous chapter, had been made at different times and with different objects. Hitherto the possessors of the laws had been the priests and the prophets—the official re-positories of the religion and of the learning of the *Book not needed before.* people. The community generally had not felt the need of a book of religion. They had been able to have recourse to the priests at the local altars; they had been able to consult the prophets who spoke in the name of the Lord; they had been able to repair to the Temple at Jerusalem, where the High Priest was invested with the Urim and Thummim.

Crisis in 7th Cent. B.C. But at the beginning of the 7th cent. B.C. a crisis was evidently at hand. The efforts of Hezekiah had recently been exerted to put down the local worship at the high places. The high places were a constant obstacle to the spiritual development of the worship of Jehovah; they possibly also impeded the attempts of statesmen to reunite all Israel at Jerusalem, after Samaria had fallen. But the abolition of the high places must have seemed to

the common people like the annihilation of the constant
witness, to be found 'on every high hill,' to the reality
of their religion. The removal of the priests, who for
centuries had presided over local and family festivals,
offered the daily evening sacrifice, and decided every
doubtful point of faith or honesty or 'cleanness,' must
have seemed like the withdrawal of sentinels from their
post, and the surrender of the country-side to the mercies
of the invaders' gods. Then, too, the successes of the
Assyrian armies favoured the idea, that they were the
strongest gods that presided over the most powerful
legions. All the old tendency to idolatrous syncre-
tism received a fresh impulse from the introduction
of new thoughts and strange superstitions from the banks
of the Euphrates.

Lastly, there was present to every thoughtful and
devout mind the warning conveyed by the overthrow of
the Northern Kingdom. Was it not possible that such
a disaster was impending over Judah too? And what
was there of true vitality, which could uphold the
religion of Jehovah, if the Temple should be over-
thrown, its courts desolated, its altar laid in ashes?
If that fatal blow should come, was the life-blood of
the nation's faith to ebb at once away? Were the men
of Judah, like their brethren of the Northern Kingdom,
to be poured out like water on the sand and lost?

Then, we may suppose, one or more of the prophets of *Prophets reveal the spiritual life of the laws.*
the kingdom of Judah arose, and sought to supply the sore
religious need of their countrymen. The people's laws,
which had lain hitherto too much in the hands of the
princes and their priests, these, they resolved, should now
be made known to all. But the mere publication of
a group of laws would do little to quicken the conscience,

or inspire enthusiasm. Accordingly, the laws only constitute the framework for the real message, a setting for a great hortatory appeal. The legislation thus published was clearly not intended to be exhaustive. It was not so much a complete code as a group of excerpts from the statute-book. The legal portion furnished but the basis for prophetic teaching. Behind all, there hangs the sombre background of warning, and the denunciation based on the recollection of the captivity which had already swept away the kingdom of the northern tribes.

A people's, not a priest's, book. Thus were the old laws presented in a popular form, as the 'people's book,' combining creed and law, exhortation and denunciation. It was a prophet's formulation of ' The law of Moses,' adapted to the requirements of that later time. 'The law,' in the guise of prophecy, this might become a spiritual rallying-point for Judah and Jerusalem ; it might be the means of upholding spiritual life even in the overthrow of national hopes.

Secret of its power. Such an explanation satisfactorily accounts for the combination of the homiletic style, characteristic of literature in the seventh and sixth cent. B.C., with a formulation of laws which included some of the most ancient statutes. Nor is it difficult to understand how such a work, during the reactionary reign of Manasseh, became lost to view. That its accidental discovery in the eighteenth year of King Josiah produced so astonishing an effect can well be imagined. The evils, which the prophet writer or writers had sought to combat, had grown in intensity during the seventy or eighty years which had elapsed. The reform, so necessary before, culminating in the abolition of the high places, which Hezekiah had failed to carry out successfully, had now been long delayed: the difficulty of effecting it must have become CHAP. II. proportionately greater; the flagrant indulgence in open idolatry, under the patronage of the court, had raised yet more serious obstacles in the path of religious restoration. In a single year 'the book of the law' caused the removal of every obstacle. The laws it contained must, many of them, have been familiar, by tradition, long usage, and written codes. But in this book, laws, old and new alike, lived in the spirit of Moses, and glowed with the vehemence of prophecy. The tone in which the law was here expounded to the people was something new. It marked the close of one era; it heralded the *Its opportuneness.* beginning of another. It rang sharp and clear in the lull that so graciously intervened before the tempest of Babylonian invasion. The enthusiasm it aroused in the young king communicated itself to the people. The discovery of 'the book of the law' procured at once the abolition of the high places. The book was recognised as a divine gift, and lifted, though but for a passing moment, the conception of the nation's religion above the routine of the priesthood's traditional worship.

In the authority and sanctity assigned, at this conjuncture, to a book, we recognise the beginnings of the Hebrew Canon. And we cannot but feel, that it was no mere chance, but the overruling of the Divine Wisdom, which thus made provision for the spiritual survival of His chosen people on the eve of their political annihilation.

The generation of Hilkiah had hardly passed away, *Its historic significance.* when the deportation of the citizens of Jerusalem and the destruction of the Temple seemed to threaten the extinction of pure worship. But Josiah's reign had seen the

CHAP. II. dawn of that love and reverence for Scripture, with which the true Israelite, whether Jew or Christian, was destined ever afterwards to be identified. The coincidence is instructive. The collapse of the material power of the house of Israel contained within it the seed of its spiritual revival in the possession of the indestructible Word of God.

CHAPTER III.

THE BEGINNINGS OF THE CANON (*continued*).

The Exile.

THE degree of veneration which 'the book of the
law' received from the people at large, can hardly at any
time have been very considerable before the exile. It
certainly was not of a lasting character. Josiah's reforms
were effected, so to speak, from above downward. They
did not emanate from the people, but from the king.
Outside the court and a few sincerely religious minds
among the prophets and the priests, there were probably
not many who, after the first shock of surprise, troubled
themselves about the ascendancy temporarily obtained
by 'the book of the law.' The half century of idolatrous
government by Manasseh and his son had unfitted the
nation for the moral effort of acknowledging the claim
and submitting to the restraint of any new spiritual
authority. The verdict of the historian of the Books
of Kings makes it sufficiently evident, that Josiah's sons
and successors did nothing to promote the spiritual interests of their people. Nor, indeed, could we expect
from their short, disturbed, and calamitous reigns any
further popular recognition of the sacred authority vested
in 'the law.' And yet its influence upon those whom it

CHAP. III.

'Book of the law': influence on individuals.

was most calculated to impress has left traces clear and unmistakable. Perhaps we should not quite be justified in saying that the influence of this book is alone responsible for the so-called Deuteronomic style, wherever it is to be found in the Old Testament. For the possibility must be admitted, that the style was but characteristic of a phase in Hebrew literature, and marked the particular colouring peculiar to the prophetical writing of the century.

Distinctive in style and in treatment of national questions. But, even so, we shall probably be right to connect the prevalence of Deuteronomic thought in later writings with the feelings of veneration excited by 'the book of the law.' The appearance of the peculiar style and phraseology of Deuteronomy denotes something more than the accidental resemblance of contemporary literature. It implies that the Deuteronomic treatment of the nation's history, for some reason, commended itself in an especial way to later writers, and that, for the same reason, the stamp of its religious thought was transferred to other literature. Clearly the standard of life and doctrine, reflected in 'the book of the law,' was adopted as the truest utterance of the Spirit of Jehovah. It is a noteworthy phenomenon in the history of Hebrew literature. Can we, however, doubt as to the reason? It was because, though on a small scale, the influence of the written Word, as the revelation of the Divine Will both for the people and for the individual, had for the first time made itself felt.

Of the influence, exerted upon religious thought by this first instalment of the Hebrew Canon of Scripture, we are able to form some judgment from writings which were either actually composed, or compiled and edited, in the century following upon the discovery of 'the

book of the law,' and were afterwards admitted into the CHAP. III.
Canon of Scripture.

The two most conspicuous examples are supplied by the prophecies of Jeremiah and the Books of Kings.

Jeremiah's call to the ministry of prophecy took place *Influence* five years before the discovery of ' the book of the law ' *upon Jeremiah.* (Jer. i. 2). He was one, probably, of a small but devoted number, who recognised in this book a pledge of spiritual hope, and joined himself heartily to the efforts of religious revival on the basis of the newly-discovered, prophetic, and popular formulation of the law.

Jeremiah is an author who places himself freely under obligations to other writers. In his extant prophecies he frequently makes allusions to incidents recorded in the Pentateuch, without, however, directly citing from materials incorporated in our Pentateuch. It is the more noticeable, therefore, that such quotations as he undoubtedly derives from the Pentateuch are all to be *Jer.'s quota-* found in Deuteronomy, e.g. :—iv. 4 from Deut. x. 16 *tions from Deut.* (xxx. 6); v. 15, 17 from Deut. xxviii. 31, 49; xi. 4 from Deut. iv. 20; xi. 8 from Deut. xxix. 14, 19. It will be remarked, that he does not introduce these quotations with the formula of citation from a sacred book. But this is perhaps not surprising in the early days of the recognition of a sacred book. The time had not yet come to rely upon the authority of a quotation. The prophet was still the living oracle.

Jeremiah's testimony, in certain other respects, is full *His recogni-* of importance. He refers not only to the existence of *tion of written law.* ' the law,' but to the danger of its being perverted by the recklessness or by the wilful malice of the scribes (ch. viii. 8): ' How do ye say, We are wise, and the law of the Lord is with us? But behold the false pen of the

CHAP. III. scribes hath wrought falsely.'   Here was a peril which was especially likely to arise, when but few copies of 'the law' existed, and when the authority of the written law was not fully recognised.   In another passage, the prophet rebukes the unscrupulousness of the priests, to whom was entrusted the duty of instructing the people from the law (ch. ii. 8): 'The priests said not, Where is the Lord? And they that handle the law knew me not'; and, possibly, he is there also referring to the sacred deposit of the written law.   But the abuses which he condemns, the perversion and falsification of the written text, belong to a time which as yet was as far as possible a stranger to the awe that was eventually to gather round the text of Canonical Scripture.   Zephaniah, a younger contemporary of Jeremiah, possibly calls attention to the same neglect of the newly-established written authority, when he complains of the priests, 'they have profaned the sanctuary, they have done violence to the law' (iii. 4).

His Deuter-onomic style. Jeremiah's own devotion to 'the law' stands in marked contrast to the indifference and faithlessness of the priests he denounces. A comparison of his Hebrew style with that of Deuteronomy has justified some scholars in the assertion, that the prophet must have elaborated his oratorical prose upon an imitation of that in the book of Deuteronomy. Whether this was actually the case or not, a comparative study of the style of the two books shows how the prophet must have steeped himself in 'the book of the law,' whose words and phrases he so frequently repeats, whose teaching he so persistently enforces.

Turning to the Books of Kings, we shall, of course, notice the use of the formula of citation in the passages to which attention has already been called (e. g. 1 Kings *Chap. III.* ii. 3, 2 Kings xiv. 6), from which, as well as from the *Books of* whole narrative in 2 Kings xxii, xxiii, we gather the *Kings.* compiler's attitude towards 'the book of the law.' In these historical books, no less than in the prophecies of Jeremiah, the impress of the Deuteronomic character- istics is everywhere observable. But, while its influence may most easily be discovered in the use of particular words and phrases, it is reproduced in a more subtle form by the whole conception of Israelite history and Israelite religion, presented in the narrative of the two kingdoms. The Books of Kings apply the Deuteronomic standard of judgment, that of the Covenant relations of the people with Jehovah, to the interpretation of history.

In other books of the exilic period we may notice the same influence at work. Thus, leaving out of the question the historical framework of the Deuteronomic laws which was possibly composed at or about this time, we have only to mention the distinctly Deuteronomic portions included in Joshua and Judges[1], and to point to traces of the same influence in the language of Isaiah II, Ezekiel, and Zephaniah.

But, in spite of the influence which it thus clearly *Sacred* exercised, the Deuteronomic law was still far from play- *writing* ing the part, which Canonical Scripture occupied in *less valued* later times. For this we may see two reasons. Firstly, *than Pro-* the living voice of the prophet was still heard, and took *phet's voice.* precedence in men's minds of any written oracle. The sixth cent. B.C. saw Jeremiah, Ezekiel, the writer of Isaiah II, Zechariah, and Haggai still labouring in the midst of their countrymen. The pious Jew who listened

[1] e. g. Jos. i, viii. 30–35, x. 28–43, xxii. 1–8, xxiii ; Jud. ii. 11–23, iii. 4–6, x. 6–18, &c.

to them, and who reverted in thought to the history of the
past, could hardly do otherwise than believe, that, so long
as the spirit of prophecy remained, in it, rather than in
any writing, would be conveyed the message of the Lord
to His people. By comparison with the force of living
utterance, the authority of written law would appear
weak. And this impression would be increased, when
a prophet, like Ezekiel, could formulate a new ideal
scheme of worship (xl–xlviii), differing in many respects
from that contained in the written tradition of the law.
Moreover, in numerous details, it was not easy, and
loss of confidence would be the price of failure, to
reconcile the enactments in 'the book of the law' with
the words of a yet older tradition, or to adapt them
to the changes in the outward circumstances of the
people consequent on the Captivity and the Return.

'The Book of the Law' insufficient. Secondly, a national Scripture, consisting only of the
Deuteronomic law, carried with it its own evidence of
insufficiency. The recognition of such a Canon could
not fail to be followed by a demand for its expansion
and enlargement. The Deuteronomic 'book of the law'
presupposed a knowledge of the older laws; it presupposed also a knowledge of the early history of the
Israelite race. The veneration in which the Deuteronomic formulation of the law was itself held, must have
added to the popular regard for those other documents,
without a knowledge of which so many of the allusions
in the Deuteronomic Scripture would have been un-
intelligible. Now the writings on which Deuteronomy
rests, both for historical facts (e.g. Deut. i. 9–17, cf. Ex.
xviii; Deut. ii. 26–32, cf. Num. xx, xxi) and for laws
(cf. Ex. xx–xxiii), are the Jehovist and Elohist narratives,
which, for some time before the beginning of the seventh

cent. B. C., had been united into a single composite
work.

In a century of great literary productiveness, of which we have a few extant examples in the prophecies of Jeremiah, of Ezekiel, of Isaiah II, of Obadiah, of Zechariah, and of Haggai, in the compilation of the Books of Kings, not to mention the possible composition, in the same era, of Job, Lamentations and certain Psalms, it was almost sure to happen, that the heightened veneration for the most ancient records would result in some endeavour to connect them with 'the book of the law' that was so dependent on them. We conjecture, therefore, that the Deuteronomic law having received its definitely historical setting (Deut. i–iv, xxxii–xxxiv), the Book of Joshua was added to it by the scribe, or redactor, who so freely edited the Jehovist-Elohist version of the Joshua narrative in the spirit of the Deuteronomic Scripture; and that then, or about the same time, a redaction of the whole Jehovist-Elohist compilation was prefixed to the Deuteronomic laws. Such a step may at first have been taken for private edification, or, conceivably, for convenience in public reading. In any case, it was a natural step. We need not go far to find the motives for it. Imagine the reverence with which the pious Jew, in his Babylonian exile, would regard the archives that recorded the beginnings of his nation and the foundation of his faith. He saw his people threatened with extinction in the land of their captivity; the ancient records told him that the founder of his race was summoned alone by the voice of God from this very land of the Chaldees, and preferred before all the princes of Babylonia. He saw the Jews lying helpless in the grasp of the mightiest empire in

Western Asia; the history described to him a deliverance, which was the very birthday of Israel's nationality, when they emerged from a condition of servitude under Pharaoh, more intolerable than ever Nebuchadnezzar had thought of imposing.

He saw in Babylon the most elaborate worship of heathen deities, Bel, Nebo, Merodach and a host of others, a worship performed with infinitely greater splendour than was probably ever witnessed at the Temple of Jerusalem, which now lay in ruins, and yet attended with depths of moral degradation that made Babylonian shamelessness a proverb. He read in the ancient records of his race, how Jehovah had manifested Himself to the Patriarchs, to Moses, and to the prophets, in purity and love as well as in power; and he realized something of that pure and simple spiritual revelation of Jehovah, which, through the teaching of the Prophets, had ever been lifting Israel up to higher and nobler conceptions of man and his Maker. These were thoughts which shed a new light upon the Divine purpose served by the nation's earliest writings; they revealed the possibility that the pen of the scribe would transmit the expression of Jehovah's Will in a more enduring form than even a prophet's voice.

Conjectured acceptance of joint narrative and law. The exact manner in which the Deuteronomic laws were thus revised, and the Jehovist-Elohist writings conjoined with them, will never be known. It was, as we have said, an age of literary activity. Annals were being collected, histories compiled, prophecies transcribed and edited, everything, in short, was being done to preserve the treasures of Hebrew literature and the memorials of Hebrew religion, which had been threatened with extinction in the national overthrow.

The addition of the Jehovist-Elohist writings to the Deuteronomic was but one instance of the collecting and compiling process that was going on. But the use of this larger literary work would not have commended itself all at once for general acceptance. For all we know, it may have had to compete with other similar compilations ; and have survived them on account of its intrinsic superiority.

Conceivably the institution of the Synagogue, or the germ of that institution, promoted the process of its reception into special favour. Exiles in a foreign land would there have gathered not only to hear the exhortations of the prophet, but to listen as some priest or Levite read aloud the traditions of the past, that recorded the former mercies of Jehovah and His everlasting purpose toward His chosen people.

But yet another process of compilation must have been *Compilation* going on, of which we only know that a commencement *of Priestly* was made at the beginning of the exilic period. This was *Laws during Exile.* the gathering together of the numerous groups of Priestly Laws. That the Priestly Laws existed in any one complete compilation before the time of the exile, so that they could be referred to, for literary purposes, as a code well known to the people at large, is hardly any longer possible to be maintained ; but that the customs and institutions, with which these laws are concerned, had most of them existed for centuries, and were provided for by appropriate regulations, is not denied.

The disasters of the exile doubtless stimulated devout priests to collect and group together laws and precedents, with which hitherto the priestly families had alone been thoroughly conversant. For, after the destruction of the Temple, the tradition both of the Temple ritual and of religious ceremonial generally was in peril of being forgotten. Desuetude was likely to be more fatal in its influence than wilful neglect.

Ezekiel and the Priestly Laws. It is in the writings of Ezekiel that we first find unmistakable signs of acquaintance with a collection of Priestly Laws that we can certainly identify. His language shows so close a resemblance to the Law of Holiness, that some scholars have even maintained that the prophet was the author of Lev. xvii–xxvi. That view is now generally rejected, but the resemblance is best explained on the supposition that the *collection* of 'the Laws of Holiness' had not long been formed when Ezekiel wrote. The individual laws themselves were, of course, most of them very much older than his time; but the prophet was not only, as a priest (Ezek. i, 3), accurately acquainted with their contents, he was also deeply penetrated with their spirit, he assimilated their distinctive phraseology, he adopted their special formulas. Jeremiah too was a priest (Jer. i. 1); but he was unaffected by 'the Law of Holiness.' The inference is obvious. In the land of the captivity the priests grouped together and formulated in writing the priestly regulations, to save them from being lost. Hence it is Ezekiel, who was one of the exiles ' in the land of the Chaldeans,'—and not Jeremiah who remained in Palestine,—that testifies to their existence. But though he was acquainted with 'the Law of Holiness' as a separate collection, it is unlikely that the other Priestly Laws, in their present form, were, in Ezekiel's time, finally codified. It is true his knowledge of their technical terms is undeniable; but this is only what we should expect from a priest well versed in the phraseology which had become traditional among the members of the priestly caste[1]. As compared with the mass of the Priestly Laws in the Pentateuch, the Priestly Laws sketched by Ezekiel (cf. xliii. 13–xlvi. 24) indicate a slightly earlier stage of ritual development. The arguments of critics, who, while acknowledging the antiquity of the institutions themselves, have pointed out signs of their being represented in a somewhat more ornate and developed form in the Priestly Laws of the Pentateuch than in Ezekiel, cannot well be resisted[2].

If so, we may regard the 'Law of Holiness' in its present literary form as a compilation of ancient ceremonial laws in conformity with the tradition at the beginning of the exile, and as illustrating the process by which the Priestly Laws generally were afterwards collected. The Book of Ezekiel shows with what freedom a prophet could handle the priestly tradition. It shows that he could not have regarded it as a fixed code admitting of no substantial alteration. Changes so complete as those which he contemplates in his Vision would bring with them changes in worship, and he has no compunction in propounding them.

The work of compiling the Priestly Laws was probably carried on at Babylon, which, as we know, was the scene of a vigorous literary activity among the Jews. At a time and place which witnessed the redaction of Judges, of Samuel, and of Kings, an analogous process applied to the Priestly Laws and to the version of the early narratives, which embodied the teaching and tradition of the priests, is only what we should expect. That this work had been completed, or

Priestly Laws, codified not published.

---

[1] Cf. Smend's *Ezekiel, Introd.* p. xxvii.
[2] See Driver, *Introd. Lit. O. T.* pp. 132, 133.

that, if completed, the Priestly Code had as yet been recognised as authoritative Scripture by the side of the Deuteronomic 'book of the law' when the Jews returned from exile, may well be doubted. On the face of it, we should expect that some interval would elapse between the process of compiling the laws of the priestly caste and the expression of a desire to unite them with writings which had been, perhaps, for a generation or more, the accepted means of popular religious instruction. It is, therefore, noteworthy that Zechariah in his prophecy makes no appeal to it; and that Haggai (ii. 11–12), when speaking of the priestly authority to decide on matters of cleanness, represents the priests delivering their sentence upon their own authority, not prefacing it, as the scribes of a later day would have done, by the formula, 'It is written.' The priests' authority was based, no doubt, on their Priestly Law, written or oral; but the prophet's words suggest that the requirements of the Priestly Law were not known to the nation generally, and existed in no other form than that of a private code in the hands of the priests themselves [1].

[1] The objection that Ezra iii. 2 seems to indicate acquaintance with the codified priestly law is only an apparent difficulty, and is not really *ad rem.* Critical analysis has clearly shown that the chapter in question does not come from the pen of Ezra, but from the chronicler (see my commentary on 'Ezra and Nehemiah,' *Introd.* § 4, in the 'Cambridge Bible for Schools,' Cambridge, 1893), who, writing in the third century B.C., everywhere assumes that the completed priestly code underlay the whole Israelite constitution from the earliest days of the monarchy. The passage cannot therefore be alleged as evidence dating from the period of the return, of which the narrative tells. It is only an instance of the chronicler's belief that the priestly worship of the Temple, with which he was himself acquainted, had never varied—a position which is now known to be untenable.

CHAPTER IV

THE COMPLETION OF THE FIRST CANON.

The Law.

THE Jews who returned from the exile (536 B.C.)
formed at Jerusalem a religious rather than a political
community. To them the first object to be achieved
was to restore the Temple worship and to rebuild the
House of God. For the achievement of that object, and
for that only, had Cyrus granted them his merciful
decree. (Ezr. i. 1–4.) A small number only of the
children of Israel returned to their own land. A century
later the nation had become a sect, their constitution
a Church, their 'law' a Bible.

During all the first years of privation and hardship
endured by this community, the only Scripture, recognised as such by the people, seems to have been the
Deuteronomic law. It was on the strength of this law
that Ezra took action against marriage with the 'strange
women' (Ezra ix. 1, 2, x. 3)[1]; and it is the teaching and
phraseology of Deuteronomy which colour the language
of Ezra's confession in Ezra ix. 6–15, and of Nehemiah's
prayer in Neh. i. 5–11. Undoubtedly an oral tradition of
priestly and ceremonial law was kept up by the priests

---

[1] Cf. Neh. xiii. 1–3 with Deut. xiv. 2, xxiii. 3–6.

CHAP. IV. who ministered at the restored Temple.   But either this had no close resemblance to the completed priestly code familiar to us in the Pentateuch ; or, if it had, it was most negligently and carelessly administered by the priests.   There is no escape from the alternative.   At least, this would appear from Neh. viii. 13–18, where

Neh. viii. 13-18. *The people ignorant of complete code of law.*

we learn, that until the people received instruction from Ezra they had been ignorant, or had been kept in ignorance, of the right way to celebrate the great Feast of Tabernacles.   Such a degree of ignorance on the part, not of the common people only, but of the heads of the great houses, and even of the priests and the Levites, would be to us incomprehensible, if we could suppose that the completed code of Priestly Laws had all along formed part of the sacred Canon of Scripture.   On the supposition, however, that the Priestly Laws had hitherto been mainly orally transmitted, and then perhaps only fragmentarily and too often negligently, the contrast between the defect of custom and the requirement of the letter becomes in some degree intelligible.   The Deuteronomic law (Deut. xvi. 13–17) had said nothing of the celebration of the Feast of Tabernacles by dwelling in booths.   The construction of booths is required, in the precepts of the Priestly Law, as a distinctive symbolic feature of the feast.   Until Ezra made it known, the requirement had not been observed.   Was it that the custom had been forgotten by the people?   If so, the Priests had either neglected to teach the people the Law, or they had failed to preserve the tradition of the Law faithfully.   The conclusion is almost certain, with this striking example before our eyes, that the full Priestly Law could not have been, at least popularly, known in Jerusalem before the year 444 B. C.

It will be remembered that we have already regarded it as probable that the compilation of the Priestly Laws had gradually taken place among the Jews in Babylon, and that with them there had also been combined the great Jehovist and Elohist narrative and the Deuteronomic writings.   The possession of the combined work would acquaint those who studied it with a complete scheme of Israelite worship and ceremonial based upon the tradition derived from earliest times.   Whether or no *Its posses-* such a tradition occasionally contradicted itself on certain *sion a new source of* details, was immaterial, so long as whatsoever was pro- *power.* nounced to be ancient, and whatsoever of sacred custom, was faithfully committed to writing.   It is clear that such a work would place any careful student, who took the trouble to master its contents, upon a footing of equality with, and even of superiority to, priests who only relied upon the memory of individual families, upon local tradition, and upon personal usage.   He would be possessed, in a compact form, of all that a single priestly memory could retain, and, in addition, of all that survived of cognate interest, to be derived from other sources.   The minute study of the priestly as well as of the other national laws would thus enable any devout Jew, ardent for religious reform, to occupy an unassailable position both in rallying the people to a standard of purer worship, and in combating any tendency to negligence or unfaithfulness arising from the ignorance or worldliness of the priesthood.   But, before arraigning the priesthood, the reformer would have to assure himself of the sympathy of the people.   Until he could gain a hearing, it would be labour lost to invoke the national enthusiasm for the stricter observance of the ancient laws.

Ezra the scribe, as we are told, 'went up from Babylon, and he was a ready scribe in the law of Moses' (Ezra vii. 6). He was 'the scribe of the words of the commandments of the Lord, and of his statutes to Israel' (Ezra vii. 11). The law of his God was in his hand (Ezra vii. 14).

On the strength of the words just quoted, Hebrew legend of later time told how Ezra was inspired to dictate from memory all the twenty-four books of the Hebrew Canon of Scripture, that had been destroyed by the Chaldeans at the destruction of Jerusalem (4 Esdras xiv. 39–48). On the strength of the same words, it has been suggested in modern times, that Ezra himself was the author of the Priestly Laws, which, with the help of Nehemiah, he succeeded in imposing upon the Jews of Jerusalem. For the Jewish legend there is, as we shall see, no foundation in historical fact[1]. There is scarcely more solid foundation for the other wild specula-

Ezra not the writer of the Priestly Laws.

tion. The extant portions of Ezra's own memoirs (Ezra viii–x) show no resemblance whatever to the characteristic style of the Priestly Laws. The latter, as we have already pointed out, consist of various groups of regulations, which, dealing, as a rule, with different subjects, every now and then reintroduce topics that have already been handled; and, in such cases, the obvious variations, not to say contradictions, between one passage and another, cannot be reconciled with any theory of unity of date or unity of authorship (e. g. Num. iv. 3, &c. with Num. viii. 23–26; Lev. iv. 13–21 with Num. xv. 22–26). It has, indeed, been objected that the sameness of the style that runs through the Priestly Laws, coupled with the occurrence of late forms of Hebrew,

[1] See Excursus A.

might be regarded as an argument in favour of the view that a single writer, if not Ezra himself, at least one who was of Ezra's period, should be credited with their composition. But the general sameness of style is a characteristic that arises not so much from unity of authorship as from the continuous use of technical language relating to a special class of subjects. As to the occurrence of late Hebrew forms, their presence must be admitted, though not in the degree claimed for them (e. g. by Giesebrecht, Z. A. T. W., 1881, 177–276). They are to be regarded as evidence of the date at which the work of compilation was performed ; they are fatal to the maintenance of the antiquity, not of the laws, but of their medium, the vocabulary, by which they have been transmitted to us.

It appears to me quite useless to attempt to ascribe to any one man this work of compilation and redaction. Such a process would have been long and gradual. It had probably been going on continuously ever since the beginning of the exile. Whether, therefore, Ezra, 150 years later, had any direct share in the work, is a question upon which it would be vain to speculate. He was a scribe ; and, so far, it is just possible he may have been directly connected with the last phases of the process. So much, or rather so little, can be granted of the alleged connexion of Ezra with the formation of the Canon of Scripture.

With the history of its acceptance, however, his direct connexion is proved by unequivocal testimony. The completed compilation, which had been executed by the scribes of Babylon, had not found its way to Jerusalem before the arrival of Ezra (457 B. C.). The possibility suggests itself, that Ezra's mission to Jerusalem

Possibly their pro- mulgator in Jerusalem.

was undertaken for the purpose of promulgating the completed Book of the Law, and, at the same time of establishing the religion of Jehovah, once for all, upon a footing of publicity and of immutability from which it could not be dislodged by any unscrupulousness, treachery, or neglect on the part of the priesthood. From the Memoirs of Ezra and Nehemiah it is evident that an influential section of the priests was not to be trusted.

We are told that Ezra started upon his journey to Jerusalem having as his object in life, ' To seek the law of the LORD and to do it, and to teach in Israel statutes and judgments' (Ezra vii. 10). For upwards of thirteen years he apparently made no attempt to publish to the people the Book of the Law. No sooner, however, did Nehemiah arrive, as governor, than Ezra took steps to make it known. We are left to conjecture the motive for his delay. Was it due to the opposition that his first measure of reform encountered (Ezra ix, x)? or was he content quietly to devote himself to the task of completely mastering the details of the Law, before venturing to promulgate it, resolved deliberately to wait, until the opportunity of popular enthusiasm, joined with the certainty of official support, should absolutely assure him of success?

Neh. viii-x.
*Ezra and
the Law.*
The account of the occasion, on which he made known to the people the contents of the completed ' Law,' is narrated in a document written by one who was almost, if he was not actually, a contemporary of the event. The Chronicler has inserted the description in the middle of the Memoirs of Nehemiah (Neh. viii-x). Into the various questions, relating to that scene and its narrative, this is not the place to enter with any minuteness. So much, however, is quite clear: (1) that the Book of the

Law, introduced by Ezra, and publicly read by him and the Levites before the Temple and in the presence of the assembled people, was to the mass of his countrymen a new book; (2) that the fulfilment of its requirements apparently caused alterations in usage, which—and it can hardly be an accidental coincidence—correspond with variations that, in a comparison between the Deuteronomic and the Priestly Laws, are distinctive of the latter and, we believe, the more recently formulated code (e.g. observance of Tabernacles, Deut. xvi. 13–17, Num. xxix. 12–38; payment of tithe, Deut. xiv. 22–29, Num. xviii. 21–32)[1]; (3) that, in the promulgation of this book, the Levites were more conspicuously associated with Ezra than the priests; (4) that, from henceforward, the requirements of the Priestly Laws are unquestionably complied with in the events recorded by the historian and by Nehemiah, and are presupposed in all Jewish literature later than the time of Ezra.

The following brief explanation, it is hoped, will suffice to make the circumstances clear. Assured of the favour and active support of Nehemiah, Ezra published to the people the law which was ' in his hand.' It consisted, as we suppose, of the final expansion of the people's Book of the Law; with Deuteronomist law and Jehovist-Elohist narrative had now been combined the Priestly Narrative and the Priestly Laws. The publication of the work heralded a radical change in the religious life of the people. The People's Book was no longer to be confined to the prophetic re-formulation of laws, which had once so deeply aroused Jewish thought and influenced Jewish literature. The priesthood was no longer alone to possess the key of knowledge as to the clean and the un-

[1] Cf. Neh. viii. 14–17; x. 32, 38.

G

CHAP. IV. clean, the true worship and the false (cf. Ezek. xliv. 23, 24). Their hereditary monopoly was to be done away. The instruction of the people was to pass from the priest to the scribe. Not what 'the law' was, but what its meaning was, was henceforth to call for authoritative explanation. The Law itself was to be in the hands of the people.

A Crisis.
The conjuncture was a critical one for the history of Judaism. There was a sharp division between the High Priest's party and the supporters of Ezra. The records of Ezra and Nehemiah leave us in no practical doubt on the point. The priests were foremost in supporting a policy of free intercourse with the heathen, of fraternizing, for the sake of material advantages, with the leaders of the Samaritans (cf. Ezra ix. 1, 2, x. 18–22, Neh. vi. 10–14, xiii. 4–14, 28). The opposition of Ezra and the energetic action of Nehemiah averted the evil effects of this policy. But it is probable that, if the patriotic enthusiasm of the people had not been awakened by Nehemiah's successful restoration of the walls, Ezra and his colleagues would not have been strong enough, in the face of the priests, to establish upon a firm footing the public recognition of a larger Canon of Scripture. The far-reaching effect of their action may not then have been so obvious as the immediate advantage to be obtained. The immediate advantage was, that a knowledge of the Priestly Law was placed within the reach of every Jew, and that a fatal barrier was thus raised against any attempt at fusion with the stranger and the Samaritan[1]. The far-reaching effect was that a standard of holy and unholy, right and wrong, clean and unclean, was delivered to the Jews as a people, so that all Jews,

[1] From this time forward intrigues for combination with the Samaritans cease, and the Samaritans become a rival religious community.

whether of the Dispersion or in Judea, whether in Babylon CHAP. IV.
or in Alexandria or within the walls of Jerusalem, could
equally know the will of the Lord, and equally interpret
the difficulties of moral and social life by appeal to the
'Torah,' to the verdict, not given by the mouth of the
priest or the prophet, but obtained by search into the
letter of 'the Law.'

In effecting this change, Ezra, and Nehemiah gave *Priestly*
its final shape to the religious legalism of their people. *opposition.*
As to the priests, while it is probable that some, for
popularity's sake, refused, and others who favoured the
cause of Ezra did not wish, to stand aside on the
occasion of the popular acknowledgment of the Covenant,
which was ratified on the basis of the publication of this
'law' (Neh. ix. 38, x. 2–8), their attitude as a body cannot be regarded as having been warmly sympathetic.
The absence of Eliashib's name among 'those that
sealed' (Neh. x. 1, 2) has naturally, but perhaps unneces-
sarily, excited attention; it may be that his name is
included in that of Seraiah, the name of his 'father's
house': but, even so, the evident hostility which Nehemiah experienced at the hands of the High Priest's
family (Neh. xiii), coupled with the greater prominence
of the Levites in viii. 4, 7, 9, ix. 4, 38, makes it probable,
that the policy of Ezra and his colleagues was far from
having the support of the aristocratic and priestly caste.
But, in spite of all obstacles, their policy triumphed. It
was never reversed. Judaism took its rise from their
policy, that of national submission to the yoke of 'the
Law.'

That 'the Law,' thus acknowledged by the people as *Ezra's Book*
sacred and accepted as binding, was substantially the *of The Law*
our
same as our Pentateuch, is generally admitted. With *Pentateuch.*

CHAP. IV. the exception of a few possible later insertions, and of certain minor alterations, due to an occasional revision of the text, 'the Torah' has probably descended to us very little changed.

Its position, at first, undefined. Naturally the full significance and value of such a 'Canon' of Scripture would not at first be understood: Its influence would only be very gradually obtained. None could have foreseen its future absolute sway. Long habit had accustomed the priesthood to adapt the details of their regulations so as to meet the changing circumstances of their day. It was not likely that this elasticity of administration, with all the opportunities which it permitted of relieving burdens and advancing interests, would all at once be surrendered. For some time at least after the authority of 'the Law' had been accepted, divergencies in detail would be openly permitted or tacitly practised, without any thought of dishonouring the sacred Book, so long as the great principles of the legislation were safeguarded. It has been suggested that such variations in practice sometimes led to interpolations being made in the Priestly Laws, and that certain difficulties presented by different accounts of (*a*) the burnt-offering, (*b*) the Temple-tribute, (*c*) the tithe, (*d*) the age of Levitical service, as well as by the text of Exodus (xxxv-xl), are only intelligible on the supposition, that a long time elapsed before the sanctity of Scripture effected uniformity of practice, or protected the purity of the text of Scripture.

Possible later insertions.
(a) Continual burnt-offering. (*a*) The law of burnt-offering in Lev. vi. 8–13, which in language and style is apparently the most ancient extant, does not contain any enactment for an evening burnt-offering. In the history of the Monarchy we have mention of an evening meal-offering (cf. 2 Kings xvi. 15),

but not of an evening burnt-offering.   Now in the
apparently later Priestly law of Ex. xxix. 38–42, Num.
xxviii. 1–8, we find both a morning and an evening
burnt-offering commanded; and reference to a double
daily burnt-offering distinctly occurs in Neh. x. 33 and
Chronicles (e. g. 2 Chron. xxxi. 3).   The view, that the
laws of Ex. xxix. 38–42, Num. xxviii. 1–8 were inserted
after that codification of the Priestly Laws, to which Lev.
vi. 8–13 belongs, offers a solution which should not be
hastily set aside.   The same variation is patent, both in
the laws and in the narratives.   Either then the mention of 'the continual burnt-offering' in Neh. x. 33 refers
to a new practice, which was afterwards expressed in
the law of Ex. xxix, Num. xxviii. by a later insertion,
or the law in Lev. vi, supported by 2 Kings xvi, contains but a partial and incomplete statement.   Whether
we see a variety in custom in the one case, or an incomplete description in the other, we must admit that
changes in practice, real or implied, could easily arise.

(*b*) In Ex. xxx. 11–16 a poll-tax of half a shekel is
commanded in every year that a census was taken of the
Israelite populace.   From this irregular payment an
annual Temple-tax would of course differ considerably.
But it has naturally called for remark, that in Neh. x. 32
the annual Temple-tax is assessed at one-third shekel a
head, while in later times the Temple tribute-money was
half a shekel (Matt. xvii. 24), a sum obviously based
on Ex. xxx. 11–16.   Either, therefore, the one-third
shekel marked the prevailing poverty of Nehemiah's
time, or the sum mentioned in Ex. xxx. 11–16, agreeing
with later custom, marks an alteration in the Priestly
Law made after Nehemiah's time, substituting $\frac{1}{2}$ shekel
for $\frac{1}{3}$.   In either case, freedom of action, in reference to

*(b) ½ shekel
Temple-tax:*

CHAP. IV. important details contained in the law, would be illustrated by this instance.

(c) *Tithe of cattle:* (c) A yet more remarkable example is furnished by the Priestly Law of tithe. There can be very little doubt that in the earlier Deuteronomic law (Deut. xiv. 22–29) and in the regulations laid down by Nehemiah (Neh. x. 35–39, xii. 44, xiii. 5), the tithe was only supposed to have reference to the produce of the field, and consisted mainly of corn, wine, and oil.

But in the Priestly Law of tithe in Lev. xxvii. 30–33, 'the law of the tithe of the field' (vv. 30, 31) is followed by 'the law of the tithe of the herd and the flock' (vv. 32, 33). The only support for this enormous addition to the burden, laid upon the people for the maintenance of the priests and Levites, is found in the narrative of the Chronicles (2 Chron. xxxi. 6); where, however, the mention of the tithe of oxen and sheep reads suspiciously like a later gloss[1].

The difficulty is not one that admits of full discussion here. But clearly, if the tithe of cattle was a custom known in Nehemiah's time, it was not exacted; and if it was not known then, it either had dropped altogether out of usage, or it had never yet been introduced. Whether, then, it was originally in the Priestly Law and had become obsolete, or is a late interpolation, later than Nehemiah's time, we have, in this case also, proof that scruples concerning the text of Scripture did not for some considerable time arise in sufficient force to secure

---

[1] 2 Chron. xxxi. 5, 'And as soon as the commandment came abroad, the children of Israel gave in abundance the firstfruits of corn, wine, and oil, and honey, and of all the increase of the field; and the tithe of all things brought they in abundantly.' Ver. 6, 'And the children of Israel and Judah, that dwelt in the cities of Judah, they also brought in the tithe of oxen and sheep, and the tithe of consecrated things,' &c.

for it immunity from interpolation or rigid uniformity in
the observance of the letter.

(*d*) A well-known illustration of the composite nature
of the Levitical Law is presented by the requirements
for the age at which a Levite could enter upon his work
of ministration.   In Num. iv. 3, &c. the age of service is
reckoned as from thirty to fifty, but in Num. viii. 24 it
is reckoned as from twenty-five to fifty.   In Ezr. iii. 8,
and in 1 Chron. xxiii. 24–27, however, the active service
of the Levites is stated by the Chronicler as commencing
at the age of twenty.   Whether or no it is the case that
this reduction in the age arose in post-exilic times from
the difficulty of obtaining the service of any Levites at all
(cf. Ezra viii. 15), it exemplifies the freedom with which
even in the Chronicler's time (circ. 250 B.C.) variations
from the law were considered unimportant in matters of
detail.

(*e*) The strangest and most difficult problem, arising
from the freedom with which the Torah, in spite of its
sanctity, was treated in early times, is presented by the
condition of the text throughout a long section of
Exodus (xxxv–xl).   This passage, which repeats almost
word for word the substance of a previous section
(xxv–xxxi), differs considerably in the Greek text from
the Hebrew both by variety of order and by omission of
verses.   Now the LXX version of the Pentateuch was
probably composed in the third century B.C., and is the
most carefully executed portion of the Greek Bible.
How then did these variations arise?   The answer is not
apparent.   But the inference is certainly permissible,
that some time must have elapsed before the veneration
of the law effectually prevented alterations or minor
efforts at textual revision.

If occasional revision of old, no introduction of new subjects of legislation permitted: e.g. wood-offerings, Neh. x. 34.

On the other hand, the temptation to introduce fresh regulations, dealing with new subjects, seems on the whole to have been successfully resisted. A signal instance of this is afforded by the mention of the regulations for wood-offerings. Wood-offerings must, at all times, have formed an important contribution to the sanctuary; and, probably, in consequence of the wholesale destruction of wood by the Chaldeans at the siege of Jerusalem, wood had become, in Nehemiah's time, exceedingly scarce and proportionately expensive. The charge of providing the needful supply of wood, for the sacrifices of the Temple, was distributed among the leading families, who took it in turn, the rotation being decided by lot, to furnish as much as was required (Neh. x. 34). From Nehemiah's own words it is clear that that energetic governor regarded the establishment of this rule as one of the most important reforms he had been enabled to carry out (Neh. xiii. 31). It deserves notice, therefore, that, while, in Neh. x. 34, the rule itself is described by the formula, 'As it is written in the law,' no such law is to be found in the Pentateuch. The reference of the formula can hardly be limited to the mention of the law of the burnt-offering (Lev. vi. 8–13); for the reference to the burnt-offering in Neh. x. 34 is perfectly general in terms. It is more probable that, inasmuch as the regulation dealt with a subject unprovided for in existing statutes, it was decided that the introduction of such a novelty into the Law should be avoided.

Tendency towards uniform text.

Whatever freedom of treatment the Canon of 'the Law' received at first, there can be no doubt, that so soon as the Priestly Laws became public property they began to lose elasticity. It was only a matter of time. Once regarded as universal in application, they would soon

become stereotyped in form. The scribe's task of transcribing the letter and of explaining its application to
the daily affairs of life, was necessarily based on the
uniformity of the text. The multiplication of copies,
which would result from the law becoming a people's
book and ceasing to be a priest's book, soon raised a
barrier against any extensive change. The public reading of the law which seems to have been continued from
the great example of Ezra (Neh. viii) was a distinctive
feature of Synagogue worship ; and liturgical use, while
it added sanctity to the books, made it the more necessary
that copies of the book should not vary in their
contents.

That this first Hebrew Canon of Scripture consisted *First Hebrew Canon Pentateuch.*
of the Pentateuch, and of the Pentateuch only, if nowhere
directly affirmed, is implied by all the converging in-
direct evidence of which we can make use.

(*a*) It is implied, by the fact, that, from the earliest *'Torah,' (a) Always distinct group.*
time at which mention is made of the Hebrew Canon,
the Torah is mentioned separately as a distinct group
from 'the Prophets and the other writings' (cf. *Prologue
to Ecclesiasticus*).

(*b*) It is implied by the exceptional reverence paid to *(b) Object of Peculiar reverence in post-exilic Scripture.*
the Law of Moses in the post-exilic writings of the Old
Testament. The compiler of the Chronicles and of Ezra
and Nehemiah assumes the authority of the law in its
finished form throughout all the centuries of the history
which he narrates. The prophet Malachi (iv. 4) appeals
to the Law of Moses as the accredited standard of doctrine for all Israel. In the Book of the Psalms, though
it is true we have comparatively little reference to the
details of ceremonial, the veneration for the Law, expressed by the writer of such a late Psalm as Psalm cxix,

shows how unique was the influence of the Jewish Law, the earthly emblem of the Psalmist's ideal. It is only in the Book of Daniel (ix. 2), a book which, in its present literary form, was probably not composed until the second century B.C., that we first find any mention of other writings beside the Law, to which appeal could, be made as an authoritative standard.

(c) *In later*
Jewish
literature.   (*c*) It is implied in the special deference accorded to the Pentateuch by Jews of later time, in comparison with that which they paid to their other Scriptures. It is the Torah which is the subject of the son of Sirach's eulogy in Ecclus. xxii. 23; and it is the Torah, as the mainstay of Judaism, that Antiochus labours to destroy (1 Macc. i. 57). It is the translation of the Pentateuch into Greek which was not only the first instalment of the Septuagint version, but also, if we may judge from the rendering and the style, the only portion of the version which was carried out upon some definite plan, or executed with something of the accuracy and care that would be demanded for an authoritative edition. We may surely suppose, that, if at the time when the Torah was translated into Greek, it constituted the whole Scriptures of the Jews, one authoritative Greek version would have been prepared for public use in the Synagogues. The unequal and often very defective translation of the other books shows that the work, in their case, is the result of private and independent literary enterprise. It is reasonable to regard this as a proof that the sacred authority of the Prophets and Writings was not for some time recognised, not indeed until their translation had become established by common use among Greek-speaking Jews. Similarly, it is to the Pentateuch far more than to any other portion of the Hebrew Scrip-

tures, that Philo, the great representative of Alexandrine
Judaism, ascribes the highest gift of divine inspiration.

CHAP. IV.

(*d*) It is implied by the fact, that from the Torah, and
from the Torah alone, for some considerable time at least,
lessons were systematically read in the public services of
the Synagogue. It was not till a later time, as we shall see,
that lessons were added from the Books of the Prophets;
and in their case it does not appear certain, that any
systematic division into lessons was adopted until after
the Christian era (Luke iv. 17). Even in later days the
Lesson from the Prophets consisted merely of an extract,
intended to supplement and illustrate that from the
Torah. The Prophets were never read continuously
through, like the Law. The earlier use and the earlier
liturgical division of 'the Law' suggest its earlier recognition as Scripture.

*(d) In Syna-
gogue ser-
vice.*

(*e*) It is implied by the fact, that the title of 'the Law'
was long afterwards used to designate the whole Hebrew
Canon of Scripture, partly as a reminiscence of earlier
usage, partly as a tribute to the higher esteem in which the
Law was held. Cf. John x. 34, xii. 34, xv. 25, 1 Cor. xiv. 21.

*(e) Title of
Scripture,
Law.*

One piece of evidence of a yet more direct character
is offered by the Samaritan version of the Pentateuch.
The Canon of Scripture recognised by the Samaritan
community, even down to the present day, consists of
the Pentateuch alone. It has been very generally and
very naturally supposed, that the Samaritan community
obtained their Torah, which, save in a certain number of
comparatively unimportant readings, is identical with the
Jewish Torah, from the renegade Jewish priest, of the
name, according to Josephus, of Manasseh, who instituted
on Mount Gerizim a rival temple worship to that on
Mount Moriah (*Jos. Ant.* xi. 7 and 8). Josephus has

*Direct
Evidence of
Samaritan
Pentateuch.*

CHAP. IV.   placed this event in the days of Alexander the Great;
but here he is probably a victim of the strangely erroneous views of chronology, which the Jews of his own
and of later times have commonly entertained respecting
their nation's history in the interval between the Return
from the exile and the victories of Alexander. But as
Nehemiah makes no mention of the building of the
Temple on Mount Gerizim, it is very possible that that
event was considerably later than the expulsion of the
High Priest's grandson, and that Josephus' chronology
may be correct so far as regards the date of the erection
of the rival Samaritan shrine. We need have little
hesitation in connecting Josephus' account with the
ejection by Nehemiah of the grandson of the high
priest, Eliashib, who had married the daughter of
Sanballat, and had thus disgraced the family of the
high priest (Neh. xiii. 28). The latter event happened
almost exactly a century before the age of Alexander's
victories. It is hardly likely that two events, so similar
in character and yet so near in point of time, narrated
the one by Nehemiah and the other by Josephus, should
be unconnected with one another. We may safely
assume that the events are the same, and that the grandson of Eliashib is the renegade priest, Manasseh. When
this priest, at the head probably of a disaffected Jewish
faction, joined the Samaritan community and established
an exact reproduction of Jewish worship, he, or subsequent followers, may be presumed to have carried with
them the Scriptures that regulated the Temple worship
and were read in the services of the Synagogue. Now,
if the Canonical Scripture of the time consisted of the
Torah alone, we have here an explanation of the fact
that the Torah alone was adopted by the Samaritans

to be their Scripture. They adopted that which the schismatic Jews brought with them. The Scriptures, whose authority was recognised by the Jews *after* the occurrence of the schism, never found a place in the Samaritan Canon. Of course, it may fairly be contended, that the Samaritans would not be likely to adopt into their Canon any books that might appear to glorify the Temple at Jerusalem. But there were books against which they could take no such exception, as, for instance, the Book of Judges, which dealt especially with the heroic deeds performed in the northern tribes, or the Book of the prophet Hosea, who was an Ephraimite. If these had already been accepted as Canonical at Jerusalem, the Samaritans would have had no reason for excluding them at the time when they admitted the Torah of the Jews. Had they once accepted into their Canon any other books beside the Torah, the scrupulous conservatism in religious matters, which has always distinguished the Samaritan community, could not have failed to preserve either a text of the books themselves or the tradition of their usage. The limitation, therefore, of the Samaritan Canon to the Torah affords presumptive evidence that, at the time when the Samaritan worship was instituted, or when it received its final shape from the accession of Jewish malcontents, the Canon of the Jews at Jerusalem consisted of the Torah only.

The expulsion of Eliashib's grandson took place about *'The Law'* the year 432 B.C. Approximately, therefore, in this date *first Hebrew Canon of* we have a *terminus ad quem* for the conclusion of the first *Scripture before 432* Hebrew Canon of the Scripture. Before that year, its *B.C.* limits had already been practically, if not officially, determined. At that time, no other writing was regarded by the Jews as sacred and authoritative. This was the

beginning of the era of the Sopherim or Scribes. Under
their influence Jewish religion received the legalistic
character which ever afterwards clung to it. The power
of the prophets had passed into the hands of the scribes.
The religion of Israel had now become, and was destined
henceforth to remain, the religion of a book; and the
nucleus of that book was the Torah.

Appendix to Chapter IV.

It is necessary here to append a few remarks upon the Samaritan Version of the Pentateuch, the importance of which, in the history of the Hebrew Scriptures, will be apparent to every thoughtful student. Important, however, as the subject is, it will be felt to belong more properly to the province either of an inquiry into the history of the Hebrew text, or of an investigation into the history of the Hebrew characters. But in recent years the evidence of the Samaritan Pentateuch has been loudly proclaimed to be the rock upon which the modern criticism of the Pentateuch must inevitably make shipwreck. Under these circumstances an apology is hardly needed for briefly touching upon the subject.

The Samaritan Pentateuch, as is well known, has been *The old Hebrew characters of the Samaritan Version.* preserved to us in the old Hebrew, or, as some prefer to say, in the Canaanite, characters, and not in the square Hebrew, or Aramaean, characters, which are so familiar to us. Upon this interesting fact of the preservation of the old Hebrew characters in the Samaritan Pentateuch, attention has been concentrated. It is this fact which in some quarters is alleged to furnish a conclusive proof that the Pentateuch, practically in its present form, existed before the Exile. The Jews, it is said, changed their method of writing from the old style to the new while they were still in Babylon; and, accordingly, the Samaritan Pentateuch, which is written in the characters of the old style, must, it is alleged, at least have been copied from pre-exilic exemplars, written in the old characters, and may even have been derived from Israelite copies, which had survived the overthrow of the Northern Kingdom in the year 721 B.C.

Everything, according to this contention, turns upon the accuracy of the principal assertion, that the Jews changed their style of writing while they were in exile. The evidence upon which it rests consists of a legend which ascribes to Ezra the merit of devising the square Hebrew characters. We meet with this legend in the *Talmud.* Talmud: 'R. Jose said, Ezra was worthy that the Torah should have been given by his hand; but although it was not revealed through him, the characters in which it was written were altered by him[1].' But apparently the earliest mention of it in literature is to be found in the *Origen.* writings of the Fathers. Origen records the Jewish belief that Ezra, during the Exile, had committed to the Jews a different alphabet from that which had previously *Eusebius.* been in use[2]. Eusebius (if indeed it is not Jerome who inserts the statement in his translation) mentions the current belief that Ezra gave the Jews their Scriptures *Jerome.* written in a new style of writing[3]. Jerome goes into

---

[1] Jer. Meg. i. 10; b. Sanh. 21 b, quoted in Hambürger's *Real Encyklopädie*, Bd. 2, p. 1212.

[2] Origen, *Selecta in Pss.* ii. 1, 2; ii. 539, Φασὶ γὰρ τὸν Ἔσδραν ἐν τῇ αἰχμαλωσίᾳ ἑτέρους αὐτοῖς χαρακτῆρας παρὰ τοὺς προτέρους παραδεδωκέναι (ed. Lommatzsch, tom. xi. 396 f.).

[3] Euseb. *Chronicon*, Lib. i. § 5, 'Is (Esdras) enim fertur cunctas a Deo dictas Scripturas in mentem sibi revocasse, easque Judaeis tradidisse novis Hebraicarum literarum formis expressas.'

greater detail: 'The Samaritans,' he says, 'moreover *Chap. IV.* *App.* transcribe the Pentateuch of Moses exactly letter for letter; they differ only in the shapes and minor details of the characters.   And it is certain that, after the capture of Jerusalem and the restoration of the Temple under Zerubbabel, Ezra, the scribe and teacher of the law, devised these other letters which we now use.   For right up to that time the same characters had been employed by the Samaritans and the Jews[1].'   Epiphanius writes *Epipha-* *nius.* to very much the same effect: 'When Ezra went up from Babylon, his desire was to separate Israel from the rest of the nations, in order that the stock of Abraham might not appear to be mingled with those dwellers in the land (='*am haareç*) who hold the Law but who do not (accept) the Prophets (i.e. the Samaritans).   He therefore completely changed the old style of writing, giving up the pointed character, because the use of that style had already been adopted by the Samaritans[2].'

The unhistorical character of the legend is recognis- *Legend un-* *historical.* able upon its very surface.   Not a trace of it is found in the Canonical Scriptures, in the Apocrypha, or in the writings of Josephus.   Its first appearance in literature is six centuries after the period of Ezra; and Jewish legend was notoriously active with the name of Ezra, to whom it promiscuously ascribed any event or institution

[1] Jerome, *Prologus Galeatus*, 'Samaritani etiam Pentateuchum Moysi totidem literis scriptitant, figuris tantum et apicibus discrepantes.   Certumque est Ezram Scribam legisque doctorem post capta Hierosolyma et instaurationem templi sub Zorobabel alias literas reperisse quibus nunc utimur, cum ad illud usque tempus iidem Samaritanorum et Hebraeorum characteres fuerint.'

[2] Epiphanius, *De xii Gemmis* (Versio Antiqua, tom. iii. 255; ed. Migne, iii. pp. 358, 359): 'Hesdra ascendens a Babylone, volensque discernere Israel a reliquis gentibus, ut genus Habrahae non videretur esse permixtum cum

connected with the interval between the return from the
Captivity and the victories of Alexander.   In assigning
Ezra to the period of the Captivity and the generation
of Zerubbabel, the legend betrays the untrustworthy
character, and shares the chronological confusion of
late Jewish tradition respecting post-exilic events.   The
intrinsic improbability of the story that Ezra should
have originated an alphabet in order to separate his
countrymen from the Samaritans is sufficient to condemn
it.   That at a period when the literature of the Jews
enjoyed a well-established position and inherited the
treasured productions of former centuries written in the
old characters, any one individual should have succeeded
in abolishing the old alphabet and in imposing upon his
people another, for the purpose of accentuating a racial
hostility, will appear to every reasoning mind to the last
degree improbable.

But, indeed, there is scarcely need to consider the
story seriously.   A short review of the history of Hebrew
writing will at once show the real character of the legend,
and dispose of the popular assumption which has arisen
out of it.   An element of truth will, in this as in other
similar cases, be found to lurk in a seemingly unlikely
legend ; and to this we shall call attention after review-
ing the testimony supplied by our existing knowledge of
the history of Hebrew writing.

habitatoribus terrae, qui tenent quidem legem, non tamen et prophetas,
immutavit pristinam formam relinquens *deessenon* (= כתוב רעץ, read sometimes in Jewish authorities כתוב רעץ), propter quod ea forma a Samari-
tanis praeoccupata jam fuerat.'   The fancifulness of the legends respecting
Ezra and the Samaritans may be illustrated from another passage in
Epiphanius *Advers. Haereses*, Lib. i. tom. i, *Haeres.* vii ; i. 23 : Ἐπαίδευε
τοίνυν Ἔσδρας καὶ οἱ μετ' αὐτοῦ τὸ γένος τὸ ἐν τῇ Σαμαρείᾳ, καὶ ἐκλήθησαν
Σαμαρεῖται οἱ τὸν νόμον διὰ τοῦ Ἔσδρα τοῦ ἀπὸ Βαβυλῶνος ἥκοντος διαδεξά-
μενοι.   Διῆλθε δὲ χρόνος ἐτῶν τεσσαράκοντα ἄλλων, καὶ ἡ αἰχμαλωσία ἀνείθη.

The old Hebrew, or Canaanite, character of Israelite writing has been preserved to us from the age of Hezekiah (circ. 700 B. C.) in the Siloam inscription, in which the letters have a general resemblance to the characters in Mesa's inscription upon the so-called Moabite Stone (circ. 900–850 B. C.). This ancient style of letter, which is called in the Talmud *Kethob Ibri*, or 'Hebrew writing,' continued in use for a long period. There is no trace of its use being affected by the Exile. In Ezra iv. 7 the words, 'And the writing of the letter was written in the Syrian *character*,' probably indicate that the Jews, in the days of Artaxerxes (465–424 B. C.), were obliged to have recourse to the Aramaean characters for purposes of official correspondence with the authorities of the Persian empire, but they also imply that the Aramaean characters were still regarded as part of a foreign usage. In the second century B. C. the coins of Simon Maccabeus (143–135 B. C.), and so late as the second century A. D. the coins of Bar-Cochba (135 A. D.), retain the old Hebrew lettering; and it may fairly be claimed that the lettering of the coinage of a native dynasty or of a patriotic leader must above all things be legible by the people and acceptable to them. Possibly these coins may retain certain archaic forms; but they furnish evidence of incontestable force that, so late as the second century A. D., the old letters were preferred by patriot Jews to the square Aramaic characters. How completely this disposes of the legend of Ezra's inventing a more sacred form of alphabet, need hardly be pointed out.

Turning now to the square Hebrew characters, it appears that they represent a development of an archaic Aramaean alphabet, traces of which are preserved in Assyrian weights, &c. of the eighth century B. C., and in

The old Hebrew characters: in the Monarchy;

in the second century B. C. and second century A. D.

The square Hebrew characters: Aramaean origin.

H 2

CHAP. IV.
APP.

the famous *stele* of Teima in Arabia dating from the sixth century B.C. The spread of this alphabet throughout Western Asia was gradual and continuous throughout the last four centuries before the Christian era. In our Lord's time the square characters had apparently become very generally accepted. They are found in inscriptions belonging to that era. Our Lord Himself clearly refers to their use, when He speaks of the 'Yod' (*lôτa*) and of 'the tittle' (*κεραία*) or horn of a square Hebrew letter (Matt. v. 18). By the Rabbins it was called either the 'square writing,' *Kethob merubba*, or the Assyrian writing, *Kethob Asshuri*. A subsequent development of the square characters is to be found in the Palmyrene and Nabataean inscriptions of the second century A.D.

Used in the first century A.D.

Such, then, are the chief facts that are known as to the history of Hebrew writing. But the further question when the Jews dropped the old Hebrew characters and adopted the square characters in the transcription of the sacred rolls containing the Books of the Law, cannot be answered with any certainty. The most ancient Hebrew inscription in which the first signs of the change from the old Canaanite letters to the square Aramaean are discernible, is that which is known as Arak-el-Amir on the ruins of the castle of Hyrcanus on the east side of the Jordan, belonging to the year 176 B.C. On the other hand, the earliest Hebrew inscription written in pure Aramaean characters is that on the so-called Tomb of St. James, in the valley of the Kidron, which is assigned to the first century B.C. There can be no manner of doubt that the two characters were in use at the same time, and that the Aramaean only very slowly drove out the Canaanite style.

So far as the Samaritan Pentateuch is concerned, the

characters in which it is written are described by palaeo-
graphists as a *late* modification of the old Hebrew
writing. As such, it may be attributed, in the forms
that have been preserved, to the ultimate stage in the
development of the old Hebrew alphabet, before the
final adoption of the square Aramaean form [1]. And in
support of this view I may adduce the authority of one
of the most eminent Orientalists, the late Professor
W. Wright (*Comparative Grammar of the Semitic Races*,
Cambridge, 1890, p. 39): 'This alphabet is still found,
with slight modifications, upon the Maccabee and other
Jewish coins; and is known to us in its latest shape as
the *Samaritan* alphabet. It began, however, to be dis-
used by the Jews even before the commencement of our
era, and to be supplanted by a modified form of the
Palmyrene character, the so-called square character,
כְּתָב מְרֻבָּע. Some of the extant inscriptions of this type
belong to the century preceding our era.'

Jewish and Samaritan writings were probably therefore
alike composed in the old Hebrew characters until the
fourth or third century B.C. From about that time
forward it appears probable that the Aramaean characters
began to compete with the old Hebrew in Jewish literature. This is what we might expect, bearing in mind
the general diffusion of the Aramaean characters in Syria
and Babylonia, and the spread of Jewish population
throughout Western Asia. Under the influences of 'the
Dispersion' and the pressure of trade, the movement in
favour of a change of character from the old Hebrew to
the square Aramaean must have been immeasurably

---

[1] See Benzinger's *Hebräische Archäologie* (Freiburg, 1894), pp. 286–288 ;
Nowack's *Hebräische Archäologie* (Freiburg, 1894), pp. 284–288.

stronger in the Jewish community than it could have
been in the more limited and more deeply Hellenized
Samaritan people. With the Jews the two styles of
handwriting must have for some time competed side by
side. Patriotism preferred the old Hebrew letters ; but
the interests of commerce, the influence of the scribes of
Babylonia, and the tendency towards a uniform simpler
style of writing, proved too strong a combination, and
prevailed. The Samaritan Church, however, preserved
the old characters unaltered. Greek had probably in-
vaded all Samaritan literature save that of worship.

*General
conclusion.*   As a result, then, of this slight sketch, it appears that
the use of the old Hebrew characters in the Samaritan
Pentateuch simply furnishes the evidence that at the
time when the Samaritans received from the Jews their
Torah, the style of writing had not yet undergone the
change which it was destined to undergo among the
Jews. ' Unfortunately,' as Buhl says (p. 41), ' we possess
no tradition respecting the time at which the Samaritans
received the Law. Those, however, who do not admit
that the Pentateuch was subjected to any substantial
revision after the time of Ezra, can scarcely entertain a
doubt that this took place at the time when the Samaritan
Church and worship were set up upon Mount Gerizim.'

While the available evidence points to the probability
of the view which has been advocated above, that the
Samaritans received their Torah at the close of the fifth
or at the beginning of the fourth century B.C., the palaeo-
graphical testimony, supplied by the traditional forms of
the Samaritan alphabet, makes it practically certain,
*that the Samaritan MSS. of the Torah have been derived
from an exemplar, or exemplars, written at a later period
than the fourth century B.C.* The supposition therefore

that the characters in which the Samaritan Pentateuch CHAP. IV,
is extant furnish any argument against the legitimacy APP.
of the main outlines of Pentateuchal criticism, is due to
a misapprehension of the facts.

The legend which, with so little probability, ascribes *The signifi-*
a change of literary characters to the unique influence *cance of the*
of Ezra, is not altogether lacking in significance. The *legend con-*
Jews were apt to personify important incidents or *cerning*
institutions by connecting them with famous names of *Ezra.*
the past. In the present instance the selection of Ezra
was not otherwise than happily made. Ezra was the
typical scribe. He impersonated to the Jews the age
of the Sopherim. The gradual transformation of the
Hebrew characters from the Canaanite to the Aramaean
was begun during the epoch of the ascendency of the
scribes. To assign this change to the commanding
influence of the typical scribe was doubtless to overstep
the limits of strict historical accuracy. But the poetical
licence of legendary fiction has thus enshrined the recollection of a great and impressive change in the literary
history of the Hebrew Scriptures—a change which may
possibly have been expedited by the traditional hatred
of the Samaritans, and by the desire to distinguish the
Torah-rolls of the Jewish synagogues from those that
were copied on Mount Gerizim; but which may, with
even more probability, be considered to have been
promoted by the influence of the Rabbinic Schools of
Babylon, by the spread of Jewish synagogues in Syria
and Mesopotamia, and by the gradual adoption, on the
part of the Jews, of the Aramaic dialect in preference to
the Hebrew of their forefathers.

CHAPTER V.

THE SECOND CANON, OR THE LAW AND THE PROPHETS.

CHAP. V.
———
The Canon of 'the Law' insufficient.

IN the latter half of the fifth century B.C. the Torah had received its final recognition as Holy Scripture. The popular veneration for this 'Canon,' quite apart from the teaching of the scribes, must have been largely due to the fact, that its contents dealt with the origin of the Hebrew race and with the foundation of the Israelite religion. But, in an even greater degree, its association with the Temple ritual, its perusal in Synagogue services, and its growing use as the test of conduct and doctrine in social and private life, had the effect of exalting it above all other Hebrew literature, and of enhancing its value in the estimation of every devout Jew. And yet it was impossible for 'the Law' to remain the whole 'Canon' of Jewish Scripture. It lacked the representation of that very element which had been the most important factor in the growth of the pure religion of Jehovah, the element of prophecy. Without prophecy, as has been said, 'the Law was a body without a soul[1].' And although the prophetic spirit breathes in the *teaching* of the Torah generally, and in particular in that of Deuteronomy, nevertheless the Torah, as a whole, did not represent either the fulness or the freedom of prophecy.

[1] Cf. Dillmann, *Jahrb. f. deutsche Theol.* 1858, p. 441.

It would not be too much to say that the life and purity of Israel's faith had hitherto depended upon the testimony of the prophets. It was to the prophets that the people owed the revelation of the Lord's will. In a sense they had been the true mediators of the law. The consciousness of the inseparableness of the spirit of prophecy from that of 'the Law,' expressed in such different passages as 2 Kings xvii. 13, Zech. vii. 12, and Neh. ix. 26, was sure, sooner or later, to make itself felt in the worship of the nation. For centuries 'the Word of God' had been declared to the people by the prophet in the form of 'instruction' or Torah. But now the work of the prophet was over; 'Torah' was identified with a written law, it was no longer the prophet's spoken word. Prophecy had ceased; and the question was, whether 'the Law' alone could permanently fill the gap which had thus appeared in the religious life of the community?

Chap. V.
Prophecy and the Law.

Instinctively our answer is, that it could not. And because it could not, we shall see that, after an interval of time, the writings called in the Hebrew Canon the 'Nebiim' or 'Prophets [1],' gradually received such recognition in the Jewish Church as caused them also to be set apart as Canonical Scripture, although never probably, in Jewish opinion, estimated as of equal honour with 'the Law.'

The 'Nebiim.'

The steps by which these additions to the Canon of 'the Law' were made are, indeed, in a great measure hidden from our view. The scanty evidence at our

---

[1] A group consisting, in our Hebrew Bibles, of the two divisions, (a) 'the Former' or historical prophets, represented by the four books, Joshua, Judges, Samuel, and Kings; (b) 'the Latter' or prophetical, represented by the four books, Isaiah, Jeremiah, Ezekiel, and the Twelve Minor Prophets. See p. 11.

command points, as we hope to show, to the conclusion, that the canonicity of all 'the Prophets' had been recognised, before any of the writings of the last group, or Hagiographa, were included in the national Scriptures.

I. Causes of Selection.
II. Period.
III. Limitation. For this purpose, it is necessary, firstly, to consider briefly the circumstances under which these writings tended to obtain such special recognition as at once separated them from other literature and associated them with the sacred 'Law'; secondly, to investigate the limits of the period within which it seems probable that the canonicity of 'the Prophets' was determined; and thirdly, to consider whether other writings, besides those included in the traditional group of the Nebiim, received at the same time the stamp of canonicity.

I. In the first place, we consider the circumstances which led to the selection of 'the Prophets' and their association with 'the Law.' Attention has already been frequently called to the literary activity which prevailed among the Jews of Babylon during and after the exile. The desire to preserve the ancient memorials of the race would have led to many works of compilation. Of such, a few only have survived, and they entirely owing to their having afterwards become 'Canonical' Scripture.

It would be a mistake, however, to suppose that 'the Prophets,' historical and prophetical, represent only the surviving specimens of Israelite literature, that were rescued from the wreck of the civil community by the energy and industry of a few devout men. The work which led to the formation of the Canon was not merely conservative; it was also constructive and selective, constructive from the point of view of the historian of Old

Testament Theology, selective from the point of view of *CHAP. V.* the historian of Jewish literature.

To the earlier part of the exilic period should pro- *Joshua,* bably be referred the compilation of the materials of the *during* Book of Joshua, which, based on the narratives of the *Exile.* Jehovist-Elohist Writing, were edited in the spirit of the Deuteronomic law, and eventually combined with our Deuteronomy. The combination did not long outlast the formation of the Hexateuch (p. 69). To the close of the period of Nehemiah is to be ascribed the action of the scribes, by which our Book of Joshua was separated from the Deuteronomic portion of the 'Torah.' The ground of the separation must have been, either that its narrative did not contain direct religious teaching, or, as seems more probable, that the Book of the Law seemed to close more appropriately with the death of the great Lawgiver. The close literary union of Joshua with *Jos. and* Deuteronomy is, on grounds both of the style and of the *Deut.* continuity of the subject-matter, placed beyond all doubt. The fact that the books are separate, and, further, that they appear in two different groups of the Hebrew Scriptures, at once becomes intelligible, when we realise that an interval of time elapsed between the recognition of the 'Torah' and the final acceptance of ' Joshua.'

When we pass to the Book of Judges, we find signs *Judges;* that its compilation probably belongs to the same period. *three sources of,* It is well known to every careful reader, that the book *when com-* consists of three clearly marked portions, which differ in *piled.* style and treatment, and represent extracts from different sources of narrative. In the first of these sections (i. 1– ii. 5) it is probable that the narrator borrowed from the same ancient literary source that supplied material for the compilation of Joshua ; e. g.

Judges i. 10–15 = Joshua xv. 13–19.

       „   21 =   „   63.

       „   27, 28 =   „   xvii. 12, 13.

       „   29 =   „   xvi. 10.

In the second (ii. 6–xvi), which contains some of the oldest fragments of early Jewish literature, it is equally evident, from the style, that they have been compiled or edited by one who writes in the spirit of the Deuteronomic Law. Clear proofs of his handiwork are to be seen in such passages as ii. 11–23, iii. 7–11, vi. 7–10, x. 6–17.

In the third portion (xvii–xxi), containing two distinct narratives, as well as in the first, 'no traces are to be found of the hand of the Deuteronomic redactor of the middle division ; there are no marks either of his distinctive phraseology or of his view of the history as set forth in ii. 11–19. Hence it is probable that these divisions did not pass through his hands ; but were added to the book as he left it (ii. 6–xvi) as an introduction and appendix respectively by a later hand.' (Driver, in the Jewish Quarterly, Jan. 1889.)

The compilation of the whole work belongs therefore to the literary energy of a period later than that of the Deuteronomic editor. To attempt to decide the date of the compiler with any precision would be out of the question. Perhaps we should assign his work to the latter part of the exilic period.

Books of Samuel.

The Books of Samuel are a compilation, which contains some most ancient elements. The influence of Deuteronomy is not so clearly marked in them as in the Book of Judges, although its presence may probably be detected in 1 Sam. ii. 1–11, 27–36, vii. 2–viii, x. 17–26, xii, xv, 2 Sam. vii. The work of compilation may therefore have taken place in the exilic period. The materials, however, which are incorporated in the Books of Samuel were comparatively little modified by the compiler. But either the sources from which they were taken survived for a considerable period, and occasioned the variations of text which appear in the LXX version; or the books were current in a different recension, before they received recognition as Sacred Scripture.

The Books of Kings terminate with the mention of events that occurred about 560 B.C. In them, more conspicuously than in any of the other narrative books, is to be seen the influence of the Deuteronomist. Some scholars have supposed this effect to be due to the first vivid impression produced by the publication of the Deuteronomic law, and have therefore placed the first compilation as early as the last decade of the seventh cent. B.C. (610–600). They have suggested that, half-a-century later, various additions were made and the last chapters of the history appended.

The composite character of the narrative is obviously expressed by the writer's reference to ' The Book of the Acts of Solomon' (1 Kings xi. 41), and by frequent allusions to ' The Book of the Chronicles of the Kings of Israel and Judah,' as well as by the clearly marked excerpts from a narrative history of the prophets, especially of Elijah and Elisha (e. g. 1 Kings xvii–xix, xxi, 2 Kings i–viii, xiii. 14–19). The date of its compilation can hardly be placed earlier than the close of the sixth cent. B.C.

Now from the composite character of the historical books we may infer the existence of abundant narrative material at the period when their compilation took place. But we can gather from the books themselves what the

Distinctive feature of narrative books.

qualities were, which led to their being selected and eventually preferred above all other historical memoirs dealing with the same events. Over and above the truthfulness, the dignity, the beauty, the vividness, the simplicity of their narratives, stands one pre-eminent characteristic, which at once explains the mould in which they were cast and imparts to their narrative its wonderful power to teach. This was the spirit of Hebrew prophecy interpreting to us the course of history in accordance with the eternal principles of Divine Revelation. The four narrative books of 'the Prophets' are no mere catalogues of facts, they are not even a continuous uniform history. They unfold the workings of 'the law of Jehovah' in the history of Israel, both in their description of the nation's internal development and in their picture of its relation to other nations.

If now the historical books were finally selected, because in a special manner they set forward the history of Israel's past, judged by the law of the Lord, and in the light of the spirit of prophecy, it is natural to ascribe the beginning of their separation from other literature to a period, when the work and teaching of the prophets were, for some reason or other, attracting especial attention, and claiming peculiar veneration.

Witness of Prophets, during Monarchy, not popularly acceptable.

Before the exile, the prophets of Jehovah found themselves, as often as not, in opposition to the dominant form of religion. Their sayings were perpetuated either orally or in the writings of their disciples; but their testimony, if preserved in the recollection of the people, as in the instance of Micah the Morashtite (Jer. xxvi. 18), did not at once obtain any hold over the religious thought of the nation in a literary form. The acquaintance, however, of the prophets with the words of their own predecessors

in the ministry of prophecy is openly avowed. Jeremiah
borrows largely from other sources. Ezekiel appeals to
the predictions of the prophets (Ezek. xxxviii. 17) which
the people had disregarded.

Towards the close of the exile, the power and prestige *Change pro-*
of the prophets must have been greatly enhanced, in *duced by*
the estimation of their countrymen, by the evidently *Exile and*
approaching fulfilment of the predictions of Jeremiah. *Return.*
The prophet Zechariah could appeal to the fulfilment of
the words of ' the former prophets ' (cf. Zech. i. 4, vii. 7,
12). Both the catastrophe of the exile and the joy of
the return confirmed the confidence of the faithful, and
removed the doubts of the wavering, in respect of the
mission of the prophets. The descendants of the generation that had sought to put Jeremiah to death rallied to
the exhortations of Haggai and Zechariah (Ezra v. 1).
The reverence for the prophets was heightened, as it
became increasingly evident, that the gift of prophecy
was becoming more rare and threatened to become
extinct. Zechariah foresees the time at hand when the
claim to prophecy shall betoken imposture (Zech. xiii. 3).
In the days of Nehemiah, the old prophets are referred
to as the ministers of Jehovah, who had witnessed in the
past to a stubborn disobedient race and had been disregarded (Neh. ix. 26, 30). Modern prophets were
largely intriguers (Neh. vi. 7, 14). And if one more voice
of prophecy was to be heard, it was to testify, that the
day was past for that form of delivering Jehovah's
message, and to express the belief, as it were, in its
last breath, that, through the witness of no new prophet
but only through the return of Elijah, the prototype of
prophecy, could be brought about the regeneration of so
corrupt a people (Mal. iv. 5, 6).

It was, then, at the time when the Canon of the Law was already recognised, that the veneration for prophecy grew apace, and made the people deplore its decay and resolve, so far as possible, to preserve the words of the ancient prophets from perishing. It is, therefore, important as well as interesting, to find that one of the few traditions, respecting the collection of the Jewish Scriptures, connects the task of forming a library, in which prophetical and historical works are especially mentioned, with the labours of Nehemiah. The tradition is contained in a certain letter, prefixed to the Second Book of Maccabees, which purports to be addressed by Jews in Palestine to their countrymen in Egypt in the year 144 B.C. The letter is generally, and on good grounds, considered by scholars to be spurious; but even so, the possibility remains, that the traditions which are contained in the letter may have been obtained from other sources

An Ancient tradition: 2 Macc. ii. 13. of a more trustworthy kind. The tradition which here concerns us mentions a current report, 'how (Nehemiah) founded a library and gathered together the books (or, things) concerning the kings and prophets, and the (books) of David and letters of kings about sacred gifts' (2 Macc. ii. 13)[1]. These words throw no light upon the recognition of any portion of the Canon. But they connect with the memory of Nehemiah, and therefore, probably, with the whole generation which he personified, the preservation of public documents, and of historical records and court memoirs of national interest.

As we have before had occasion to observe, the preservation and collection of writings mark the stage in the history of the canonical writings which is preliminary to their especial selection for liturgical use and

[1] See Excursus D. v.

religious purposes generally. While, therefore, we have CHAP. V.
no right to assume, as has often been done, that the
writings referred to in the Epistle are to be identified
with 'the Nebiim,' with 'the Psalms,' and with ' Ezra and
Nehemiah,' there is fair reason to suppose, that, in Nehemiah's time, some such a collection of books and documents
was made, and that amongst them were possibly some
of the books afterwards embodied in the Canon, some,
too, of the older documents on which they were based.

II. Having, then, reached this probable conclusion, that *When were*
in the days of Nehemiah a special interest had been *regarded as*
aroused in the preservation of the writings and sayings *Scripture?*
of the prophets, we have next to consider within what
limits of time we should place the process, by which they
came to be recognised as authoritative Scripture.

We might naturally assume that such recognition
would not take place, until some time had elapsed after
the acceptance of the Law as the people's Scripture. The
sanctity and dignity of ' the Law' must at first have over-
shadowed everything else. A possible illustration of its
influence may be found in the historical sketch contained
in the prayer of Ezra and the Levites (Neh. ix). The *The Law at*
details of the sacred narrative are there all drawn from the *first over-shadowed*
Pentateuch (vv. 6–25); and, though allusions are made *all other writings.*
to events of later history (e. g. vv. 27, 30), these are expressed only in vague outline and in the most general
terms, and the great names of Joshua, of Gideon, of
Samuel, of David, of Solomon, of Elijah are conspicuously absent. Whether the historical Psalms cv,
cvi. belong to this date or not, we cannot say. But it is
noticeable, that in them, as in Neh. ix, reference to the
merciful dealings of God with His people Israel is, for the
most part, limited to the events included within the range

I

of the Pentateuchal literature.   And the explanation is probably this, that these religious songs are based upon the Canon of the 'Torah,' made familiar to the people by the service of the Synagogue.

Turning for a moment to the books of the prophets, we can possibly glean hints from some of them as to the date of the revision, which presumably immediately preceded their admission to the rank of Holy Scripture.

Isaiah, date of compilation.   *Isaiah.* In our book of Isaiah, the first portion (i–xxxv) consists of collections of prophecies written, most of them (i–xxiii, xxviii–xxxiii), by Isaiah himself.   Several of them, however, the best scholars judge to be derived from a much later time.   Now, if the period of the exile prove to be, as is very probably the case, the date of chaps. xxxiv, xxxv, and if a post-exilic date be assigned to the group chaps. xxiv–xxvii. (see Ewald, Delitzsch, Dillmann, Driver)[1], we perceive at once, that the compilation of this first portion only—to which have been appended both an extract from the Book of Kings (2 Kings xviii–xix) and the song of Hezekiah (xxxviii. 9–20), obtained probably from some independent collection of national psalms—can hardly have taken place much before the period of Nehemiah.   It may be conjectured, that the addition of the concluding section (xl–lxvi), which makes no claim to Isaianic authorship, but indisputably reflects the thought of the closing years of the exile, was added at a time when the prophetical writings were being collected and edited by the scribes, and when, the recollection of the authorship of this section having been forgotten, it could, not unnaturally, be appended to the writings of Isaiah.

[1] See however, 'An Examination of the Objections brought against the genuineness of Is. xxiv–xxvii,' by W. E. Barnes, B.D. (Cambridge, 1891).

Jeremiah. In the case of the Book of Jeremiah, we CHAP. V.
have clear evidence that some interval of time elapsed *Jeremiah,*
between the decease of the prophet and the age in which *evidence of*
his prophecies were edited. This may be shown by the *structure.*
fact that chap. xxxix. 1–13 is condensed from 2 Kings
xxv. 1–12, and that the concluding chapter (lii) is derived
from 2 Kings xxiv. 18, &c., and xxv. 27–30. It would
also appear from the dislocated order of the prophecies.
The existence, again, of great variations in the text of
the LXX version points to the probability of Jeremiah's
prophecies having once been current in some other form,
as, for instance, in smaller collections of prophecies. This
variation in form would probably be earlier in date than
their final recognition as sacred Scripture, after which
event it is not likely that any important changes could
be introduced.

Minor Prophets. In the collection of the Twelve *Minor*
Minor Prophets, we have possible indications of the limit *Prophets.*
of time, before which it is at any rate improbable that
these writings were received as sacred Scripture. It is
likely enough that they already formed a distinct collection, and were already treated as a single work, when
they were first raised to Canonical dignity. For it
appears, that to the editor who combined them are due
not only the headings prefixed to Hosea, Joel, Amos,
Micah, but also the title given to the three last groups
of prophecy, irrespective of their different authorship,
'The burden of the word of the Lord,' Zech. ix. 1, xii. 1,
and Mal. i. 1.

As to the date of their compilation, we gain some idea *Malachi.*
from knowing that Malachi was composed at or about
the time of Nehemiah's governorship (445–433 B.C.). A
collection of prophetical writings which included that of

CHAP. V. Malachi, could hardly have been made until some time had elapsed from the date of its composition. We cannot suppose, that popular opinion would have approved the incorporation of recent, or almost contemporary, work in the same collection with the older prophets. Many years would have to slip away, before it was fully realised that Malachi was the last of the great series. Perhaps nearly a century had passed, before his countrymen learned to class his words with those of his honoured and more venerable predecessors.

Jonah. If, as seems very possible from the evidence of the language, the Book of Jonah is an allegory written, for a didactic purpose, at the close of the fifth century B.C., it would hardly, we think, have been admitted at once among the earlier prophets of Israel. Some time must have elapsed since it had been composed, the popularity of the work must have become assured, and the hero of the story been generally identified with the prophet of Gath-hepher (2 Kings xiv. 25), before it obtained its unique position, corresponding to the date of the supposed writer, of a narrative among the Minor Prophets.

Zechariah. The writings of Zechariah (i-viii) received an extensive addition (ix-xiv) of uncertain date and unknown authorship from the hands of a compiler. This must have been effected, when the recollection of what were and what were not Zechariah's writings, had become indistinct; probably, therefore, later than the fifth century B.C.

From the indications thus given by the contents and structure of the books themselves [1], we infer that, in the case of 'the Prophets,' if the process of special collec-

---

[1] The evidence of Joel has been purposely omitted, on account of the great uncertainty, whether the post-exilic date, ascribed to it, can be considered to have been substantiated.

tion was begun in the time of Nehemiah, that of their
selection and recognition as sacred Scripture can hardly
have begun until a century later. This is an impression for which we derive some support from the
condition of the text of the Septuagint version. The
marked divergency between the Hebrew and the Greek
text, in the Books, for instance, of Samuel and the prophet Jeremiah, points to the existence of different Hebrew
recensions current not long before the Greek translation
was made in Alexandria, or to a different text being
recognised by the scribes in Palestine from that which
was best known in Egypt. Differences of recension were
not likely to have been permitted after the books had
once obtained a special recognition. So long as varieties
of texts existed side by side, so long, we may assume,
the books had not been invested by the Jews with any
strict ideas of canonicity. The particular recension of
the book, which happened to receive canonical recognition from the scribes, would be that which in after time
suffered least from the accidents of transmission, because
its preservation had been the object of special care. It is
possible, however, that a Hebrew text, representing the
recension which accompanied the admission of the book
within the precincts of the Canon, may preserve to us a
text differing more widely from the original than that of
the Septuagint version. It is possible, in other words, that
the existing Hebrew text may represent a poorer text
from the fact that it has been more studiously 'revised'
by the scribes. Against that, however, must be set the
undoubtedly greater freedom with which the Jews in
Alexandria handled the national Scriptures. Interpolation in Egypt may be set off against 'redaction' processes in Palestine and Babylon.

CHAP. V.   We assume, therefore, that the Greek translation
of 'the Prophets' was for the most part completed
before their Canonical character had been determined,
or recognised, in Alexandria. On the other hand,
the evidence of the 'Prologue to Ecclesiasticus' is conclusive, that the Canonicity of 'the Prophets' had
been accepted there since the beginning of the second
century B.C.

It deserves passing notice that the Chronicler, writing
about the beginning of the third century, and making
large extracts from the Books of Samuel and Kings,
makes no sign of consciousness that he is borrowing
material from any peculiarly sacred source.

If our general line of argument be admitted, the date
which we assign for the *terminus a quo* of the period,
within which the Canonicity of the prophets was recog-

Influences;
Alexan-
der's
Victories,
reaction
against
legalism.
nised, will be not earlier than 300 B.C. Was it the spread
of Hellenic culture that followed in the wake of Alexander's victories, which contributed the crowning impulse
to the desire of the Jewish community to expand the
limits of their sacred literature, and to admit the writings
of the Prophets, for purposes of public reading, into the
'ark' of the Synagogue? It is a thought fruitful in
interesting speculation.   It cannot be affirmed upon
the basis of any direct evidence, but it surely is a not
improbable suggestion.   Whether also 'something like
a reaction against the spirit of Ezra [1]' may partly account
for the elevation of 'the Prophets' to the rank of Holy
Scripture by the side of 'the Law,' is also a question
which, if, for lack of evidence, it admits of no certain
answer, is certainly a suggestive conjecture.   It is an
interesting thought, that the fascination of the new

[1] Cheyne, *The Origin of the Psalter*, p. 363.

Hellenic literature and the spiritual sterility of the interpretation which the Jewish scribes applied to 'the Law,' may have been forces operating together, though from opposite sides, to bring about the inclusion of 'the Prophets' within the Hebrew Canon.

The task of determining a *terminus ad quem* for this period is, perhaps, not so difficult. At least, the evidence which is here at our disposal is of a more definite character; and it tends to show that, at the beginning of the second century B.C., the Prophets had already, for some time, occupied the position in the Hebrew Scriptures which was assigned to them by later tradition. Before the beginning of the second century B.C., the second stage in the formation of the Canon had ended; and the limits of 'the Law and the Prophets' had been determined.

(i.) The first evidence to this effect that we have to notice is that which is supplied by the writings of Jesus, the son of Sirach, whose collection of proverbial sayings is contained in the book, known to English readers as Ecclesiasticus, which was composed about the year 1·80 B.C. In his celebrated eulogy (ch. xliv–l) upon 'the famous men' of Israel, he refers to events as they are recorded in the Books of Joshua, Samuel and Kings[1]. When he refers to Isaiah, he expressly ascribes to him the comforting of 'them that mourn in Zion' (Isaiah lxi. 3). Shortly afterwards, he makes mention of Jeremiah, using of him language borrowed from his own prophecies (Jer. i. 5–10). He proceeds, next, to speak of Ezekiel, refer-

Ecclesiasticus, The Wisdom of Jesus, the son of Sirach, circ. 180 B.C.

---

[1] The Judges are dismissed in a couple of verses (Ecclus. xlvi. 11, 12). For Joshua, see ch. xlvi. 1–6; for the Books of Samuel, see ch. xlvi. 13–xlvii. 11; for the Books of Kings, see ch. xlvii. 12–xlix. 3. Isaiah is mentioned, ch. xlviii. 20–25; Jeremiah, ch. xlix. 6, 7; Ezekiel, ch. xlix. 8, 9; the Twelve Prophets, ch. xlix. 10; Zerubbabel and Jeshua, ch. xlix. 11, 12; Nehemiah, ch. xlix. 13.

ring especially to his mysterious vision (Ezek. i. 28). He then makes mention of the 'Twelve Prophets,' who 'comforted Jacob and delivered them by assured hope.' He speaks of Zerubbabel and Joshua, and, although his notice of them may be based on the writings of Haggai (ii. 3) and Zechariah (iii. 1), it is clear from his references to Nehemiah, that he was acquainted with the substance of Ezra and Nehemiah. In, at least, one passage he makes allusion to the Books of Chronicles (xlvii. 9, cf. 1 Chron. xvi. 4). In other passages he makes use of language in which have been noted parallelisms with the Psalter, with the Book of Proverbs, with the Book of Job, and, though this is very doubtful, with the Book of Ecclesiastes.

The writer alludes, therefore, to other books besides those which are included in 'the Law and the Prophets.' It is not, however, possible for us to infer anything more from this than that 'the son of Sirach' was well acquainted, as we might have expected, with the literature of his countrymen, with books which undoubtedly existed in his day, were largely read, and afterwards included within the Canon.

The 'famous men' mentioned in order of Scripture.   The two most important features in his testimony are (*a*) the systematic order of his allusions to 'the famous men,' and (*b*) his mention of the 'Twelve Prophets.' (*a*) In his list of 'the famous men' he seems to follow the arrangement of the books of the Law and the Prophets, to which, we might suppose, were popularly added, by way of appendix, the writings from which he derived his mention of Zerubbabel, Jeshua, and Nehemiah. Towards the close of his reference to the Books of Kings, he naturally introduces his mention of Isaiah in connexion with the reign of Hezekiah. After he has finished his review of the historical books, he mentions in

succession Jeremiah, Ezekiel, and 'the Twelve Prophets,' CHAP. V.
and he appends the names of the heroes of the Return
from the Captivity, before passing on to describe the
glories of his own great contemporary, the high priest
Simon. (*b*) The fact that he mentions the 'Twelve *The Twelve-*
Prophets,' proves that, in his time, this title was given *Prophets.*
to a group of prophets, whose writings had long been
known both in the form and with the name of a separate collection, clearly identical with that in which they
appear according to the tradition of the Hebrew Canon.

We have said that his mention of Zerubbabel, Jeshua,
and Nehemiah seems to imply his recognition of the
books Ezra and Nehemiah as a kind of appendix to the
historical books of the Prophets. It is possible that
other books may have occupied a similar position. But
that a clearly marked line of separation was drawn
between such books and those that were regarded as
Canonical is probably implied by the writer's omission *Significant*
of Ezra, Job, Daniel, Esther, and Mordecai from the *omissions;*
Ezra, Esth.,
list of the 'famous men'[1] of Israel. The omission of *Dan.*
Ezra, regarded by itself, would not have had any such
significance; for the mention of Nehemiah shows the
writer's acquaintance with the latter portion of the
Chronicler's work. But when we recollect the position
that Ezra occupied in later Hebrew tradition, when we
remember, too, the popularity which the stories of Esther
and Daniel obtained in later times, it is hardly possible
to suppose that, in so striking a list of the heroes and
champions of his people mentioned in Jewish Scripture,
the author would have omitted these great names, if he
had known that his readers were familiar with their story,

---

[1] Ecclus. xliv. 1, 'Let us now praise famous men, and our fathers that
begat us.'

CHAP. V.   or if their story had, in his day, been found in the Jewish
Canon.

(ii.) The next piece of evidence to be noticed is that
which is supplied by the Book of Daniel, which, in all
probability, was compiled, if not actually composed, in or
Dan. ix. 2.   about the year 165 B.C.   We find in chap. ix. 2 a reference
to the prophecy of Jeremiah, which the writer speaks of
as forming a portion of what he calls 'the books.'   His
words are, 'In the first year of his (Darius') reign I
Daniel understood by *the books* the number of the years,
whereof the word of the Lord came to Jeremiah the
prophet for the accomplishing of the desolation of Jerusalem, even seventy years.'   The author here refers to a
group of writings which included the prophecies of
Jeremiah, and which for some reason he designates 'the
Sephârîm,' or '*the* books.'   It is a natural supposition—
when we recollect that the Book of Daniel itself never
had a place among 'the Prophets'—that the writer or
compiler of Daniel wrote these words when the Canon
of 'the Prophets' had already been determined.   It
appears probable, at any rate, that the writer of Daniel
was here referring to this group of the Hebrew Scriptures.
By the title which he gives to them, equivalent almost to
the later term 'the Scriptures,' though hardly yet employed in so technical a sense, the writer testifies to his
knowledge of certain important and sacred books set
apart for religious use, and evidently expects his readers
to know what 'The Books' were, to which he refers, and
in which were included prophecies of Jeremiah.

Greek Pro-   (iii.) Lastly, we take the evidence supplied by the
logue to Ec-
clesiasticus;   Greek Prologue to Ecclesiasticus, written by the grand-
132 B.C.   son of Jesus, the son of Sirach, about the year 132 B.C.[1]

[1] See Chap. VI, and Excursus D.

Three times over he there makes mention of 'the Prophets' as a second group in the tripartite division of the Hebrew Scriptures. There is practically no reason to doubt that 'the Prophets' thus mentioned are identical with the group that has become familiar to us in the traditional arrangement of the Canon. Be this as it may, the evidence of the Prologue is sufficient to show that, in the writer's opinion, one division of the sacred books of his people was known by the name of 'the Prophets,' and was, in his time, part of a well-established arrangement, which he could assume his readers in Alexandria to be perfectly acquainted with.

On the basis, therefore, of the external evidence, coupled with the testimony of the books themselves, we arrive at the probable conclusion that the formation of the group of 'the Prophets,' having been commenced not earlier than the year 300 B.C., was brought to a completion by the end of the same century. We may conjecture that the conclusion of the second Canon, viz., 'the Law and the Prophets,' may have been reached under the High Priesthood of Simon II (219–199 B.C.). Having first been added as a kind of necessary appendix to the Law, 'the Prophets' had gradually grown in estimation, until they seemed partially to fill the gap, which the people never ceased to deplore in the disappearance of the prophetic gift (Ps. lxxiv. 9, 1 Macc. iv. 46, ix. 27, xiv. 41, Song of Three Children, 15). Before the close of the third cent. B.C. they ranked as Scripture, after 'the Law,' and above all other writings.

The 'Prophets' selected, 300–200 B.C.

In this we should surely reverently acknowledge the guiding hand of Providence. For, thus, it was divinely overruled that, on the eve of the great crisis, when Antiochus Epiphanes, seconded only too skilfully by

The value of their witness, in the reign of Antiochus Epiphanes.

CHAP. V. the turpitude of the Jewish high priests, Jason and Alcimus, sought to obliterate the religious distinctiveness of the Jewish people, to break down the wall of separation, and to reduce their religion to the level of a local variety of Hellenic paganism, another bulwark had been opportunely raised in the defence of the pure religion of Jehovah. The veneration of 'the Law' was deepened in the hearts of 'the Pious' (the *Khasidîm*) by the recognition of the prophets. The temper which reckoned 'the Prophets' as part of the inspired Scriptures of the people was a pledge of the success of the Maccabean revolt.

III. One question remains to be asked. Did the group, called 'the Prophets,' in this second stage of the development of the Canon, include any book which is not found in the traditional order of the Hebrew Scriptures? Did any of the books which are now included within 'the Hagiographa' originally belong to 'the Prophets'?

Other books known, not recognised as Scripture. We have already noticed the probability, that, at the beginning of the second century B.C., other highly venerated writings formed a kind of appendix to the Prophets, without being as yet actually included in the Canon. Thus, besides the historical writings of Chronicles, Ezra and Nehemiah, collections of Psalms and Proverbs were doubtless familiarly known. But there is little ground for supposing that these writings were ever combined in the same group with the writings of 'the Prophets.' The collection of 'the Prophets,' if we may judge from its contents, was evidently intended to be homogeneous. Purposes of public reading in the Synagogue had, we may well imagine, determined their selection. In this case, writings, differing widely from one another in character, differing also, for the most part, from 'the Prophets' in style and subject-matter, were not likely to be associated with them. They would require the formation of a new and distinct group of Scripture.

The Books, however, of Ruth and Lamentations have occasioned some little uncertainty. Much doubt has been felt as to which group they originally belonged to, 'the Prophets' or 'the Writings.' In the Septuagint Version, the Book of Ruth follows the Book of Judges, *Ruth and* and the Book of Lamentations follows that of Jeremiah. *Lament. not in* By many it has been thought that the Septuagint Ver- *'Nebiim.'* sion has thus preserved their original position; in other words, that the two books already ranked as Scripture when the Canon of the Prophets was closed. According to this supposition, the Books of Ruth and Lamentations were not transferred to their place in the Hagiographa of the Hebrew Bible, until the arrangement of the Jewish Scriptures was finally decided upon by the Jewish doctors of the middle ages. We hope, however, to show, in the course of the following chapter, that there are good reasons for regarding 'Ruth' and 'Lamentations' as having, from the first, been completely separate works from 'Judges' and 'Jeremiah,' and, therefore, as never having been included among 'the Prophets,' except where the influence of the Alexandrian Version may be detected. The principle upon which the books of the Septuagint Version are arranged in the extant copies will fully account for the position assigned in them to Ruth and Lamentations respectively. No account is taken of the separateness of the two groups of the Hebrew Scriptures, the Prophets and 'the Writings.' Regard is apparently only paid to connexion of subject matter, or to con-

CHAP. V. siderations of chronological sequence, as roughly determining the order of their arrangement. But even then
no uniformity of order is observed; and the fact of the
extant MSS. being Christian in origin deprives their
evidence of any real value, when they are found in conflict, as is the case in this question, with the uniform
testimony of Jewish tradition.

'The Prophets' in the Syna-gogue Services. With the recognition of the Prophets we naturally
associate their use in public worship. Probably, there-
fore, during the third century B.C., the lesson from the
Prophets (the *Haphtarah*) was added by the scribes to
the lesson from the Law (the *Parashah*)[1]. It was an
ingenious suggestion, but one without a word of support
from early literature, and first made in all probability by
Elias Levita, that the introduction of a lesson from 'the
Prophets' arose during the persecution of the Jews by
Antiochus Epiphanes. According to this conjecture,
when Antiochus made the possession of a copy of 'the
Law' punishable by the heaviest penalties (1 Macc. i.
57), it was necessary to hide 'the rolls of the Laws';
the scribes, therefore, determined to select the Synagogue lessons from the writings of 'the Prophets'
instead of from 'the Law'; and from that time forward
the use of the prophetic lesson retained its place in the
public services. Unfortunately for this conjecture, no
confirmation of it has yet been found in any early
testimony. It is far more probable, that the adoption
of a lesson from 'the Prophets' corresponded with the
period of their admission into the Canon; and that
their occasional liturgical usage, having from time to
time found general approval, facilitated their reception

---

[1] Parashah = 'division,' or 'section.' Haphtarah = 'conclusion' or
'dismissal' (cf. 'Missa').

as Scripture. Whether they were suited for reading in the Synagogue services, may very possibly have been the test which decided the admission of a book into the group of the Nebiim. It is possible that the practice of reading portions in the Synagogue first led to the idea of setting apart, as sacred, other books besides the five books of the Law.

But the reading of 'the Prophets' was not at first arranged upon the same systematic plan as the reading from 'the Law,' nor until some time after the Christian era. In the New Testament, we have mention of the reading, in the Synagogues, from 'the Prophets' as well as from 'the Law' (Luke iv. 16, 17, Acts xiii. 15, 27); but from the passage in St. Luke's Gospel (iv. 16, 17), we rather gather that our Lord read a passage from Isaiah, which He either selected Himself, or read in accordance with the chance selection of the Synagogue authorities.

We do not find, until several centuries after the Christian era, any mention of other writings being *systematically*[1] read in the Synagogue besides those included in 'the Law and the Prophets,' and in this Synagogue tradition we seem to have a confirmation of the view that 'the Prophets' were received into the Canon before the Hagiographa. Also, in connexion with this subject, it may be remarked that the Aramaic Paraphrases, or Targums, of the Law and the Prophets are much earlier in date than those which exist of the Hagiographa; and that, while the Targums of the Law and the Prophets appear to have been prepared for the

---

[1] That extracts from the Hagiographa were from time to time read in the Synagogues, before the present Jewish Lectionary came into force, is a very probable supposition. But later usage favours the view that the reading of such extracts was for the purpose of brief and informal comparison with the Lessons from the Law and the Prophets.

CHAP. V.   purpose of public reading, those of the Hagiographa seem rather to have been intended for private use.

The Law and the Prophets.   Whether or no a recollection of the time, when the Hebrew Canon consisted only of the Law and the Prophets, is preserved in the frequent use of the phrase, 'the Law and the Prophets,' may be disputed. But the possibility of the explanation may be acknowledged; and, if so, an illustration of this earlier stage in the history of the formation of the Canon survives in the language of the New Testament (e. g. Matt. v. 17, vii. 12, xxii. 40, Luke xvi. 16, 29, 31, Acts xiii. 15, xxviii. 23).

CHAPTER VI.

THE THIRD CANON.

The Law, the Prophets, and the Writings.

THE earliest intimation that we have of a third group of writings being included among the Hebrew Scriptures is obtained from the Prologue to Ecclesiasticus, which was referred to in the previous chapter. The Prologue, as we saw, was written in Greek, and was prefixed to the Greek translation of the 'Wisdom of Jesus, the son of Sirach,' that his grandson made in Egypt about the year 132 B.C. Three times over in the course of this Prologue he speaks of the sacred Scriptures of the Jews, calling them at one time 'The Law and the Prophets and the others who followed after them,' at another 'The Law and the Prophets and the other Books of our Fathers,' at another 'The Law, the Prophets, and the rest of the Books.' The employment of these terms justifies us in supposing that the writer was acquainted with a recognised tripartite division of Scripture. But the expression, by which he designates the third group, certainly lacks definiteness. It does not warrant us to maintain, that 'the Writings' or 'Kethubim' were all, in their completed form, known to the writer. What, however, it does warrant us to assert, is that the writer fully recognises the fact that other books could take, and some had already taken, a 'tertiary' rank by the side of 'the Law

K

and the Prophets.' He is addressing himself to the Greek-speaking Jews of Alexandria; he is translating a work written in Hebrew by a devout Jew of Palestine; and, as he does not add any words either of qualification or of explanation to his mention of this third group, we may fairly assume that the beginning of the formation of a third group of Sacred Books had been known for some time, and that, in his day, it might be taken for granted as known by Jews whether in Palestine or in Egypt.

Books, known but not regarded as Scripture, 200 B.C.

When now we come to consider the history of this third group, we cannot, perhaps, hope to determine, with any degree of precision, the origin of its formation. But we can conjecture, with some show of probability, what the circumstances were that led to its commencement. We may remember that, at the time when the group of 'the Prophets' was in all probability closed, there existed among the Jews an extensive religious literature outside the limits of the Canon. The author of Koheleth (Ecclesiastes), writing probably in the third century B.C., sighs over the number of books and the weariness of the flesh resulting from their study (Eccles. xii. 12). The great historical narrative of the Chronicler, comprising our Books of Chronicles, Ezra and Nehemiah, had probably been completed in the early part of the same century (cf. Neh. xii. 11, 22). Perhaps from the same period had come the Book of Esther. The Books of Job and Proverbs had long been well known to Jewish readers, and the influence of the Book of Proverbs, in particular, has left its mark upon the Wisdom of Sirach. Large portions of the Psalter were doubtless well known, especially through the Temple services. The Book of Lamentations was commonly supposed to record the

elegy of Jeremiah over the destruction of Jerusalem. In *CHAP. VI.*
the Song of Songs had come down one of the most perfect specimens of early Hebrew poetry ; and in the Book
of Ruth a charming idyll of early prose narrative. These
writings, which are so well known to us, were probably
only samples, though doubtless the choicest ones, of an
abundant literature to which every Jew at the end of the
third century B.C. had access.

It is very possible, as has already been suggested, that, *An appen-*
at the close of the third century B.C., some of the writ- *dix to*
'the Law
ings we have just mentioned occupied so conspicuous a *and the*
Prophets.'
position as to constitute an informal appendix to the
Canon of 'the Law and the Prophets.' Informal only ;
they were not yet admitted to the full honour of
canonicity. In that reservation we have the only satisfactory explanation of the peculiarities which naturally
call for remark in 'the tripartite division' of the Hebrew
Scriptures. Why, it is asked, are not the Books of Ezra
and Nehemiah, of Ruth, of Esther, and of Chronicles,
found among the narrative books of the second group ?
Why, again, are not the Books of Lamentations and of *Anomalies*
in tripartite
Daniel found among the prophetical writings of the *division of*
Scripture
same Canon ? The only probable answer is that supplied *explained.*
by the recognition of development in the formation of
the Hebrew Canon. When the collection, called by the
name of 'the Prophets,' was being completed, the
writings that we have just referred to had not yet
obtained the degree of recognition, which alone could
cause them to be regarded as Scripture. When we ask
ourselves why they failed to obtain recognition, our
answer will be different in almost every instance. Some
would be excluded because in the treatment of their
subject-matter they differed so widely from the books

K 2

CHAP. VI. included in the prophetic group; among these would
be Lamentations, the Song of Songs, Ecclesiastes, and
Ruth. Others, which closely resembled the writings of
the second group, failed to find admission on account of
the recency of their composition; among these would
be Chronicles, Esther, Ezra and Nehemiah. In the case
of two others, it is probable that their *compilation* had
not yet been completed at the time when the Canon of
the Prophets was concluded; these were the Psalter and
the Book of Daniel. Books, unfitted, on such grounds,
for reading in the Synagogue services, would not be
admitted to 'the Nebiim,' the contents of which were
probably selected for that purpose principally.

Mediaeval Jewish Explanations inadequate. The explanations which Jewish writers in later times
put forward to account for the peculiarities of the tripar-
tite division are for the most part little else but fanciful
trifling, or, at the best, baseless speculation. Thus, for
instance, it was little else but trifling when they asserted
that the Books of Daniel and Esther, having been
written on foreign soil, did not merit a place among the
Prophets; or that Daniel, not having been called to the
office of a prophet, could not have his writings placed in
the prophetical group. But, for the most part, Jewish
explanations of the three divisions of Scripture were
based on the assumption that they represented three
descending degrees of inspiration, an opinion, which, it
is needless to say, is destitute of any support from
historical evidence. The three grades of inspiration
were themselves merely the result of speculation based
upon the fact of the tripartite division. The tripartite
division of Hebrew Scripture accounts for the Rabbinic
theory: the Rabbinic theory is no evidence as to the
origin of the tripartite division.

It is indeed strange to find the astounding theory put
forward in an English commentary that the tripartite
division of the Hebrew Canon was derived from the
words, quoted above, in the Prologue to Ecclesiasticus
(cf. *The Speaker's Commentary*, Apocrypha, vol. ii.
pp. 5, 38). It is, I think, quite incredible that words
occurring in a *Greek* preface to the translation of a
Hebrew work should have produced so lasting an effect
upon all subsequent *Hebrew* tradition as to have permanently influenced the arrangement of the Books of
the Hebrew Canon. It is, too, I think, quite incredible
that the thrice repeated formula, employed in the
Prologue, should have been an invention of the Greek
Translator, and not rather the description of the
Hebrew Scriptures commonly used among the Jews.
The theory, indeed, hardly requires refutation; and
while it could only have had its origin in the inability to
recognise the historical growth of the Hebrew Canon, it
illustrates the straits to which scholars are driven who
are unable to accept the view of the gradual formation
of the Canon, and are yet compelled to discover some
other plausible explanation for the origin and apparent
anomalies of its tripartite division.

We turn now to the subject of the formation of the
third group. We must pass in review the events which
occurred in Jerusalem, between the conclusion of the
Second Canon and what seems to have been, approximately, the time of the commencement of the Third.
During this interval, men like Jason and Alcimus, had
brought the High Priesthood to the lowest stage of degradation. Their corruption and treachery had been
followed by the persecution of Antiochus Epiphanes.
The latter tyrant, finding himself unable to bend, with

CHAP. VI. a rapidity sufficient to please him, had endeavoured to break, at a single blow, the obstinacy of the Jewish people. The horrors of his persecution had been followed by a wild outbreak. The seemingly hopeless struggle for freedom had been led by the patriotic sons of Mattathias B.C. 167 (cf. Dan. xi. 34). Little by little, in the face of overwhelming odds, the cause of the Jewish patriots had triumphed. First of all, religious freedom had been won; then, after a time, civil liberty had been obtained, foreign garrisons were withdrawn, the old borders restored. Under the successive High Priest-

Jonathan 161–143 B.C. Simon 143– 135 B.C. hoods of Jonathan and Simon, the brothers of Judas · Maccabeus, it appeared as if complete independence had been attained, and as if the Jewish people had once more entered upon a career of national greatness, united by the ties of devotion to the religion of Jehovah.

The edict of Antiochus 168 B.C.: its effect. It appears a not unnatural supposition, that the enthusiasm of that unique religious revival originated the movement, which sought to expand the Canon of the Hebrew Scriptures by the addition of another, a third, group of writings. The impulse for such a movement would not be far to seek. The subtle, but impolitic, command of Antiochus went forth to destroy the copies of the Jewish Law (1 Macc. i. 56, 57 [1]). He divined their influence, but he misjudged his power to annihilate it. His order enhanced, in the eyes of the patriot Jews, the value of the treasure which they possessed in their national writings. The destruction of books of the law would probably be

---

[1] 1 Macc. i. 56, 57, 'And when they had rent in pieces the books of the law which they found, they burnt them with fire. And wheresoever was found with any the book of the testament (*better*, covenant), or if any consented to the law, the king's commandment was, that they should put him to death' (A. V.). Cf. Jos. *Ant.* xi. 5, 4 ἠφανίζετο δὲ εἴ που βίβλος εὑρεθείη ἱερὰ καὶ νόμος.

accompanied by the indiscriminate destruction of any CHAP. VI.
other ancient and carefully-cherished Hebrew writings.
On whatsoever documents the ignorant and brutal
soldiery of Antiochus could lay hands, they would treat
all alike as 'copies of the law' in order to gain the reward
of their destruction. The pillage of Jerusalem and the
profanation of the Temple by the Syrian army must
have occasioned the loss of many a precious literary relic
of the past, which might otherwise have come down
to us. But the persecution of Antiochus, like that of
Diocletian 303 A.D., only succeeded in revealing to the
possessors of Scripture the priceless character of their
heritage. The blow of the persecutor ensured the
preservation of the Sacred Books. The power and
sanctity of Scripture were realised, when it was seen that
the arch-enemy of the nation sought to destroy the
religion of the Jews by destroying their books.

Amid the general revival of religion, of which the
renewal of the Temple services and the restoration of the
Temple fabric would be the most conspicuous signs, we
may be sure that a heightened veneration for the national
Scriptures played a significant and an important part.
It is, therefore, with feelings of special interest that we
come upon the traces of a tradition which connected a
movement, undertaken for the recovery, collection, and
preservation of ancient Jewish writings, with the great
name of Judas, the Maccabee. The tradition is to be *An import-*
found in the same spurious letter prefixed to the Second *ant tradi-*
Book of Maccabees that we had occasion to mention in *tion:*
the last chapter. The passage runs as follows: 'And in *2 Macc. ii. 15.*
like manner Judas also gathered together for us all those
writings that had been scattered by reason of the war
that we had; and they remain with us' (2 Macc. ii. 14).

CHAP. VI. The spurious character of the Epistle, in which the
passage occurs, makes it, of course, impossible for us to
put implicit confidence in its statements.   But its references to the Maccabean age are, by comparison with
its mention of Nehemiah, proportionately more trustworthy, as the writer may be presumed to rely upon
a more nearly contemporary source of information.
Judas was a man, not of letters, but of action ; and
his death followed shortly after his greatest victory
(161 B. C.).   Probably, therefore, if a movement for the
preservation of ancient Hebrew writings was set on foot
at this time, it was only by later popular legend impersonated in the name of the great hero, with whom the
war of Jewish independence, and everything connected
with it, were apt to be identified.   Among the writings
'that had been scattered by reason of the war,' we may
well imagine that the majority of the 'Kethubim' are to
be included.   At this, as at the other stages in the formation of the Canon, the process of collection and of
reverent preservation is preliminary to that of admission
within the sacred limits.   The religious leaders of the
patriotic party were not likely to delay long.   In raising
to the dignity of Holy Scripture writings which had thus
escaped destruction, they would make a selection of those
which had exerted the greatest influence over the spirit
of the devout Jews during the time both of the great
national rising and of the humiliation which preceded it.
To invest them with the rank of Canonical Scripture
would be the best means of ensuring their preservation
and of perpetuating their spiritual ascendency.   They
would be entrusted to the special charge of official
scribes ; the whole nation would at once be enlisted in
their protection and veneration.

When, however, was the first step taken? It is, perhaps, only a conjecture; but when we remember that the
recognition of, at least, some portion of the 'Kethubim'
is referred to in a writing not much later than 132 B. C.
(*Prol. Ecclus.*), we can hardly place it later in the century
than the important epoch of the revival under Jonathan
and Simon, who in turn succeeded to the leader-
ship of the Patriotic party, after the death of Judas
(161–135 B. C.).

The *Psalter* is the most important book of the 'Kethubim,' at the head of which it stands in our Hebrew Bibles.
We have little doubt that the Psalter was the first book
in the third group to obtain admission to the rank of
Scripture. The Psalter had hitherto been used as the
service book of the Temple singers[1]. Henceforward it
was to become the hymn book of Israel. Whereas it
had been the sacred book of poetry for the priests and
Levites, it was now to minister to the spiritual thought
of the whole nation. Its final revision, which probably
immediately preceded its admission into the rank of
Scripture, was subsequent to the persecution of Antiochus—if it be true, as is very generally supposed,
that the influence of the Maccabean era is to be traced in
Psalms xliv, lxxiv, lxxix, if not in others to which critics
have assigned a similar late date. The time of its final
promulgation in its present form and of its first recognition as part of the people's Scriptures, may well have
been that of the great religious revival that accompanied the success of the Maccabean revolt, and the
downfall of the Hellenizing party among the Priests
and nobles.

[1] For the use of the Psalter in the Temple services cf. the Titles of Pss.
xxiv, xlviii, xciii, xciv, in the Septuagint Version.

The influence of the Psalter as a book of Scripture soon made itself felt. Accordingly, whereas it is doubtful whether the Psalter is ever directly quoted by the son of Sirach, it is noticeable that in the First of Maccabees, a book written at the close of the same century, a quotation from the Psalter occurs, which is introduced with the formula of citation from Scripture (1 Macc. vii. 16; cf. Psalm lxxix. 2, 3). It is not for a moment denied that collections of Psalms had been in existence, and had been commonly known and used, long before. Of this we may be satisfied without stretching the interpretation of 'the Books (or things) of David' (2 Macc. ii. 13), which Nehemiah is said to have collected, so as to make it mean necessarily the Psalms of our Psalter.

The Chronicler makes free extracts from Psalms, mingling them together (1 Chron. xvi. 8–36); but he gives no sign of taking them from a sacred collection.

Evidence, to show that the Psalter had been finally compiled, or was treated as authoritative Scripture, is lacking before the Maccabean era. After that epoch, the evidence is forthcoming. May we not suppose, that its use by the devout and patriot Jews, during the three or four years, when the Temple worship was suspended (168–165), led to its general recognition immediately afterwards? Withdrawn from special priestly usage, it became at once the people's book of devotion.

An argument which has sometimes been brought forward in order to prove that the Psalter had been current in a completed form before the Maccabean era is based upon 1 Chron. xvi. 36. It is alleged that the Chronicler must have been acquainted with the Psalter in its division into five books, in order to

quote the doxology that concludes the cvi[th] Psalm. CHAP. VI.
The argument, however, is not so convincing as it
would appear to be at first sight. On the one hand,
it is maintained by some, that the doxologies that
appear at the close of the Books of Psalms were not, as
the above-mentioned argument would pre-suppose, added
at the time when the Psalter was finally edited ; but
that those Psalms were selected to conclude the various
books of the Psalter which happened to terminate
with a suitable doxology. On the other hand, Professor 1 *Chron.*
Cheyne suggests, 'it is not certain that any part of *xvi. 36.*
Psalm cvi. is quoted in 1 Chron. xvi ; vv. 34–36[a] consist
of liturgical formulae which were no more composed
solely for use in Psalm cvi. than the doxology attached
to the Lord's Prayer was originally formulated solely
to occupy its present position. It is highly probable
that a doxology was uttered by the congregation at the
close of every Psalm used in the Temple service, and
there is no reason why not only the doxology in verse 36,
but the two preceding verses, should not have been
attached by the Chronicler to the Psalm which he had
made up simply as liturgical formulae' (Cheyne's *Origin
of the Psalter*, p. 457). The division of the Psalter into
five books was more or less arbitrary. The compiler adds
to the concluding Psalms of the first four books (xli, lxxii,
lxxxix, cvi) a liturgical formula. The formula in Ps. cvi.
46 differs from the others, and its concluding verse is
longer by one clause than the parallel passage in 1 Chron.
The Chronicler would have had no object in omitting
it. But the editor of the Psalter may have adapted
the new words from the text of the Chronicler in
1 Chron. xvi. 36[b].

If now it be asked what other books were admitted

*Books undis-
puted and
disputed.*

into the Canon at or about the same time as the Psalter, we should reply, although with the reserve due to the necessary element of conjecture in our reply, Proverbs, Job, Ruth, Lamentations, Ezra and Nehemiah, and, very possibly, the Book of Daniel. With respect to the Books of Ecclesiastes, Song of Songs, Esther, and Chronicles, there are grounds for supposing that, in their case, admission was more tardy. At least, it is natural to surmise that objections, which were felt and expressed in later days, to the retention of some of these books within the Canon, very possibly reflect something of the hesitation that preceded their acceptance as Scripture. There are also other reasons, which I shall shortly mention, that make it unlikely that these four books were admitted at the earliest possible opportunity. They constitute what we may venture to call the 'Antilegomena' of the Old Testament. They are the 'disputed' books of the Hebrew Canon.

A few words are here necessary upon each of the books included in this last group of the Canonical writings. We shall be able to gather from our inquiry something of the nature of the writings themselves, and therefore judge better of the principles upon which they were admitted. The *Psalter* has been already noticed.

Proverbs.

The *Book of Proverbs* is a clear instance of a work that has been gradually compiled. From the title of chapter xxv we gather that the group of proverbs collected in chapters xxv–xxix, in the time of Hezekiah, was added when one, if not both, of the other main groups already existed (chaps. i–ix, x–xxiv). Unfortunately, the date at which the collection, made by the men of Hezekiah's reign, was thus appended has not been told us; but it is evident that to this combined work

were also added, at a much later time, the concluding
groups of proverbs (chaps. xxx and xxxi. 1–9, 10–31).
Three or four stages are thus clearly revealed by the
structure of the compilation. The latter groups, forming a sort of appendix, were probably added at the
time when the whole book was issued in its present
literary form, very probably not earlier than the fourth
century B.C. Its moral strength, the brightness and
variety of its maxims, the antiquity of its contents, and
the name of Solomon associated with the authorship of
its earlier portion, combined to place it in the highest
repute[1]. A book, however, which was so evidently
compiled for purposes of private religious edification
and so little adapted for purposes of public reading,
would have had no appropriate place among 'the
Prophets,' the group which, as we have seen, seems to have
been intended especially for public reading in the synagogues. But the Book of Proverbs would be among the
first to receive recognition in the formation of a more
miscellaneous group of religious writings. The practical
philosophy of Jewish wisdom (*Khokmah*) was by it
represented in the Hebrew Canon.

The *Book of Job*, which was, in all probability, com- *Job.*
posed during the period of the exile, belongs to a vein
of religious thought which, as may be shown by a
comparison of Job with the contents of Isaiah xl–
lxvi, seems to have exercised a profound influence
upon the religious conceptions of that epoch. Obviously of a very different class of writing from the
Prophets, it was not likely to be admitted into the
Canon until the formation of the 'Kethubim' allowed

[1] Its influence has left a strongly marked impression upon the Wisdom
of Sirach. Cf. Montefiore in the *Jewish Quarterly Review*, 1890, p. 490.

CHAP. VI. room for poetical and philosophical writings. The group of 'the Prophets' had been occupied with the consideration of national events and the national religion. The Book of Job appeared to deal with the troubles of individual experience. From the earliest times it was undoubtedly treated by the Jews as a strictly historical work (cf. Davidson's *Job*, Cambridge Bible for Schools, p. xiii). Whether a work of biography or imagination the Book of Job supplied a new element in the discussion of one of the great problems of life, viewed from the aspect of individual consciousness. It dealt with speculative questions. It had no fitting place in the Canon save in the mixed group of 'the Kethubim.'

Ruth. The *Book of Ruth*, in its simplicity and picturesqueness, is one of the most attractive writings that have come down to us from the pre-exilic literature. The pedigree of David (Ruth iv. 18–22) was probably appended long after its original composition, but may possibly have facilitated the admission of the little book into the Canon, either along with, or soon after, the Psalter with which the name of David was inseparably associated. In connexion with this suggestion, it is noticeable that in the Talmudic order (*Baba Bathra*, 14 b) the Book of Ruth stands immediately before the Psalter, the book of David's genealogy preceding the book of his Psalms. (See Chapter XII.)

It has already been mentioned that by some scholars the Book of Ruth is considered to have originally formed part of the Book of Judges. In support of their view, they appeal to the traditional position of the book in the Septuagint version, and to the statements of Jerome respecting the Hebrew custom of his day. But Jerome's opinion in the matter adds nothing, as we shall see later on,

to the evidence of the Septuagint ; while the arrangement CHAP. VI.
of the books in the Septuagint version, according to
subject-matter, deprives the juxtaposition of Ruth to
Judges of any real significance. With this exception,
the Hebrew tradition is uniform, that the book belonged,
from the first, to 'the Kethubim.' And this is what we
should gather from a comparison of the style and contents of the Book of Ruth with the concluding chapters
of the Book of Judges. The quiet idyllic picture which it
gives of Palestine stands in sharp contrast to the wild
scenes of disorder described in Judges xvii–xxi. Nor can
we ignore the thought, that in the Book of Judges, which
deals for the most part with events of national interest
and political importance, transacted also generally in
the northern part of the country, we should not expect
to find a quiet domestic tale, of which the scene is laid
at Bethlehem, a town of Judah. Ruth has more resemblance to Samuel than to Judges.

The *Book of Lamentations* has occasioned a similar Lamenta-
difficulty. In the Septuagint version, it has a place tions.
immediately after Jeremiah, and a preface is prefixed to
it stating that it is the composition of Jeremiah. Jerome
affirms that in the Hebrew Scriptures 'Lamentations' was
reckoned with Jeremiah among 'the Prophets.' The
tradition of Jeremiah's authorship, commonly current
among Jews and Christians alike, would be sufficient to
account for the position of the book in the Septuagint
version, and for the tradition that it once had a place
amongst the 'Prophets.' Leaving out of the question
the matter of authorship, which is very far from being
certainly ascertained, it will be sufficient here to point
out the improbability that the Book of Jeremiah, which
closes with the historical narrative of chapter lii,

ever had a poetical section appended to it.   If it be objected that the writings of Isaiah furnish an exact parallel, the concluding section (Isaiah xl–lxvi) having been appended to the historical narrative (xxxvi–xxxix) which concludes the prophecies of Isaiah I, we may reply that the analogy is a misleading one. There is all the difference in the world between a long prophetical section like Isaiah xl–lxvi and the little group of poems, some of them containing acrostic poetry, comprised in the Book of Lamentations. Such poetry partook little of the character of writing adapted for inclusion among 'the Prophets'; Isaiah xl–lxvi seemed exactly to coincide with it. If, again, 'Lamentations' had been appended to the writings of the prophet at or before the time of the formation of the second Canonical group, I can see no sufficient reason for its separation at a later time, nor any likelihood that Jewish scribes would have permitted so innovating a change. It is more natural, I believe, to suppose that the poetical character of the work, which excluded it from 'the Prophets,' caused it to be introduced, at the same time with the Psalter and with Job, among the miscellaneous books of 'the Kethubim.'

Ezra and Nehemiah.   The *Books 'Ezra' and 'Nehemiah'* form one work in the Hebrew manuscripts; and there is no reason to doubt that they were not only originally united, but that they originally formed the concluding portion of the Books of Chronicles. The fact of their having been separated from the Books of Chronicles and of their occupying a position, in the traditional order of the Hebrew Bible, in front of, instead of, as we should expect from chronological reasons, after, the Books of Chronicles, is at first sight a strange circumstance, and

difficult to account for. But it receives a satisfactory CHAP. VI.
explanation from the probable history of their admission into the Canon. The narrative contained in 'the
Prophets' had closed with the middle of the exile
(2 Kings xxv. 27). We may well fancy how essential
it would seem, that some record of the return from the
exile, of the restoration of the Temple, of the rebuilding
of the city walls, of the first reading of 'the Law,' should
be included in the writings of the Jewish Scriptures.
The latter portion of the Chronicler's work, which seems
to have been compiled not earlier than the beginning
of the third century B.C., offered just what was required.
If now we adopt the conjecture, that a portion, identical
with our books, Ezra and Nehemiah, was separately
admitted into the Canon, and that, at some later time,
the remaining portion, i.e. the Books of Chronicles, received similar recognition, we are able to reconcile the
phenomena of the identity of style and structure (cf.
2 Chron. xxxvi. 22, 23, Ezra i. 1-3) with the difficulty
presented, at first sight, by the position assigned to Ezra
and Nehemiah, separate from and yet in front of Chronicles. That Ezra and Nehemiah had already been detached
from the Chronicles in the days of Jesus, the son of Sirach
(B. C. 180), is certainly possible, and is, perhaps, favoured
by the reference made to the name of Nehemiah in Ecclus.
xlix. 13 (cf. Neh. vii. 1). The allusion in the same passage to Zerubbabel and Joshua is probably derived from
Haggai and Zechariah (Hag. i. 12, 14, ii. 2, 4, 21, 23; Zech.
iii. 1-9), and is therefore inapplicable for this argument.

The Book of Daniel. The present is not the place to Daniel.
enter into details of the thorny controversy respecting
the date and authorship of the Book of Daniel. For
our purpose, however, it is important to call attention

L

CHAP. VI. to one point.   We may put it in the form of a question.
Supposing that so remarkable a work, dealing in a
spirit of prophecy with the destiny of the great empires
of the world, had been well known to the Jews at the
time that the group of 'the Prophets' was formed, is it
probable that it would have failed to receive a place in
that portion of the Canon?   It is, I believe, most improbable.   The inference is obvious.   Either the book
was not known at the conclusion of the third century
B. C.; or it had not yet been compiled.   Of the two
alternatives, the former, I confess, seems to me the
more improbable; the latter has a good deal to be said
in its favour.   (a) It would be difficult to suppose that
a book of such importance could remain in obscurity.
(b) The character of the Hebrew in which it is written
favours the hypothesis of a late date.   (c) The absence
of any reference by the son of Sirach to Daniel, in his
list of the 'famous men,' would be most surprising, supposing that he had been acquainted with our Book of
Daniel.   In a somewhat similar list, enumerating the
heroes of the Jewish race, which occurs in a book composed less than a century later, we find allusion made
both to the Three Children and to Daniel in the den
of lions (cf. 1 Macc. ii. 59, 60).   (d) To some readers a yet
more convincing proof of the date of composition is
afforded by the contents of chaps. viii, ix, xi, in which the
incidents described evidently correspond with details of
history, politics, movements of armies, treaties, and royal
marriages, that belong, during the first half of the second
century B.C., to the mutual relations of Syria, Egypt, and
Palestine.   Judging by analogy, such detailed description has less resemblance to the style of prediction of
the future than to that of the apocalyptic narration of

the past. (*e*) It may also be noted, that while no quotation from, or allusion to, the book occurs in writings of an earlier date than the Maccabean era, references to it are frequent after the middle of the second century B. C. The oldest portion of the Sibylline Oracles (iii. 396–400), written possibly about 130 B.C., shows acquaintance with it. Its contents are referred to by the author of 1 Maccabees (i. 54, ii. 59, 60); and the rise of Jewish apocalyptic literature, which was so largely coloured by imitation of Daniel, has never been attributed to a date earlier than the latter half of the second century B. C. But whatever conclusion be come to upon the question of its date, its admission to the Canon was evidently not long delayed after the commencement of the formation of the Kethubim group[1].

That the remaining books, which I have called the '*Antilegomena*' of 'the Kethubim,' were admitted with great hesitation, and after considerable delay, and that, even after their admission to Canonical rank, they were, for a long time, viewed with suspicion and but little used, seems to be a natural conclusion to be drawn from the dearth of reference to them in the Jewish literature of the next two centuries (100 B.C.–100 A.D.), and from the rumours of opposition, more especially to the Song of Songs, Esther, and Ecclesiastes, of which we find echoes in later Hebrew tradition.

'Antilegomena.'

The *Song of Songs* is derived from the best period of Hebrew literature. At a time when the poetry of the Psalms, Job, and Lamentations was being received into

The Song of Songs.

---

[1] The dependence of the first portion of Baruch (i–iii. 8) upon Daniel (chap. ix) is clearly shown by Baruch i. 15, 16, 17, 21, ii. 1, 9, 11, 19. But the composition or re-edition of Baruch (1) belongs to a much later date than that traditionally assigned to it: cf. Schürer, *Gesch. des Jüd. Volks*, 2ter Theil, p. 721, and *Psalms of Solomon* (ed. Ryle and James), pp. lxxii–lxxvii.

CHAP. VI. the sacred Canon, it would have been natural to include so exquisite a poem, which was popularly ascribed to Solomonic authorship. Having once been admitted, however, grave objections seem to have been raised against it. Jewish scholars were perplexed by the difficulty of discovering a suitable interpretation to its seemingly secular theme. Allusions to the book are not found in literature before the Christian era. It is included in the list of Hebrew Scriptures recorded by Melito (170 A. D.). According to Jewish tradition, its canonicity formed the subject of discussion among the Jewish doctors of the first and second centuries A. D.[1]

Ecclesiastes. *Ecclesiastes*, which had been written probably in the third cent. B. C., contained much that must have sounded strangely in the ears of Jews, much that, we know, gave offence to some readers. But its inclusion in the Canon had very probably taken place, before these objections were fully realised. The name of Solomon had possibly contributed to its admission into the group, which already included the Proverbs and the Song of Songs. Its place in the Canon represents one phase of the spirit of Jewish wisdom, or Khokmah, in an age of intellectual questioning. As we shall see, its methods of dealing with the problems of life gave rise to grave doubts among the Jews, as to whether its statements could be reconciled with the 'Law,' and, therefore, whether it could be retained within the Canon. But it is everywhere implied in these discussions, that the book was already in the number of the Scriptures, and, according to a Talmudic story[2], it was

---

[1] See Chap. ix.

[2] See Jer. Berakoth, Chap. vii. 2 (fol. 11[b]), 'The king (Jannaeus) said to him, "why didst thou mock me by saying that 900 sacrifices were required, when the half would have sufficed?" "I did not mock thee,"

quoted as Scripture by Simon ben Shetach in the reign of Alexander Jannaeus (B. C. 105–79). Along with the Song of Songs, its canonicity, according. to Jewish tradition, was discussed and ratified at the Council of Jamnia (90 and 118 A.D.). See Cheyne, *Job and Solomon*, pp. 279 seq.

The *Book of Esther*, the composition of which may *Esther.* very probably be assigned to the third century B.C., became in later days one of the most popular writings of the Kethubim. But its admission to the Canon was either so long delayed, or was afterwards, for some reason, regarded with such disfavour, that in some quarters among the Jews of the first century A.D., as we shall see later on, it was omitted altogether from their list of sacred books (e.g. Melito, cf. chap. xi). The doubt about its acceptance may possibly have arisen in connexion with the Feast of Purim. The book contains the explanation of the origin and observance of that feast. Was objection taken to the book on the ground of its inculcating a feast not commanded in the Law? Or did the observance of the feast on the fourteenth of Adar (Esth. ix. 19) appear to add undue importance to the festival which commemorated the victory of Judas Maccabeus over Nicanor on the thirteenth of Adar (B.C. 161), and was it thus capable of being regarded with suspicion and jealousy by the Pharisee faction, who, throughout the greater part of the first century B.C., were at deadly enmity with the Asmonean house? Or, was it that the fast commanded to be observed on the thirteenth of Adar, in commemoration of Haman's attempt to destroy the Jews on that

replied Simon, "thou hast paid thy share, and I mine . ... Verily it is written (Eccles. vii. 12): *For wisdom is a defence, and money is a defence.*"'

day (Esth. iii. 13, ix. 1), conflicted with the feast-day of Nicanor, and therefore gave offence to the populace? Such are some of the various suggestions that have been made. Yet another ground of objection may have been found in the absence of the sacred Name. This peculiar feature, which it shares with 1 Maccabees (in the best text), may be accounted for, either by the exaggerated dread of profanity in the frequent use of the sacred Name, or, as Riehm suggests (*Einleit.* ii. 341) by the writer having intended his work not for religious usage, but for reading on occasions of secular festivity. The same explanation, which accounts for the absence of the sacred Name, will account for the hesitation to place the work on a level with the rest of Scripture.

'The day of Mordecai' was observed in the days of the writer of 2 Maccabees (xv. 36). Whether, in consequence, we should be justified in inferring the general recognition of Esther among the sacred books at the beginning of the first century A.D., is obviously a very doubtful question. All we can say is, that it was recognised among the sacred books by Josephus, who, when speaking of the Canon of Scripture, evidently had the Book of Esther in view, as the last book, in point of date of composition, that had been admitted into the sacred category (Joseph. *Contr. Ap.* i. 8).

The temper and tone of the book, perhaps, commended it to the choice of a generation which still smarted under the recollection of the cruelties perpetrated by Antiochus Epiphanes, and may account for its acceptance in the second century B.C.; but, with equal probability, it may have incurred unpopularity with the more thoughtful spirits among the teachers of the people in the first century B. C. Was it the recrudescence of per-

secution that revived the popularity of the book? Did
the attitude of the Roman Empire recall the savage
purpose of Haman, and restore the narrative of Esther
to favour? Or, was it the resemblance between Haman,
the Agagite, and Herod, the Idumean?

We mention the *Books of Chronicles* last of all, not *The Books of Chronicles.*
because, in their case, canonicity has been more disputed
than in the case of the three last-mentioned books, but
because in the traditional order of the Canon they present the appearance of being added as an appendix. The
detachment of Ezra and Nehemiah from the main work,
their admission into the Canon as a separate narrative,
and their position there immediately in front of Chronicles, form a line of probable evidence, that the canonicity
of Chronicles was recognised at a considerably later
date than that of Ezra and Nehemiah. But at what
date did this take place? In our Saviour's time, the
Canon of Hebrew Scripture very probably concluded
with Chronicles. The real pertinency of the argument
which has been alleged in favour of this view, based
upon our Lord's appeal to the whole category of
innocent blood shed 'from the blood of Abel to the
blood of Zachariah,' is only then understood, when it is
seen that He is not referring to the limits of time, from
Abel to Joash (Matt. xxiii. 35, Luke xi. 51, cf. 2 Chron.
xxiv. 20-22), but to the limits of the sacred Canon,
from Genesis to Chronicles—from the first to the last
book in Hebrew Scripture: it was equivalent to an
appeal, in Christian ears, to the whole range of the Bible
from Genesis to Revelation.

We have nothing further to go upon than probability,
in assuming that the four last-named books, Song of
Songs, Ecclesiastes, Esther, and Chronicles, were accepted

CHAP. VI. into the Canon at a later date than the other writings of the Hagiographa.   If so, they may have occupied, for some time, the position of ' Antilegomena,' or disputed books, accepted by some Jews, and rejected by others. The books of the Hagiographa were not continuously read in the Synagogues.   They were not, therefore, estimated by the same test of public usage.   It would be possible, I should think, for a book to hover a long time in suspense, having been admitted into the sacred list at a time of popular religious enthusiasm, but having afterwards incurred suspicion, in consequence of doubts as to its orthodoxy, raised by the factious jealousy or officious zeal of learned scribes.   But, once admitted, a book was never likely to be excluded.   The dread of novelty, which protected the Canon against encroachment, helped also to appease the resentment against writings that had already received a quasi-recognition. The fact of a book having once been received within the list of the national Scripture never failed to outweigh, in the long run, the scruples that were felt at its doubtful orthodoxy.

There are unfortunately wide gaps in the external evidence, which stretches over more than two centuries of Jewish literature, from the Prologue to Ecclesiasticus, written about 132 B. C., down to the *Contra Apionem* of Josephus, written at the close of the first century A. D. But the external evidence requires separate consideration, and we must devote to it the following chapter.

CHAPTER VII.

THE THIRD CANON (*continued*).

1. *The Greek Prologue to Ecclesiasticus.* This writing has already been referred to; and attention has been drawn to the importance of its testimony, the earliest that has come down to us, respecting the 'tripartite division of the Canon.' The vagueness of the writer's words, in designating the third division, stands in sharp contrast to the precision with which he describes the first two divisions by the very names that have traditionally been attached to them. The vagueness, such as it is, is probably due to the hitherto undefined character of the canonicity, granted to the miscellaneous contents of the new group. But the suggestion which has sometimes been made, that the writer of the Prologue considered his grandfather's work could ultimately take rank with those 'other' writings, among the Scriptures of the Jews, is not justified by the language of the opening sentence. Its importance makes it desirable I should quote it here *in extenso*, rambling and obscure though it is.

'Whereas many and great things have been delivered unto us by the law and the prophets and by the others that have followed upon them, for which it is due to commend Israel for instruction and wisdom; and since it behoves those who read not only to become skilful themselves, but also such as love learning to be able to profit them that are without, both by speaking and writing ; my grandfather Jesus, seeing he had much given himself to the reading of the law and the prophets and the other books of the fathers, and had gotten therein sufficient proficiency, was drawn on also himself to write something pertaining to learning and wisdom, to the intent that those who love learning might, after giving their attention to these *words* also, make yet further progress in their life according to the law.'

The exact meaning of the last sentence may be obscure ; but there is no thought of putting the Wisdom of Sirach into competition with the writings 'of the fathers.'   It is affirmed that the author's sole object was to assist others to a closer walk in accordance with the law, and that his assiduous studies in 'the law, prophets, and the other books' especially fitted him for the task of counselling them.   The translator concludes the Prologue with the remark, that he intends his version 'for those also who, living abroad, are wishful to be learners, being engaged in a moral reform leading to a strict life according to the law.'

The translator, if he were like the rest of his fellow-countrymen, would certainly not have placed 'the other' writings on the same level with 'the law and the prophets'; still less, we believe, would he have regarded any work, so recent as that of his grandfather, as deserving of a place among 'the books of the fathers.'

His view of 'the other books' may be thus explained.   He was aware of the two divisions of Holy Scripture, 'the law and the prophets,' which had long stood over against, and separate from, the great mass of Hebrew literature.   But he was aware also that certain other writings had recently been gradually raised above the rest of Jewish literature and had become separated from it, reverence, affection, and usage causing them to be treated as similar, though not to be reckoned as equal, in holiness, to 'the law and the prophets.' Whether this third group already contained in 132 B.C. the whole of the Kethubim, may reasonably be doubted.

2. *The Septuagint Version.* It is disappointing to *2. The Septuagint Version.* find how little evidence to the Canon is to be derived from the LXX version. The version must have been com- *begun circ. 250 B.C.* menced by the translation of 'the Law' about the year 250 B.C. The translation of other books followed; but, outside 'the Law,' there seems to have been no unity of plan. The books were translated by different hands, and at different times. Versions of the same book competed, as it were, for general acceptance. Those were accepted which found most general favour. With the possible exception of the Pentateuch [1], the version contains simply those renderings of books which, having in course of time most recommended themselves to the Jewish residents in Alexandria, outlived, because they were preferred to, all other renderings.

We infer from the Prologue to Ecclesiasticus that in *possibly complete, circ. 132 B.C.* 132 B.C. a Greek translation already existed of 'the Law and the Prophets and the other writings.' 'For the same things uttered in Hebrew, and translated into another tongue, have not the same force in them: and not only these things (i. e. the Wisdom of Sirach), but the law itself and the prophets, and the rest of the books have no small difference, when they are spoken in their own language.'

The translation of some disputed books of the Hagiographa had clearly taken place before the year 132 B.C.

---

[1] That a Translation of the Torah was executed at the request or at the expense of an Egyptian prince is the least that may be inferred from the Jewish tradition underlying the Letter of Aristeas and the statements of Josephus (*Ant.* xii. 2, *Cont. Ap.* ii. 4) and Philo (*Vita Mosis* ii. 5).

Whether all of them had been then translated, we cannot pretend to say for certain. It appears that the Greek
translation of the Books of Chronicles was known to
Eupolemus, the historian (circ. 150 B.C.)[1], and that, according to the subscription to the Book of Esther, the translation of that book may possibly be dated at 178 B.C. But
the mere fact of the translation of a book does not convey
anything to us as regards its position in the Canon.

The inclusion of the so-called Apocryphal Books in
the LXX version is sometimes alleged to be a proof, that
the Alexandrian Jews acknowledged a wider Canon of
Scripture than their Palestinian countrymen. But this
is not a legitimate inference. Our copies of the LXX
are derived from Christian sources ; and all that can
certainly be proved from the association of additional
books with those of the Hebrew Canon, is that these
other books found favour with the Christian community. Doubtless, they would not thus have found
favour with the Christians, if they had not also enjoyed
high repute among the Jews, from whom they were obtained along with the undoubted books of the Hebrew
Canon.   The fact, however, that, neither in the writings
of Philo, nor in those of Josephus—Jews who both make
use of the LXX version—have we any evidence favouring
the canonicity of the Apocryphal Books, is really conclusive against their having been regarded as Scripture by
Greek-speaking Jews before the second century A.D.

The testimony of the LXX version has chiefly a negative value. The translation of the books by different
hands, and apparently without concert, would hardly
have taken place when the Canon was fully determined.
The only considerable portion of the translation done at

---

[1] Cf. Freudenthal, quoted by Schürer, ii. p. 733.

the same time and by the same hands is the Pentateuch ;
and the Pentateuch, as we have seen, was probably the
only certainly recognised Canon at the middle of the
third cent. B.C.   The want of uniformity, the inequalities
and inaccuracies which characterize the rest of the translation, show that its execution was not part of a sacred
duty, nor even carried out in deference to any official
requirement.   It may fairly be questioned, whether the
Alexandrine Jews could have had any idea of the
canonicity of such books as Daniel and Esther, when
translations of these books were made, in which the text
was allowed to differ so widely from the original as in
the LXX version, and Haggadic variations were freely
interpolated.   Unfortunately we do not know when the
renderings were made.   The resemblance in the style of
the LXX version of Ecclesiastes to that of the version of
Aquila has been remarked upon.   But it is unreasonable
to build upon this resemblance the theory that the LXX
version of Ecclesiastes was rendered by Aquila himself.
It belongs to the same school ; but the improbability [1] of
the suggestion that Ecclesiastes was not translated before
the end of the first century A.D., needs no demonstration.
Yet, even if this were shown, the date of the Greek
translation would prove little as to the date at which
the canonicity of the Book was determined.

3. The *First Book of Maccabees*, which was composed *3. 1 Macca-*
probably at the close of the second cent. B.C. or early in *bees.*
the first cent. B.C., contains a reference to the Psalms,
introduced with a formula of quotation from Scripture,
'Whereupon they believed him ; howbeit he took of
them threescore men, and slew them in one day *according to the words which he wrote,* "The flesh of the saints

[1] See pp. 148 f.

CHAP. VII. have they cast out, and their blood have they shed round about Jerusalem, and there was none to bury them "' (1 Macc. vii. 16, 17 ; cf. Ps. lxxix. 2, 3).

We also find in this book (ch. ii. 59, 60) a mention of Ananias, Azarias, and Mesael, who 'by believing were saved out of the flame,' and of Daniel who 'for his innocency was delivered from the mouth of the lions.' Their names are commemorated after the mention of Abraham, Joseph, Phinehas, Joshua, Caleb, David, and Elijah. It is *probable* that the speech of Mattathias is intended to pass in review a list of heroic names, familiar to his hearers through the writings contained in the Canon of Scripture. But, though it proves that the contents of the Book of Daniel were well known, it cannot be claimed as establishing anything more than the *probability* of the book being at that time regarded as Canonical. The reference in 1 Macc. i. 54 to Daniel's words in Dan. ix. 24–27 is undoubted ; but proves nothing more for our purpose than acquaintance with the book.

4. Philo.   4. The writings of *Philo*, who died about 50 A.D., do not throw very much positive light upon the history of the Canon. To him, as to other Alexandrine Jews, the Law alone was in the highest sense the Canon of Scripture, and alone partook of divine inspiration in the most absolute degree.

Philo's writings, however, show that he was well acquainted with many other books of the Old Testament besides the Pentateuch. He quotes from Joshua, Judges, Samuel, Kings, Isaiah, Jeremiah, the Minor Prophets, Psalms, Proverbs, Job, and Ezra. According to some scholars he is said to show acquaintance with books of the Apocrypha. But this is very doubtful ; and, even if it be granted, he certainly never appeals to

them in support of his teaching in the way that he does
to books included in the Hebrew Canon, and never
applies to them the *formulae* of citation which he employs, when referring to the acknowledged books of the
Jewish Scriptures. By comparison with his quotations
from the Pentateuch, his quotations from the other
sacred writings are very scanty; but it is observable that
even in these few extracts he ascribes an inspired origin
to Joshua, Samuel, Kings, Ezra, Psalms, Proverbs, Isaiah,
Jeremiah, Hosea, and Zechariah. The negative value of
his testimony is strong, though not conclusive, against
the canonicity of any book of the Apocrypha, or of any
work not eventually included in the Hebrew Canon.
On the other hand, the absence of any reference in his
writings to Ezekiel, Daniel, Ecclesiastes, Song of Songs,
Esther, Ruth and Lamentations, to which some would
also add Chronicles, must also be taken into account [1].
Undoubtedly we have no right to expect that every
book of the Old Testament will be quoted in the writings
of a single author. Personal prejudices and predilections,
the absence of any point of contact between a book of
Scripture and the author's particular subject, may often
account for an apparent silence. But, in the case of a
religious writer so voluminous as Philo, and possessed
with so ardent a veneration for his people's Scriptures,

[1] Whether or not Chronicles (1. vii. 14) is quoted in *De Congr. erud. gr.*
§ 8, its acknowledgment is practically implied in the quotation from Ezra
(viii. 2, cf. *De confus. ling.* § 28). On the subject of Philo's quotations
I may perhaps venture to refer the reader to my own book, *Philo and Holy
Scripture* (Macmillan, 1895), in which all Philo's citations from and
allusions to the books of the Old Testament have been extracted and
arranged.

N. B. The quotations from Hosea (xiv. 8, 9, cf. *De plant. N.* § 33) and
Zechariah (vi. 12, cf. *De confus. ling.* § 14) are sufficient attestation to his
use of the Minor Prophets, which were treated as one book.

we are conscious that we are hardly justified in ascribing to merely accidental causes the total absence of any allusion to six, or seven, of the books of the Hagiographa. Considering the strange treatment accorded to the Books of Daniel and Esther in the LXX version, it is more than probable that Philo, like other Jews in Alexandria, had not learned to attach to them the value of Canonical Scripture. The doubts, too, which were elsewhere felt respecting Ecclesiastes, Song of Songs, and Esther, may very reasonably incline us to suppose that Philo's silence respecting them was not altogether accidental. The possibility that Ruth is to be included with Judges, and Lamentations with Jeremiah, may fairly be taken into account.

De Vita Contempl. § 3, doubtful evidence. A famous passage in Philo's *De Vita Contemplativa* § 3 (ii. 475), which so clearly speaks of the tripartite division of the Hebrew Canon, 'laws and oracles, delivered by prophets, and hymns and the other (books) by which knowledge and piety are mutually increased and perfected,' deserves mention, on account of its having been so often referred to in connexion with the history of the Jewish Canon. But doubts have been entertained as to the genuineness of the passage. The treatise in which it occurs has been supposed by some recent students of Philo's works to have been written in the third or fourth cent. A.D.[1] Whether this be so or not, we are precluded from adducing it, with any confidence, as evidence to the Jewish thought of the first cent. A.D. As, however, the passage only relates to the division of the sacred Canon, for which we have plenty of evidence elsewhere, and does

---

[1] Lucius, *Die Therapeuten* (1879). On the other side, see Edersheim, *Dict. Christ. Biog.*, s. 'Philo'; and Massebieau, *Le traité de la Vie Contemplative et la question des Thérapeutes*, Paris, 1888.

not affect its contents, the fact of its genuineness being
disputed is not a matter of any vital importance.

5. *The New Testament.* The writings of the New Testament furnish clear evidence to the 'tripartite division'
of the Hebrew Canon of Scripture. Our Lord's words
'that all things must needs be fulfilled which are written
in the Law of Moses, and the Prophets, and the Psalms
concerning me' (Luke xxiv. 44), can hardly be understood on any other supposition; but they do not warrant
the assertion, which has sometimes been made, that they
prove the completion of the Hebrew Canon in our Lord's
time. Our Lord appeals to the Messianic predictions
contained in the three divisions of Jewish Scripture.
He does not, however, apply the title of 'Psalms' to the
whole group of 'the Kethubim.' He singles out the
Psalter, we may imagine, from among the other writings
of this group, because the Messianic element in it was
conspicuous, and because, of all the writings outside
'the Law and the Prophets,' this book was the best
known and had produced the deepest impression upon
the religious feeling of the Jews. Our Lord's reference
to the group of 'the Prophets' (John vi. 45) is not in-
consistent with acquaintance with the three divisions of
the Canon; and similar evidence may be derived from
the Acts of the Apostles (vii. 42, xiii. 40).

Quotations are found in the writings of the New
Testament from all the books of the Old Testament,
except Obadiah, Nahum, Ezra and Nehemiah, Esther,
Song of Songs, and Ecclesiastes. The absence of any
reference to Obadiah and Nahum does not affect the question of the canonicity of these books; the whole collection
of the Twelve Minor Prophets was by the Jews treated *en
bloc* as one canonical work, while the brevity of the two

CHAP. VII. books in question will quite account for their not having chanced to furnish appropriate material for quotation.

When we turn to the books of 'the Kethubim,' the absence of any citation from, or reference to, Ezra and Nehemiah does not call for remark, as affecting the question of the canonicity of these books, seeing that reference to the Chronicles is undisputed (Matt. xxiii. 35, Luke xi. 51), and the recognition of Chronicles presupposes that of Ezra and Nehemiah.

Esth., Song of Songs, Eccles., not referred to; not strange. The three 'disputed' books, Esther, Song of Songs, and Ecclesiastes, receive from the New Testament no support, either by quotation, or by allusion, for their place among the Canonical Scriptures. On the other hand, it would be rash to infer from their contents not being mentioned or referred to, that the writers of the New Testament did not regard them as canonical. For it cannot be said that the contents of these books were at all especially likely to supply matter for quotation or illustration in the New Testament writings. If we ask ourselves, whether, supposing these three books to have been included in the Canon, there would be anything improbable in their not being referred to in the New Testament, considering the peculiar character of each of them, there can be little doubt what an unprejudiced reply would be.

Groups to which they belong, recognised. It is perhaps more to the purpose, in order to arrive at a perfectly fair judgment respecting the 'silence' of the New Testament, to have regard not so much to the fact that individual books are not quoted or referred to, as to the fact that the groups of books to which they belong are very definitely recognised. The testimony of the New Testament to the latest written book of the Canon, 'Daniel,' is very explicit (Matt. xxiv. 15); and the

allusion to the Book of Chronicles in Matt. xxiii. 35,
Luke xi. 51, admits, as has been mentioned before, of
a most suitable explanation, when it is regarded as an
appeal to the last book in the completed Hebrew
Scriptures. If so, the recognition of the last book in
the sacred collection may possibly imply the recognition
of all the others, even though they are not all directly
cited. Thus Song of Songs and Ecclesiastes may reasonably be imagined to have long been popularly associated
in men's minds with the writings of Solomon, and the
Book of Esther with Daniel and Nehemiah, and all
three, therefore, to have naturally been included in the
Canon. Of course, this is purely hypothetical; but all
three disputed works may well have belonged to the
Canon, without either becoming the favourite literature
of the New Testament writers, or furnishing material
which in any way affected their style, or influenced their
thought, or lent itself naturally for uses of quotation.

Against the hasty reasoning that, because these three
disputed books are not referred to in the New Testament, they were, therefore, not reckoned in the Hebrew
Canon by the first Christian writers, it must be urged,
(1) that these same books were apparently regarded
as canonical, at the close of the first century A.D., by *N. T. pre-*
the author of 4 Esdras and by Josephus, and (2) that *supposes*
the references in the New Testament to the Old Testa- *completed*
ment Scriptures lead the unprejudiced reader to sup- *Canon.*
pose, that the Jewish Scriptures were regarded in the
middle of that century as a complete and finished collection, the sanctity of which would utterly preclude
the idea of any further alteration. This latter point is
probably one that will have often impressed itself upon
readers of the New Testament. Allusions and appeals

to ‘the Scriptures,’ ‘the holy Scriptures,’ ‘the sacred writings,’ leave a conviction upon the mind, which is probably as strong as it is instinctive, that the writers refer to a sacred national collection which had been handed down from ages past, and whose limits could never be disturbed by addition or withdrawal (e.g. Matt. xxii. 29, Acts xviii. 24, Romans i. 2, 2 Tim. iii. 15).

Apocryphal books, not treated as Scripture.

The assertion has sometimes been made (cf. Wildeboer, pp. 44–47) that the New Testament writers took a somewhat lax view of the limits of the Canon of Hebrew Scripture, and were ready to extend it to a wider circle of writings than is comprised in ‘the Law,’ ‘the Prophets,’ and ‘the Writings.’ When we come to examine more closely what this statement means, we feel quite at a loss to discover how such a startling conclusion is reached. It is possible, nay, more probable than not, that some of the writers of the New Testament were acquainted with some of the books of the Apocrypha. But the parallelism of such passages as Heb. i. 3 with Wisdom vii. 26, and Jas. i. 9, 19 with Ecclus. iv. 29, v. 11, is not so very remarkable as even to make it certain, that the New Testament writer was in each case the borrower of the phrase, common to him and the Apocryphal writer. But, granting that this was the case, it would show nothing more than that the New Testament writer was acquainted with the contemporary literature of his people. In no case can it be said that a New Testament writer appeals to an extra-canonical work for support of doctrine or statement, although references for purposes of illustration may be admitted. I scarcely believe that any tendency to enlarge the borders of the Hebrew Canon can seriously be thought to be implied by the possible

reference in Heb. xi. 35, 36 to the contents of 2 Macc. vi.
18–vii. 42, in Heb. xi. 37 to an unknown passage in the
Ascension of Isaiah, in 2 Tim. iii. 8 to an unknown
work in which the magicians Jannes and Jambres figured,
in Jude 9 to a passage possibly[1] contained in the
Assumption of Moses, in Jude 14 to the Book of Enoch.
Reference to contemporary literature is not incompatible
with strict views as to the Canon. Surely, to suggest that,
because reference is made to such works as those just
mentioned—works which, so far as is known, never had
the slightest possibility of being included within the
Canon—the New Testament writers must therefore have
held very lax views on the subject of canonicity, argues
a strange incapacity to treat the New Testament writers
as rational human beings, or as Jews of Palestine in the
first century A.D.

There remains to be noticed a group of passages (Matt.
xxvii. 9, Luke xi. 49, John vii. 38, 1 Cor. ii. 9, Ephes.
v. 14, Jude 14–16), in which it has been alleged that
citations occur that cannot be identified with any passage in the Old Testament, and, therefore, can only have
been made from Apocryphal writings[2]. A reference to
any good commentary will show that, whatever explanation be adopted of the difficulty presented in Matt.
xxvii. 9 and Luke xi. 49, the theory of their containing
an appeal to the authority of an Apocryphal book rests on

---

[1] Cf. Origen, *De Princip.* iii. 2. 1.

[2] Jerome (*Comm. in Matt.* xxvii. 9), 'Legi nuper in quodam Hebraico
volumine, quod Nazarenae sectae mihi Hebraeus obtulit, Jeremiae apocry-
phum, in quo haec ad verbum scripta reperi.'

Origen on 1 Cor. ii. 9, 'In nullo regulari libro invenitur, nisi in secretis
Eliae prophetae.' (*Comm. in Matt.* xxvii. 9; iii. 118; ed. Lommatzsch,
tom. v. 29.

The passage in Jas. iv. 5, 6 has only, by a mistranslation, been supposed
to contain a direct quotation.

CHAP. VII. no trustworthy foundation and is to be rejected. The quotations in John vii. 38, 1 Cor. ii. 9, are to be explained as giving the substance and combined thought of more than one passage of the Old Testament. The words in Eph. v. 14, if not to be explained in the same way, may very possibly have been derived from some early Christian liturgical source. Only in Jude 14–16 do we find a clear case of quotation, and that from the Apocryphal Book of Enoch, a pseudepigraphic apocalypse of great value, which exerted on Jewish thought considerable influence[1]. In the Epistle of Jude it is regarded as the genuine work of Enoch the patriarch; and it is only fair to say that it is quoted in the same respectful way, as canonical books of Scripture. But there never seems to have been any idea among Jews that the Book of Enoch might be included within the Canon; and we can hardly consider the fact of its being quoted by Jude as a proof that its claims were ever gravely considered[2].

If the greater freedom, which the New Testament writers are alleged to have shown in their treatment of the Hebrew Canon, did not permit them to express more clearly than they did their recognition of the important works of Ecclesiasticus and Wisdom, it is scarcely likely that a quotation from Enoch, occurring in the Epistle of St. Jude, can be accepted as proving

[1] As may be seen e.g. in the *Book of Jubilees* and the *Testamenta* XII. *Patr.*

[2] Origen quotes it, *De Princip.* iv. 35, 'Sed in libro suo Enoch ita ait.' But elsewhere he says, 'De quibus quidem hominibus plurima in libellis, qui appellantur Enoch, secreta continentur et arcana: sed quia libelli isti non videntur apud Hebraeos in auctoritate haberi, interim nunc ea, quae ibi nominantur, ad exemplum vocare differamus' (*Hom. in Num.* 28. 2. ed. *Lomm.* x. 366). Cf. *C. Cels.* v. 54. Tertullian, 'Scio scripturam Enoch . . . non recipi a quibusdam, quia nec in armarium Judaicum admittitur.' (*De cult. fem.* i. 3.)

a general statement, for which the other arguments when Chap. VII. taken in detail break down so completely[1].

6. *The Fourth Book of Esdras.* This apocalyptic work 6. 4 *Esdras, circ.* 90 A.D. was written not long after the destruction of Jerusalem, possibly in the last decade of the first cent. A.D. The author, who purports to narrate the visions granted to Ezra, contemplates, under the veil of this imagery, the condition of the Jews in his own time, predicting the days of the Messiah and the overthrow of the Roman empire. The book is, of course, devoid of any historical value for the period of Ezra. But, for the history of the Canon in the first cent. A.D., it contains important testimony. It relates the legend that Ezra was inspired to recall to memory the sacred books of his people which had been destroyed by the Chaldeans[2], and that, for the space of forty days, he dictated their contents to five men who had been gifted with divine understanding for the express purpose. The words to which attention must be especially drawn occur in chap. xiv. 45–48 : 'In forty days they wrote ninety-four books. And it came to pass when the forty days were fulfilled that the Most High spake, saying, "The first that thou hast written

---

[1] 'But the quotation from the Book of Enoch is quite unequivocal and it definitely prevents us from saying that no Apocryphal Book is recognised by a Canonical writer. In this, as in so many other things, it is impossible to draw a hard and fast line, though in any case the use of the Apocrypha bears a very small proportion to that of the Old Testament, and in respect to spiritual authority enters into no sort of competition with it.' Sanday, *Inspiration* (Longmans, 1893), p. 95.

[2] 4 Esd. xiv. 21, 'Thy law is burnt.' The *Speaker's Comm.* makes the extraordinary suggestion: 'Perhaps with an allusion to Jehudi's (*sic*) cutting to pieces and burning the roll of the Law (Jer. xxxvi. 26). But comp. iv. 23, above.' On this note, we observe, (1) it was not the act of Jehudi, but of the king Jehoiakim (Jer. xxxvi. 28), (2) it was not 'the roll of the Law,' but the prophecy of Jeremiah, (3) the passage is not ver. 26, but ver. 23. The ref. to iv. 23 is correct.

CHAP. VII. publish openly, that the worthy and the unworthy may read it; but keep the seventy last that thou mayest deliver them only to such as be wise among the people; for in them is the spring of understanding, the fountain of wisdom, and the stream of knowledge." And I did so [1].'

We have here the mention of two groups of writings, the one consisting of seventy, whose contents were to be made known only to those especially worthy, the other of twenty-four (?) which were to be made known to all. It has generally been understood that the writer intends, by his group of seventy, the class of mystic writing which only those initiated in esoteric literature would understand and profit by. By the books which should be published for the benefit of all, scholars are agreed that, if the reading 'ninety-four' is correct, the allusion is undoubtedly to the Books of the Hebrew Canon of Scripture; for their number, as we shall see, according to later Hebrew tradition, was almost invariably reckoned as 'twenty-four.' It must, however, be admitted that the reading is uncertain. Instead of 'ninety-four,' the Vulgate reads 'two hundred and four.' 'Ninety-four' seems to be the common reading of the other (Eastern) versions, the Syriac, Ethiopic, Arabic, and Armenian. But the MSS. of the Latin show the utmost variation, one reading giving 'nine hundred and four,' another 'nine hundred and seventy-four,' another 'eighty-four' (Wildeboer, p. 35). Assuming, however, that 'ninety-four' is the right reading, the reference to the contents of the Hebrew Canon is unmistakable, and the passage must be held to be one of great interest and importance for our purpose. (a) It testifies to the virtual closing of the Canon, and as to

[1] See Excursus A.

a familiarly known fact, that it consisted of twenty-four Chap. VII.
sacred writings. (*b*) As the number ' twenty-four ' agrees
with the computation of later tradition, and as there is
no reason to suppose that any early computation of
the twenty-four books would have made them different
from the twenty-four accepted at a later time, we may
infer that all the ' disputed ' books, including ' Esther,'
were contained in the list of canonical books recognised
by the writer of 4 Esdras [1]. (*c*) It is the first occasion
on which the number of the sacred books is mentioned.

7. *Flavius Josephus.* The last testimony we here adduce 7. Flavius Josephus, 37 —circ. 110 A.D.
to the formation of the Canon is supplied by the great
Jewish historian. In completeness and directness it surpasses the evidence which we have so far reviewed.

Antiquities of the Jews. Indirectly Josephus throws Antiquitates Judaicae, circ. 93 A.D.
light, in the course of his History (*Antiquities*), upon
the Canon of Scripture received in his time by the Jews.
But if we only had to rely upon his use of Scripture in
the construction of this narrative, we should not be much
further advanced upon our way. Josephus, generally,
makes use of the LXX version of the Old Testament,
and he does not hesitate to embellish the Biblical narrative with untrustworthy legends. He makes use of the
Books of Ruth, Chronicles, Daniel, and Esther; but in the

---

[1] The suggestion made by Prof. Robertson Smith, *Old Testament in the
Jewish Church*, p. 408 (ed. 1; but omitted in ed. 2), that ' if 94 is original,
it is still possible that 70 = 72 (as in the case of the LXX translators) leaving
22 canonical books,' hardly helps matters. (*a*) If 70 = 72, it is nevertheless
expressed very definitely as 70 (' the seventy last '), leaving a balance of 24.
(*b*) For the 72 translators, there was a clear reason, i.e. 6 for each tribe.
Here there would be no reason for 72 books. But for 70 there would
be a good reason, in its being a round number, and typical of perfection
(10 × 7). See commentators on Gen. xlvi. 27, Ex. xv. 27, Num. xi. 25,
Luke x. 1. Such a mystical figure the writer would apply to the literature,
of which his own apocalypse was probably a typical specimen.

CHAP. VII.   Book of Esther he employs the Greek version, and has recourse to the apocryphal 1 Esdras with as much readiness as to the Books of Ezra and Nehemiah (cf. *Antiq.* xi. 3). In the history of the Maccabean period he relies upon 1 Maccabees. Beyond, therefore, showing acquaintance with all the narrative literature that is contained in the Hebrew Canon, the Antiquities fail to give us any definite information as to either the date of the conclusion, or the limit of the contents, of the Jewish Scriptures[1].

In his description of Solomon, Josephus makes no allusion to his being supposed to have written the books of Ecclesiastes and Song of Songs; nor, on the other hand, to his having been the writer of the Book of Proverbs. The truth is, he writes his History without any pretence of literally restricting himself to the limits which his countrymen, for purposes of their religious use, had set to the contents of their Scriptures. Thus, in his Preface to the *Antiquities* (chap. 3), he only uses rhetorical language, which it would denote a complete misconception of his style to interpret literally, as if it were the expression of a laxer conception of the sacred Canon than that generally entertained by his countrymen, when he says, 'our sacred books, indeed, contain in them the history of five thousand years.' Similarly, at the close of the *Antiquities* (xx. 11), after stating that 'these Antiquities contain what has been handed down to us from the time of the Creation of man to the twelfth year of the reign of Nero . . . . . .' he goes on to claim that he has 'accurately recorded . . . everything according to what is written in our sacred books.' But it is evident that he is here using

[1] The language of Josephus respecting the Book of Daniel and its position among the sacred writings deserves especial notice (*Ant.* xi. 11. 7).

the language of rhetorical exaggeration. No one would
have the temerity to suggest, that Josephus, or, indeed,
any Jew of his time, would have reckoned among
'the sacred books' the chronicles which recorded the
history of the Jews in the reigns of Augustus and
Tiberius Caesar, or would ever have associated the
historical treatises of a Demetrius and an Artapanes
with the Books of Samuel and Kings. Josephus merely
means that he makes full use, as long as he can, of the
acknowledged sacred books, and continues their narrative
down to contemporary times. He certainly does not
intend to suggest that the other Jewish authorities, to
which he had recourse for historical materials, were
reckoned either by him or by his countrymen as worthy
to rank in the same category with Scripture. He may
be guilty of laxity of language; there is nothing to
justify the supposition that he was more liberal in his
conception of a sacred Canon.

The Dialogue against Apion. But our attention must *De Judaeo-*
now be directed to the important passage in another *rum Vetus-*
tate sive
work of Josephus, the *Contra Apionem.* In the open- *Contra*
Apionem,
ing chapter of that treatise he repeats the rhetorical *circ.* 100 A.D.
language with which he had concluded his history.
'These Antiquities contain the history of five thousand
years, and are taken out of our sacred books and
written by me in the Greek tongue' (chap. 1). He
then proceeds to defend, at some considerable length,
the accuracy of the materials for Jewish history, and
to maintain their superior credibility in comparison
with the histories of other nations, of the Greeks
more especially (chap. 4). In the following remarkable words he asserts the accuracy of the Jewish
Scriptures, and rests it upon the ground of their divine

CHAP. VII.   inspiration : 'It has not been the case with us that all
alike were allowed to record the nation's history ; nor
is there with us any discrepancy in the histories recorded. No, the prophets alone obtained a knowledge of
the earliest and most ancient things by virtue of the
inspiration which was given to them from God, and
they committed to writing a clear account of all the
events of their own time just as they occurred ' (chap. 7).
He then proceeds to give a description, in greater detail,
of these inspired writings.   He points out that, because
they were divinely inspired, they were able, although
only twenty-two in number, to convey a perfect and
complete record.   His words are : 'For it is not the

Chap. 8.   case with us (i. e. as it is with the Greeks) to have vast
numbers of books disagreeing and conflicting with one
another.   We have but two and twenty, containing the
history of all time, books that are justly believed in[1].
And of these, five are the books of Moses, which
comprise the laws and the earliest traditions from the
creation of mankind down to the time of his (Moses')
death.   This period falls short but by a little of three
thousand years.   From the death of Moses to the
(death[2]) of Artaxerxes, King of Persia, the successor
of Xerxes, the prophets who succeeded Moses wrote the
history of the events that occurred in their own time, in

---

[1] The usual reading, ' believed to be divine,' is probably a gloss.   'Θεία
ante πεπιστευμένα, add. Euseb.'   (Niese. in loc.)

[2] If ἀρχῆς is only a gloss, τελευτῆς must be supplied.   The reference to
' Artaxerxes ' might suggest that the Book of Ezra and Nehemiah is thought
of, did we not know that in *Antiq.* xi. 5 the Artaxerxes of Ezra and Nehemiah is called by Josephus 'Xerxes,' and that in xi. 6. 1 the Ahasuerus of
the Book of Esther is called ' Artaxerxes.'   (' After the death of Xerxes the
kingdom came to his son Cyrus, whom the Greeks called Artaxerxes.')
The Artaxerxes of our passage, therefore, is Ahasuerus, whom Josephus took
to be the son of the Persian king that favoured Ezra and Nehemiah.

thirteen books. The remaining four documents comprise
hymns to God and practical precepts to men. From
the days of Artaxerxes to our own time every event has
indeed been recorded. But *these recent* records have not
been deemed worthy of equal credit with those which
preceded them, on account of the failure of the exact
succession of the prophets[1]. There is practical proof
of the spirit in which we treat our Scriptures. For
although so great an interval of time (i.e. since they were
written) has now passed, not a soul has ventured either
to add, or to remove, or to alter a syllable ; and it is the
instinct of every Jew, from the day of his birth, to consider those (Scriptures) as the teaching of God, to abide
by them, and, if need be, cheerfully to lay down life in
their behalf.'

Before examining the full bearing of this important
passage upon the history of the Canon, we must realise
the context in which it stands. (1) We must remember *Josephus:*
that Josephus writes as the spokesman of his people, in *Spokesman of Jews.*
order to defend the accuracy and sufficiency of their
Scriptures, as compared with the recent and contradictory histories by Greek writers (cf. ch. 2–4). In
this controversy he defends the judgment of his people. He does not merely express a personal opinion,
he claims to represent his countrymen. (2) We must *Uses LXX.*

[1] The usual translations of this clause fail to give the full meaning, e.g.
'Because there has been no exact succession of prophets' (Robertson
Smith, O.T.J.C., p. 408, ed. 1 ; but corrected in ed. 2, p. 164, to ' because
the exact succession of prophets was wanting ') ; ' Because there was not
then an exact succession of prophets' (Shilleto's Whiston). The position
of the article shows that Josephus has in his mind *the* unbroken succession
of prophets whose writings had supplied the Holy Scripture. The line of
prophets failed; and the failure of the prophetic spirit brought to a close
'the succession' of inspired writings. Josephus echoes the lament of his
people that since Malachi the prophets had ceased.

remember that he is addressing foreigners, and that he writes in Greek to Greeks. He cannot assume that his readers would be acquainted with Hebrew; but he may reasonably expect them to know the Alexandrine version. His own habit in the *Antiquities*, his previous work, had been to refer to the LXX version. We may be sure, therefore, that, in the present treatise, he will speak of the sacred books of his race, as they would be accessible to Greek-speaking readers. In other words, he writes *Belief in inspiration.* with the LXX version before him. (3) We must remember that he has just explained his view of the inspiration which the Jewish prophets partook of. The books he here describes are those only 'that were justly believed in.' He has in his mind the sacred, but limited, library of the Jews, exclusive of their miscellaneous literature from which he had borrowed in the composition of his Antiquities.

How then does he describe the Sacred Books?

His Canon, 22 books. (1) He mentions their number; he speaks of them as consisting of twenty-two books. He regards them as a well-defined national collection. That is to say, Josephus and his countrymen, at the beginning of the second cent. A.D., recognised a collection of what he, at least, calls twenty-two books, and no more, as the Canon of Holy Scripture. This Canon it was profanation to think of enlarging, diminishing, or altering in any way.

Standard of Canonicity. (2) He records a test of their canonicity. He mentions the standard which, apparently, in current Jewish opinion, all books satisfied that were included in the Canon. No historical writings, it seems, belonged to it which were deemed to have been composed later than the reign of Ahasuerus. The mention of this particular limit seems to be made expressly with reference to the book of Esther, in which alone the Artaxerxes of Josephus (the Ahasuerus of the Hebrew book of Esther) figures. Thus we learn that a popularly accepted test, that of date of composition, however erroneously applied, determined the question of canonicity. In the first cent. A.D., the impression prevailed that the books of the Canon were all ancient, that none were more recent than Ahasuerus, and that all had long been regarded as canonical. The same limit of date, although not so clearly applied to the poetical books, was, in all probability, intended to apply equally to them, since they combined with the books of the prophets to throw light upon the same range of history. That such a standard of canonicity as that of antiquity should be asserted, crude as it may seem, ought to be sufficient to convince us that the limits of the Canon had for a long time been undisturbed.

(3) In his enumeration of the books, Josephus mentions *Enumeration,* five books of Moses, thirteen prophetical books, and four books of hymns and moral teaching. It will be observed that he does not follow the tripartite division of the Canon, nor does he state the number of the books as twenty-four, in accordance with later Hebrew tradition, but as twenty-two. That he does not mention the Hebrew triple grouping of the sacred books admits of a natural explanation. (*a*) He is referring, in particular, *by subject,* to the *historical* books of the Jews, and he would naturally class them all together. (*b*) He had in his *as LXX.* mind the LXX version in which the Hebrew grouping is not reproduced. He was not likely to risk the bewilderment he might cause his Gentile readers by the mention of the Hebrew arrangement, which,

as it differed from the Greek, would require special explanation.

That he speaks of twenty-two, and not of twenty-four, books, admits of a similar explanation. There is no necessity to suppose he is contemplating a smaller Canon than that which has come down to us. We know that he makes use of the LXX version ; we know too that those, in later time, who reckoned the books of Hebrew Scripture as twenty-two in number, accepted the complete Canon, undiminished in size. There is little reason to doubt that Josephus' enumeration of twenty-two books is due to his reckoning Ruth with Judges, and Lamentations with Jeremiah. In later lists, e.g. those of Origen and Jerome, the number twenty-two is reached in this way (see below) ; and, in the list of Melito, 'Lamentations,' which is missing, is doubtless understood in the mention of Jeremiah.

Thirteen Books of Prophets.

If, then, we may understand the 'twenty-two' books of the Canon referred to by Josephus as the same as those included in later lists, Ruth being reckoned with Judges, Lamentations with Jeremiah, how, we may ask, does he distribute them ? What are the thirteen books of the Prophets? What the four books of hymns and practical precepts? The thirteen books of the Prophets are probably the following :—(1) Joshua, (2) Judges and Ruth, (3) Samuel, (4) Kings, (5) Chronicles, (6) Ezra and Nehemiah, (7) Esther, (8) Job, (9) Daniel, (10) Isaiah, (11) Jeremiah and Lamentations, (12) Ezekiel, (13) The Twelve Minor Prophets.

Four Books of Hymns, &c.

The four books of hymns and practical precepts are probably the following :—(1) Psalms, and (2) Song of Songs, which constitute 'the hymns ;' (3) Proverbs, and (4) Ecclesiastes, which constitute 'the practical precepts.'

Of this distribution we cannot, of course, speak confidently; but it appears the most probable. The
objection that the Book of Job is made to rank
among the historical writings is not a grave one, since
it was popularly considered to contain the history of the
patriarch. The position of Ecclesiastes is certainly suitable, while that of Daniel is very intelligible. Grätz[1],
who fancied that neither Ecclesiastes nor Song of Songs
had been received into the Canon in Josephus' time, left
these two out of the list, and then separated Ruth and
Lamentations from Judges and Jeremiah, an arrangement which happily corresponded with Grätz's own
views as to the date of Ecclesiastes and Song of Songs.
But it is impossible to reconcile with the words of
Josephus, in speaking of a long-settled Canon, the supposition that Song of Songs and Ecclesiastes were im-
ported into it shortly after Josephus wrote. Grätz's
theory finds no support in later lists, in which, if there
is any divergency from the one we have ascribed to
Josephus, it is not found in connexion with either of
the two books, Song of Songs or Ecclesiastes.

[1] Cf. *Kohelet*, p. 169.

N

CHAPTER VIII.

THE THIRD CANON (*concluded*).

Canon recognised by Josephus permanently accepted.

ACCORDINGLY, we conclude that the contents of the Canon which Josephus acknowledged, may be regarded, with some degree of confidence, as the same with the contents of the Hebrew Canon at a later time. In other words, the limits of the group of 'the Writings,' or 'Kethubim,' had practically been determined, and the Canon of Hebrew Scripture had, therefore, practically been closed, when Josephus wrote. Practically, we say; for whether the conclusion of it had been officially acknowledged, or its compass authoritatively decided by the religious leaders of the people, we cannot know for certain. Very probably there was no need for an official

70 A.D.

pronouncement before the destruction of Jerusalem by Titus. We nowhere find traces of any attempt to introduce into the early Synagogue worship a *systematic* reading from the Hagiographa. The modern Synagogue use of 'the Hagiographa' dates from a much later century[1]. The question, therefore, of the canonicity of a book would not be raised in any acute form, if the public use of it was irregular and occasional. A 'disputed book' would be used, where it met with esteem and favour; by those

---

[1] They may have been at an early date used in the Synagogue for purposes of interpretation and exposition (*Midrash*), but not of the lectionary (cf. *Jer. Sabb.* 16, fol. 15; *Tosephta Sabb.* 13).

who entertained doubts of its orthodoxy or sanctity, its *Chap. VIII.* use would simply be discontinued. It was not, we may suppose, until after the destruction of Jerusalem, that the necessity for a stricter definition of the Canon was generally felt.

Two circumstances probably conduced, after the great *Destruction* catastrophe, to make some official statement desirable *of Jeru-salem.* respecting the contents of the Sacred Collection.

(1) Firstly, the destruction of Jerusalem had broken up *Heightened* the rallying-place of the Jewish people; it had scattered *honour of Scripture.* the schools of the scribes; it had ended for ever the Temple services; it had dealt a deadly blow at the very heart of religious Judaism. As on the occasion of the previous disasters, inflicted by Nebuchadnezzar and by Antiochus Epiphanes, so now, after the great Roman catastrophe, the religion of the Jews, which the nations of the world believed to have perished among the ashes of the Temple, lived again through the power of their Scriptures. The sense of the irreparable loss they had sustained made the Jewish doctors doubly anxious to safe-guard 'the oracles' which still survived, the Holy Books. We can understand, how, henceforth, the veneration which had encompassed the books of the Canon was raised almost to the pitch of idolatry. The Scriptures were a token from Jehovah. They still survived to recall the mercies of the past; and they sufficed to infuse into the race the indomitable courage and devotion with which they faced the future. In the period that immediately followed the destruction of Jerusalem, we should expect to hear of some earnest endeavour on the part of the Jewish leaders to add, if possible, yet greater prestige to

CHAP. VIII.   the Hebrew Scriptures, to clear away doubts, where any
existed, respecting 'disputed' books, and, by a final
definition of the limits of the Canon, to prevent the introduction into the sacred list of any book which had not
stood the test of time.

Danger of Greek Version encroaching on Canon of Hebrew Scripture.   (2) Secondly, the general use and growing influence of
the LXX version among the Greek-speaking Jews of the
Dispersion threatened to lead to some misconception as
to the contents of the true Hebrew Canon.   The suggestion has been made that the Jewish community in
Alexandria formally recognised a distinct Canon of much
wider limits than that of the Palestinian Jews.   The
suggestion no doubt rested on a misconception due to the
fact that Apocryphal books (e.g. 1 and 2 Maccabees,
Sirach, Wisdom) are included in the copies of the LXX
version, and were quoted as Scripture by the early
Fathers of Alexandria.   The MSS., however, of the
LXX are, all of them, of Christian origin; and, moreover,
differ from one another in the arrangement as well as in
the selection of the books.   There is no uniform Alexandrian list.   The Christian Church derived their Old
Testament Scriptures from the Jews; but whether they
found the books of the 'Apocrypha' in Jewish copies, or
added them afterwards, we have no means of judging.
Perhaps the copies which the Christians of Alexandria
adopted, happened to contain, in addition to the Canonical Scriptures, certain other writings which the Jews in
Alexandria were more especially attached to.   We cannot say for certain.   But we do know that in Alexandria,
if we may judge from Philo and the writer of the Book
of Wisdom, the veneration for the law had been carried to such an extent, that a wider interval seemed to
separate 'the Law' from the other books of the Hebrew

Canon than that which separated the other sacred books CHAP. VIII. from the works of the great or wise men of any time or country [1]. Perhaps, in Alexandria, no formal list was recognised. Be that as it may, the line of demarcation was apt to become very slight; and the prevalent liberal tone seems to have led men not only to tolerate variation, not only to welcome, along with the recognised books of Scripture, such writings as 'Ecclesiasticus' and 'Wisdom,' but even to approve and license the addition of Haggadic legends and amplifications in the Greek versions of Job, Daniel, and Esther.

The utmost confusion was likely to arise, when the destruction of Jerusalem bereft the Palestinian tradition of Scripture of its historic centre. The number of the Hebrew-reading Jews was likely to diminish yet more, and the number of the Greek-speaking Jews to increase. If the Hebrew Canon was permanently to be preserved, it was necessary that it should forthwith be carefully defined. If a Hebrew, and not a Greek, tradition of the Jewish Scriptures was to prevail, there must be no mistake what the Hebrew Canon was. The inevitable alternative would be, that the Greek Alexandrine version of the Hebrew Scriptures, with its different arrangement and possibly its more elastic limits, would pass into general acceptance and overwhelm the tradition of Jerusalem and of the scribes of Palestine. *Less Hebrew known, more Greek spoken.*

Another cause of perplexity in connexion with the LXX, not to say of objection to its use, arose from the adoption of it by the Christian Church as their sacred Scripture. If Aquila's more literal and uniform rendering was intended to supply the place of the LXX with the stricter Jews, it affords another illustration of the *The LXX, the Christian Church, Aquila's Version.*

---

[1] Cf. Philo, *Vita Mosis,* §§ 8, 23, 24, and *De Cherub.,* § 14.

CHAP. VIII. anxiety that was felt in the second cent. A.D. concerning the Hebrew Scriptures, and of the desire to keep the tradition of the Hebrew Canon free from the influence of the Alexandrine version.

Questions of Canonicity discussed by Rabbins, end of 1st Cent. A.D. Whether we attach to these circumstances much or little importance in the last phases of the formation of the Canon, they cannot, I think, be altogether ignored. They at least tended to hasten a result, which cannot be placed much later than the end of the first cent. A.D. or the beginning of the second cent. A.D. That result we believe to have been some sort of an official declaration by the Jewish Rabbis, that finally determined the limits of the Hebrew Canon. The fact that the Mishnah, the contents of which had been current in an oral form before they were committed to writing at the end of the second cent. A.D., assumes the existence of fixed limits to the Canon of Scripture, is probably sufficient to show that a considerable interval of time had elapsed since its determination. The Mishnah records how disputes arose between Jewish Rabbis upon the canonicity of certain books, and, in particular, of books in the Hagiographa, and how the doubts were allayed through the influence of such men as Rabbi Johanan ben Zaccai and Rabbi Akiba, who died about 135 A.D. (*Yadaim*, iii. 5). The language which they are reported to have used shows, beyond all question, that they accepted the tripartite division of the Canon, and that, even while they were discussing the qualities of books whose right to a position in the Canon of Scripture was questioned by some, they never doubted that the contents of the Canon had been determined.

Synod of Jamnia. Now we happen to know that a council of Jewish Rabbis was held at Jamnia (Jabne), not very far from

Jaffa, about the year 90 A.D., and again, perhaps, in
118 A.D. Rabbi Gamaliel II seems to have presided[1],
and Rabbi Akiba was the prominent spirit. In the
course of its deliberations the subject of the Canon was
discussed. It was decided that the difficulties which
had been felt about the Book of Ecclesiastes and the
Song of Songs could be fairly answered (*Eduyoth*, v. 3).
The suggestion has been made, that we have in the Synod
of Jamnia the official occasion, on which the limits of the
Hebrew Canon were finally determined by Jewish authorities.

It may, indeed, very well have happened at this, or at
some similar, gathering about that time. In the absence
of precise information—for the Rabbinic evidence is
fragmentary and the reverse of precise—we can only say
that, as the time at which the Synod of Jamnia was held,
and apparently the subjects which occupied its discussions, are favourable to the conjecture, there is no reason
for objecting to it. As a matter of fact, the Synod of
Jamnia can be little else to us but a name ; still, as it is
a name connected with the ratified canonicity of certain
books, it may symbolize the general attitude of the Jewish
doctors, and their resolve to put an end to the doubts
about the ' disputed ' books of the Hagiographa.

We, therefore, take the year 100 A.D. as representing, *Jewish*
as nearly as possible, the *terminus ad quem* in the gradual *official conclusion*
formation of the Canon. It marks, however, only the *of Canon, about*
official conclusion. Practically, we may be sure, its *100 A.D.*
bounds had long before been decided by popular use.

The commencement of the process by which the books

---

[1] Gamaliel II succeeded Johanan ben Zaccai, and was himself succeeded
by Eleazar ben Azariah as head of the School at Jamnia. Cf. Strack, Art.
Talmud, Herzog-Plitt, R.E.[2] xviii. p. 346.

CHAP. VIII. of 'the Writings' were annexed to 'the Law and the Prophets' is probably to be ascribed, as we have already seen, to the beginning of the era of the Maccabean ascendency (160–140 B.C.). Two centuries and a half later the final results of that process received an official ratification at Jamnia or elsewhere. And yet, we have reason to believe, all the books included in the third group of the Canon had obtained some measure of recognition, either complete and undisputed, or partial and disputed, within fifty years from the commencement of the formation of the third group. The Jewish Rabbis had only, as it were, to affix an official seal to that which had already long enjoyed currency among the people.

Concerning the undisputed books, Psalms, Proverbs, Job, Ruth, Lamentations, Ezra and Nehemiah, and probably Daniel, there seems to be little reason to doubt that they were admitted almost at once into the sacred Canon. At what time the others, 'the disputed' books, received recognition, must always remain more or less a matter of obscurity, and the most different opinions will be entertained.

Canon practically closed, 105 B.C. But there are good grounds for the view that all the books eventually included in the Canon had obtained some sort of recognition before the close of the second cent. B.C., and before the death of John Hyrcanus II (105 B.C.). These grounds may, for convenience' sake, be summarised under three heads, (1) the external evidence, (2) the conditions of the Jewish Church, (3) the character of the disputed books.

Before 2nd cent. A.D.: Josephus, N.T. (1) The external evidence has already been reviewed. We gather from it, that the generation of Josephus regarded the Canon as having long ago been determined. For Josephus considered the Canon to consist of a col-

lection of writings to which a continuous series of CHAP. VIII.
prophets contributed, from Moses until the reign of
Ahasuerus; and he was evidently of opinion that the
Canon had been closed for 400 years, and that the Book
of Esther was the last thus to be acknowledged.

In the writings of the New Testament, we saw that, by
a very possible interpretation of one passage, the Books
of Chronicles were already regarded as the recognised
conclusion of the Hebrew Canon. We saw that the
absence of quotation from 'the disputed' books in the
New Testament and in Philo constituted no valid argument against their recognition as Scripture, especially as
the contents of Esther, Song of Songs, and Ecclesiastes
scarcely lent themselves to the Christian writers of the
first century A.D. for purposes of quotation. We noticed
the force of the contention, that 'the Scriptures' in the
New Testament are appealed to as a most sacred completed 'Corpus' of writings, in which any alteration
would be most improbable.

(2) To the careful student of Jewish history we venture *No change*
to think it must, on reflection, appear exceedingly un- *in 1st cent.*
B.C. proba-
likely that any fresh book would be introduced into the *ble: Jewish*
affairs,
Hebrew Canon of Scripture after the beginning of the *foreign and*
domestic.
first century B.C. The last century before the Christian
era witnessed the great civil war in Palestine, which
deluged the country in blood (92–86 B.C.), the capture of
Jerusalem by Pompey in 63 B.C., the reduction of Judea
to the condition of a Roman province, and, lastly, the
tyranny of Herod the Great (37 B.C.–4 A.D.). The religious
and social life of the Jews during all this disastrous
period was marked by two characteristic features, from
both of which we might gather how utterly futile any
attempt would be to widen or alter the compass of the

CHAP. VIII. already accepted Canon.   The first of these was the hos-

Pharisees and Sadducees. tility between the Pharisee and the Sadducee factions, which, until the arrival of Pompey upon the scene, had divided the people into two opposing camps, and continued long afterwards to be the constant cause of discord. During the whole of this century, it would be impossible to imagine any public step, intimately connected with the most sacred associations of the people, which would have received the approbation of both parties; while the action which commended itself to but one party was either doomed at once to failure, or, if attended with success, would be handed down by tradition tainted with the memory of a partisan achievement[1].

Schools of the Rabbins. Secondly, the rise of the great Rabbinic schools of Hillel and Shammai was a guarantee that a conservative attitude would be maintained towards the sacred Scripture.   The Doctors whose glory it was 'to make a fence about the law' were not likely to advocate the introduction of fresh writings within the limits of the Canon; nor, if one were bold enough to advise such a step, would

[1] The tradition recorded in the writings of the Christian fathers, Pseudo-Tertullian (*adv. Haer.* 1), Origen (*c. Cels.* i. 49 and Comm. *in Matt.* xxii. 29, 31–32), and Jerome (*in Matt.* xxii. 31, *Contr. Lucif.* 23), that the Sadducees only accepted the canonicity of 'the Law,' rests on no real foundation.   It receives no support from Josephus in his description of the Sadducees; and the fact that our Lord confuted the Sadducees from 'the Law' (cf. Matt. xxii. 23–32), which has sometimes been alleged in its favour, is no justification of the conjecture, but illustrates the regard which the Jews paid to any proofs from 'the Law' above all other arguments from their Scripture.   It is probably due to a confusion of Sadducees with Samaritans, or to a misconception of the statement that the Sadducees rejected the tissue of tradition which the scribes had woven around the precepts of the law. According to another more probable conjecture, the possibility of the admission of Ecclesiasticus and 1 Maccabees within the Canon was frustrated by the opposition of the Pharisees, who raised objections to those books, because they contained no assertion of their favourite teaching upon the subject of the resurrection.

he have escaped vehement attacks from rival teachers. CHAP. VIII.
Their work, however, was almost wholly defensive and
negative; their object, to interpret Scripture as they had
received it. We should not anticipate from the founders
of the schools of Rabbinic exegesis any favour to a more
liberal treatment of the Canon.

There is certainly no probability that any fresh book
would have obtained admission into the Canon during a
century distinguished above all others by the antagonism
of the Pharisees and the Sadducees, and by the establishment of the Rabbinic Schools.

(3) The character of the books themselves is not un- *Even
favourable to their having been received in the second 'disputed'
century B. C. The Books of Ecclesiastes and the Song of books likely
Songs were popularly ascribed to Solomon, and would to be admitted.*
naturally, therefore, be regarded as works for which room
should be found in the same group with the Book of
Proverbs. It was not as if they had only recently been
composed. The more recent of the two had existed, in
all probability, if we may judge from internal evidence,
at least for more than a century before the Maccabean
era; while the Song of Songs was the most ancient
piece of poetry not yet included in the Canon.

The Book of Esther, which was also probably composed in the third century B. C., was evidently at one
time a very favourite work. Several recensions of it
existed; and at a time when the deliverance from the
foreigner was still fresh in the memories of the Jews, it
perhaps seemed to have peculiar claims for recognition.
To the Jew of the Dispersion, it brought a special message of Divine Providence, which corresponded to the
gentler message of Ruth to the proselyte stranger.

The Books of Chronicles, from which Ezra and Nehe-

CHAP. VIII. miah were severed, would very naturally be appended to the books of Scripture. The important genealogies and the special features of its history in connexion with the Temple worship make it improbable that such a narrative would be for long excluded.

All four books are naturally associated with groups that had been received without hesitation into the Canon. Both Ecclesiastes and Song of Songs seemed to deserve their place as the writings of Solomon ; and the Song, in its poetical treatment of joy, formed the complement to the plaintive note of the Lamentations. The Book of Esther seemed to fill a gap in the history of the exile, and thus to follow upon the Book of Daniel and the Books of Ezra and Nehemiah. The Books of Chronicles received a position as the appendix of the Hebrew Scriptures, in the same group with Esther, Ezra, and Nehemiah.

In all four disputed works, the claim to antiquity was generally conceded. In this respect they would find a ready acceptance in comparison with the Wisdom of Sirach and the First Book of Maccabees, which were avowedly of recent composition.

Now if all the books of 'the Kethubim' were known and received in the first century A.D., and if, as we believe, the circumstances of the Jewish people rendered it all but impossible for the Canon to receive change or augmentation in the first century B.C., we conclude that 'the disputed books' received a recognition in the last two or three decades of the second century B.C., when John Hyrcanus ruled, and the Jews still enjoyed prosperity. The hostility between the Pharisee and Sadducee parties had then not yet assumed the proportions of an open conflict; the influence of the Rabbinic Schools was then still in an early stage.

The period, then, to which we assign the formation of the Kethubim is the interval between 160 B. C., the High Priesthood of Jonathan, and 105 B.C., the death of John Hyrcanus. According to this view, fully two hundred years had elapsed, since the Scriptural character of the last books had been, in some measure, recognised, when the Rabbins, in the generation after the destruction of Jerusalem, pronounced their official sentence upon the limits of the Canon. It was then that the Writings we have called 'Disputed Books,' which, from the peculiarity of their contents and teaching, had previously exerted little influence upon religious thought, had been little used in public and, possibly, little studied in private, seemed all at once to receive an adventitious importance. Doubts were expressed, when their canonical position was finally asserted. But no sooner were such difficulties raised and scruples proclaimed and protests delivered against their retention in the Canon, than eager voices were lifted up to defend the character of writings which, after all, had long been recognised, although, in comparison with the acknowledged books of the Kethubim, little valued and rarely made use of.

If the two periods I have indicated, the one for the admission of the last group into the category of Scripture (160–105 B. C.), the other for the final ratification of the completed Canon (90–110 A.D.), be approximately correct, their significance to the Christian student should be duly considered.

The full complement of Scripture had been arrived at, a century before the coming of Him who came not to destroy but to fulfil 'the Law and the Prophets' (Matt. v. 17). In the view of that Revelation, we need not wonder at the absence of confirmation in the New Testament for Esther, Ecclesiastes, and Song of Songs. The new Revelation taught a better spirit than that of the patriotic fierceness which is breathed in Esther. The despair of the Preacher, which expressed the unsatisfied yearning of the soul for its Redeemer, finds no echo in the books of the New Covenant. The Song of Songs told of the beauty of earthly affection; but, in the presence of the full declaration of Divine Love, its slight ray was fully absorbed like that of a candle in the light of the midday sun.

The final determination of the Hebrew Canon preceded the Church's formal acceptance of it as the Canon of the Scripture of the Old Covenant.

It was thus divinely ordered that we should be enabled to know the exact limits of those Scriptures upon which has rested the sanction conveyed by the usage and blessing of our Divine Master, and of which He spake, 'these are they which bear witness of me' (John v. 39). Thus, too, an effectual barrier was raised to protect the Scriptures of the Apostles against the encroachments of any unauthorised additions. The use of the LXX version familiarised the Christian Church with writings that never found a place in the Hebrew Canon; but, through the action of the Jewish doctors at the close of the first cent. A.D., there was never any doubt what the limits of the Hebrew Canon were. The only question which seemed to admit of two answers was, whether the Christian Church should regard the limits of the Hebrew Canon as determining the compass of the Old Testament.

CHAPTER IX.

AFTER THE CONCLUSION OF THE CANON.

THE Hebrew Canon of Scripture, whose gradual growth we have traced from its earliest stage to its final ratification, has been preserved by the Jewish community intact. Since the beginning of the second century A. D., no alteration has been permitted in the range of its contents, which, as I hope I have shown, had probably remained the same for at least two centuries. In all probability, the only modifications which it has since received from Jewish hands were changes affecting the order of the books of the Hagiographa (the present order being the work of mediaeval Jews, and dating, perhaps, from the eighth or ninth century), and the sub-division, made so late as the sixteenth century A. D., of the Books of Samuel, Kings, Chronicles, Ezra and Nehemiah.

It was natural that the Hebrew Canon, both as the Bible of the Jewish Church, and as the Scriptures acknowledged by our Lord and the Apostles, and especially sanctioned by their use, should from the first have been adopted by the Christian Church. But the prevalent use of the Septuagint version tended quickly to obliterate the distinction between the books of the Hebrew Canon and the books which, from their popularity among the Christians, were wont to be often publicly read in the churches, e. g. Ecclesiasticus, Wisdom,

CHAP. IX. 1 Maccabees, Baruch, &c. It required all the weight and learning of such men as Melito (†circ. 170), Origen (†253), Cyril of Jerusalem (†386), Athanasius (†373), Ruffinus (†410), Jerome (†420), to preserve the recollection of the true Hebrew Canon, and to maintain a preference for the testimony of its contents.

Why not in Jewish? Now, in the third and fourth centuries A.D., many of the books which we term 'the Apocrypha' had passed into general use in the Christian Church, and were constantly quoted as Scripture. Is there no analogous experience to be recorded in the Jewish Church? Did no 'Apocrypha' find their way within the sacred limits of the Hebrew books? And, if not, how was the exclusive character of the Canon so successfully secured?

In order to answer these questions, we must recall the circumstances under which the books of the Hagiographa were admitted, and under which the Canon had been closed.

Canon protected by 1. antiquity. In the first place, the impulse which led to the admission of the Hagiographa had been received from the religious revival of the Maccabean era. The revolt of Jewish patriotism against the predominance of Hellenism was based on the Revelation of Jehovah to His people in earlier times. Revelation, it was thought, had ceased with prophecy. Scripture was the embodiment of past Revelation, its claim to antiquity a recognised test of its genuineness. There was no room for recent writings, there was no confidence in their authority.

2. prestige of origin, In the second place, each of the books admitted into the Canon was invested with the prestige not of antiquity only, but also of connexion with an honoured name. Daniel, the latest work, was considered to have been written in the Captivity, and this supposition was

favoured by the words of Ezek. xiv. 14, 20, xxviii. 3 ; CHAP. IX.
Ecclesiastes, probably the next most recent, was ascribed
to Solomon. The Psalter was ascribed to David ; Proverbs and the Song of Songs to Solomon; Job to the
patriarch himself; Lamentations to Jeremiah; while
Ruth, Esther, Chronicles, Ezra, and Nehemiah were
ascribed to the famous men who wrote the narrative of
their own day, to Samuel, Mordecai, and Ezra.

In the third place, each of the books that were ad- *3. distinctive
teaching.*
mitted to the group of the Hagiographa presents a
distinct phase in Jewish religious thought. Each has
thus contributed to the representative character of Jewish
Scripture some new feature. Each reflects the light of
divine teaching from a different aspect of earthly experience. How much of the variety and the many-sided
sympathy of the Old Testament books arises from this
group! The Psalter, Job, Lamentations, and the Song
of Songs, give us Hebrew poetry of strikingly various
complexion. Proverbs and Ecclesiastes offer two very
distinct aspects of Jewish *Khokmah*. The Book of
Daniel shows us prophecy in its final apocalyptic form.
The Books of Chronicles reiterate the history of the
monarchy from the standpoint of the Temple wor-
shipper. Ezra and Nehemiah give us records and
extracts from memoirs dealing with the Return from
exile and with the foundation of Judaism. Ruth offers an
idyllic picture of Israel in days of peace ; Esther a page
of fierce intensity from the traditions of the exile. In a
literature so varied there was no side of Hebrew life and
thought which was not, so to speak, claimed and selected
to add its influence to the work of the Jewish Canon, the
work of educating, teaching, and inspiring the ' Israel of
God.'

O

Now it may well be thought that, if such writings found admission in the second century B. C., on the ground not only of their intrinsic merit but of their reputed great antiquity and, in several cases, of their reputed connexion with some great personage of the past, the conception of their antiquity and their dignity would grow more venerable and majestic as years rolled on. The separation between them and all other writings would widen with proportionate rapidity. It could not be long before the very idea of ranking any other work with the contents of the Canon would be treated as little short of blasphemy by the Rabbinic teachers.

Ecclesiasticus,
1 Maccabees.
Only in the case of two extant writings is there any probability that an attempt may have been made, in some quarters, to include them within the Canon, i. e. Ecclesiasticus and the First Book of Maccabees. In both instances there never seems to have been any real approach to success. They were neither of them recommended by the claim to great antiquity; they were neither of them stamped with the attributes of originality, or inspired with the gift of communicating any fresh fund of spiritual life and force. They were modern; for the Wisdom of Sirach did not claim to be earlier than the beginning of the second century B. C., while the First of Maccabees dated, at the earliest, from the close of the same century. They introduced no new conception of Israel's religion and history; the Wisdom of Sirach followed very closely on the lines of Proverbs, while the First of Maccabees was but a faithful chronicle of recent events.

Although they were never admitted within the Canon, they undoubtedly enjoyed high favour, and perhaps, in the opinion of some Jews, deserved a place among the

Scriptures. The Wisdom of Sirach is twice at least quoted, with the formula of citation from Scripture, in the 'Talmud' (Ecclus. vii. 10 in Erubin, 65 *a*, and xiii. 15, xxvii. 9 in Baba Kamma, 92 *b*). In a passage from Bereshith Rabba (c. 91), it is said to have been quoted as canonical by Simon ben Shetach, brother of Queen Salome, in the year 90 B.C. (For 'other Palestinian authorities' see Delitzsch, *Gesch. der Jüdischen Poesie*, p. 20, quoted by Cheyne, *Job and Solomon*, p. 282.) For three centuries or more it enjoyed a position of peculiar honour, perhaps of quasi-authority, but without the prestige of canonicity. The public reading of it is expressly forbidden by Rabbi Joseph in the Babylonian Talmud (*San.* 100 *b*).

The First Book of Maccabees never obtained such a degree of recognition. But, in the days of Josephus, it was regarded as the one trustworthy Hebrew source of history for the Maccabean period, and, in the time of Origen, it was still known in the Hebrew (cf. Orig. *ap.* Euseb. *H. E.* vi. 25).

It was not to be expected that books written in Greek would stand any chance of admission into the Palestinian Canon. On that account neither the Second of Maccabees nor Wisdom could ever have been favoured, or even have been thought of, in such a connexion. This objection did not exist in the case of Ecclesiasticus and the First of Maccabees; and the statement which has sometimes been made, that they failed to obtain canonicity, because they chanced to be no longer current in Hebrew at the time when the Canon was being concluded, is in all probability incorrect. The Book of Ecclesiasticus, probably, not only existed in Hebrew, but was also current in an Aramaised version, from

Ecclus. and 1 Macc. in Hebrew.

which the Babylonian Jews made extracts[1]. Moreover it was known to Jerome, either in the original Hebrew form or in its later Aramaic dress; and that Father affirms that it had a place along with Ecclesiastes and Song of Songs, and was designated by the title of 'Parables.' (Cf. *Praef. in libr. Sal.*, 'Fertur et Jesu filii Sirach liber . . . quorum priorem Hebraicum repperi, non Ecclesiasticum, ut apud Latinos, sed parabolas praenotatum, cui juncti erant Ecclesiastes et Canticum Canticorum [2].')

The existence of the First of Maccabees in Hebrew, in the time of Origen, is shown by the title which he gives to it—Σαρβῆθ Σαβαναιέλ (*ap.* Eus. *H. E.* vi. 25) = possibly 'the Sceptre of the Old Man are the Sons of God' (שרבים סבא בני אל), or, 'Prince of the House that God buildeth' (שר ביתא יבני אל), or, 'the Prince of Evil (and) the Mighty Men' (שַׂר בִּישְׁתָּא בְּנֵי חַיַל), i. e. Antiochus and the Patriotic Jews[3]. Jerome also states that he was acquainted with the First of Maccabees in Hebrew (*Prol. Gal.*, 'Machabaeorum primum librum Hebraicum repperi').

It was not, therefore, due to their being extant only in

---

[1] On the Hebrew quotations to be found in Rabbinic literature, see Schechter, *Jewish Quarterly Review*, July, 1891.

[2] It was recognised in the Canon of Scripture of the Nestorians, who probably derived it from the usage of Syrian Jews. (Cf. Buhl. *K. u. T. d. A. T.* pp. 52–53.)

[3] The usual text, that of Stephens, Σαρβῆθ Σαρβανὲ 'Ελ, סרבת שר בני אל (שרי), is rendered variously, e. g. Grimm, 'The History of the Prince (or Princes) of the Sons of God.' Ewald: שרבים שר בני אל = 'the sceptre of the Prince of the Sons of God.' Derenbourg: ספר בית שר בני אל = the Book of the House of the Prince of the Sons of God. (*Hist. Pal.* pp. 450–451.) Another explanation might be hazarded, שר בית סרבני (סרכני) אל = the Prince of the house of the rebels (*or*, כ for ב, chieftains) of God. Geiger (*Urschrift*, p. 205), שרבת סרבני אל 'the obstinacy of the obstinate against God' = the Syrians.

a Greek translation, that Ecclesiasticus and the First of Maccabees failed to find their way into the Canon at the close of the first century A. D.   Nor do other books of our 'Apocrypha,' which were originally composed in Hebrew —e. g. Tobit (?), Judith, Baruch i. 1–iii. 8—appear ever to have been put forward by Jewish writers as worthy to take rank with the acknowledged Scriptures of the nation.

The fact, however, that so recent a book as Ecclesiasticus should, even by mistake, be referred to with the formula of quotation from Scripture, shows that the tendency to import a favourite work into the sacred list was a real danger in the Jewish, as well as in the Christian, Church.   To guard against such a profanation, it was incumbent upon the Jewish teachers to devise some plan, by which the compass of the Canon should be rigidly preserved, and the sanctity of a book maintained, by careful tradition.   For this purpose a strangely artificial standard of canonicity was, *more Rabbinorum*, adopted.

In order to preserve the Scriptures from a profane *'Defile the hands.'* or careless handling, the Rabbins laid down the rule, that to touch the Sacred Books was to incur ceremonial defilement.   As the result of this rule, precautions were taken that the books should be kept well out of reach of common touch.   It also became necessary to declare precisely what books were included in the Canon and would therefore communicate defilement, and what books could be handled without conveying such effects.   The question of canonicity or non-canonicity soon resolved itself into the question, whether a book ' defiled the hands,' or whether it did not.   If it did, it was because it belonged to the Canon of Scripture ; if it did not, it was because it was not included in the sacred register of ' the Twenty-four.'   The remembrance of the disputes

CHAP. IX. which this test occasioned is preserved in a treatise of
the Mishnah (*Yadaim*, or 'hands')[1]. Without an explanation of the phrase, 'defile the hands,' Jewish criticisms
upon the canonicity of books of Scripture would, indeed,
convey no intelligible meaning ; but, provided with this
explanation, we gain a conception both of the freedom
with which questions of canonicity were discussed, and
of the finality with which custom had practically decided
the compass of the Canon before the Rabbinic discussions in the first and second centuries A. D.

The need was also felt of other phrases to complete
the Rabbinic definition of 'canonicity'; one, which
would convey the idea of disputed books which it was
not advisable to read publicly as Canonical Scripture,
and another for undoubtedly uncanonical or downright
heretical books, which it was advisable to eschew

Disputed or altogether.   The former idea was expressed by the term
'Hidden'
Books 'genuzim,' or 'hidden,' which was, probably, originally
(גנוזים). applied to worn-out copies of the rolls of Scriptures that
were buried or consigned to a special chamber designed
for their reception[2], and were thus put out of sight and
separated from the rolls kept, for purposes of public
reading, in the 'case' or 'théké'[3] within the 'ark' of
the Synagogue.   In this category of books preserved as
ancient, but not adapted for public reading, the Rabbins
seem to have placed the books whose canonicity was
disputed, or whose interpretation gave rise to especial
perplexity.   The *'genuzim,'* however, according to this
explanation, were quite different, in spite of the similarity

---

[1] Cf. *Yadaim*, iii. 5, 'All the Holy Scriptures defile the hands.'.

[2] Called the 'Geniza.'

[3] פִּיקֵא, פִּיק, θήκη.   The 'ark' or chest was the פִּיקָה = κιβωτός, cf
Meg. iii. 1, *Taan.* ii. 1-2, Chrys. *Orat. adv. Jud.* vi. 7 (*ed. Migne, Tom.* i.
p. 914).

in the derivation of the word, from 'Apocrypha'; the CHAP. IX.
name denotes doubt rather than final rejection. As there
is no evidence to prove that, in the first cent. A.D., a lesson
was read from the Hagiographa, we must suppose that
the relegation to the '*genuzim*' of 'disputed' books,
such as Ecclesiastes, and the Song of Songs, (see chap.
x.) implies the use of the Hagiographa, for purposes of
'Midrash,' for the public interpretation (cf. Luke iv.
17–21) of 'the Prophets' in the Synagogues.

For rejection from the Canon, the term 'extraneous,' *Extraneous*
'outside,' was used. The writings 'outside' the Canon *or 'outside'*
(*Sepharîm Khîtzōnîm*, 'books that arè outside') corre- *Books* (חיצונים).
spond more closely to our conventional conception of
'Apocrypha,' and we find designated by this term the First
Book of Maccabees ('the Megillah of the house of the
Asmoneans'), Ecclesiasticus ('the Proverbs of the Son
of Sira'), Wisdom ('the Wisdom of Solomon') as well as
books by heretics, Sadducees, Greek Philosophers, or
Christians[1]. Accordingly we find the maxim laid down
in general terms, 'It is forbidden to read in the "extraneous" books.' (*Kohel. Rabba*, 84 *c*, quoted by Weber,
Die Lehren des Talmud, Leipz. 1886, p. 81.)

But the employment of the two phrases in Rabbinic
writing is not free from obscurity. The distinction which
has here been given seems to offer the most probable
explanation (cf. Nöldeke, *Die alttest. Literatur*, 1868,
p. 238).

[1] Cf. *Sanh.* xi. 1, quoted by Fürst, *Kanon d. Alt. Test.*, p. 97. But see
Grätz (*M. G. W. J.* 1886), who renders : 'R. Akiba said, Whoso readeth
in the "extraneous" (i. e. Judeo-Christian) books, hath no part in the world
to come.   But books, like Ben Sira, written since the days of the prophets
a man may read, just as he reads a letter.' Buhl, p. 8.

CHAPTER X.

LATER JEWISH TESTIMONY.

CHAP. X.

Rabbinic evidence uncritical.

AFTER the time of Josephus, we must look to Rabbinic literature for any additional Jewish testimony. Unfortunately, very little value can be assigned to the testimony of the Talmud, and of Rabbinical literature generally, in questions of historical criticism. The Rabbinic writings abound in matter full of useful illustration; but the chronological uncertainty which envelops so much of Talmudic tradition, the fragmentary and discursive character of its contents, the indefiniteness of its allusions, the technical nature of the subjects which it handles, the unsatisfactory condition of the text, combine to make us distrust its critical worth, wherever accuracy of date is requisite.

It is, therefore, advisable to treat this branch of the subject separately, and at no great length. As evidence for our special purpose, Rabbinical statements generally tend to confirm the conclusions to which we have already come; but their principal interest consists in the light which they throw upon the attitude of Jewish teachers towards the subject of the Canon.

Two Titles of Scripture[1]. Two of the commonest titles of the Hebrew Scripture, employed in Rabbinic literature, reveal the general acceptance of the Canon both in the

[1] See Excursus E.

actual extent and in the tripartite arrangement, which, CHAP. X.
as we have seen, it most probably possessed at the close
of the first century A.D. The one title, 'the Four and *The Four*
Twenty Books or Holy Writings,' is doubly significant[1]. *and Twenty.*
It excludes the number 'twenty-two,' which, with its
transference of Ruth and Lamentations to 'the Prophets,' was adopted, probably in all cases, under the
influence of the LXX version[2] (cf. Josephus, Melito,
and Origen); and, further, as a title, it closes the door
against the introduction of any apocryphal or doubtful
books. The importance of its usage, in popularly de-
fining the limits of the Canon, receives an instructive
illustration from the sentence, 'Whoso bringeth into his
house more than the Four and Twenty Holy Writings,
brings into it confusion' (cf. *Jer. Sanhedr.* x. 1).

Another title, which became the regular designation of *Law,*
the Hebrew Bible, 'The Law, the Prophets, and the Writ- *Prophets,*
ings,' occurs so frequently in Rabbinic writings, that its sig- *Writings:*
nificance may easily be overlooked. The Jews, by adopt-
ing this somewhat cumbrous name, testified to the deep
and lasting impression produced by the gradual growth
of the Canon. They acknowledged that their Bible was
not strictly one collection, but the result of three successive collections. The name of the whole is threefold,
and of such a kind that each separate title could be
applied with justice to either of the other two divisions.
Thus, although the name 'Torah' (νόμος, Law), was
specially employed of the first division, it was capable
of being applied to the whole collection (cf. John x. 34,
xii. 34, xv. 25, 1 Cor. xiv. 21). Again, the name 'Nebiim'
was specially employed of the second division; but we

---

[1] For the early Jewish use of this number, cf. *Bab. Taanith* 8 a, *Kohel. Rabba*, fol. 116 a, on xii. 11. [2] See Chap. xii.

CHAP. X. may remember that the composition of the Pentateuch
was ascribed to one who was a prophet (Deut. xviii. 18,
cf. Ezra ix. 11), that of the Psalter to another (Acts ii.
30), that of Daniel to another (Matt. xxiv. 15). Accordingly, while the general word, 'Nebiim,' was specially
used for the second division, it might have been used
for the whole, or for any, of the writings included
in the range of the Canon. The comprehensiveness
of these two terms is illustrated by the common use
'the Law of 'the Law and the Prophets' for the whole Scripture
and the where 'the Hagiographa' were clearly not excluded
Prophets.' (e. g. in the New Testament, Matt. v. 17, vii. 12, xi. 13,
xxii. 40, Luke xvi. 16, 29, 31, xxiv. 27, 44, Acts xiii. 15,
xxiv. 14, xxviii. 23).

The third title 'Writings' was still more indefinite in
character. It may be observed that as this name was
adopted in Greek (αἱ γραφαί) and in Latin (Scriptura)
for the whole collection of sacred books, a special
designation, 'Hagiographa' (ἁγιόγραφα), had to be in-
vented for the remaining group.

The whole Hebrew title, therefore, is a combination of
three different names, each applied to a particular section,
but each capable of representing the sacred character of
the whole.

The original separateness of the three divisions is thus
reflected by the threefold name, and by the absence of
any one title. The formula ך.נ ה. T. N. K. (i. e. Torah,
Nebiim, Kethubim) belongs to a later (i.e. the Massoretic)
phase of Hebrew literature.

We turn next to the consideration of a subject which,
at first sight, would seem to be of great importance. The

canonicity of certain books of the Hebrew Scriptures, CHAP. X.
was, as we have already noticed, called in question, at *Rabbinic*
different times, by Jewish teachers. In the case of *objections to Canonicity*
Ezekiel, Jonah, Proverbs, Song of Songs, Ecclesiastes, *of*
and Esther, objections were made by various Rabbins.
Their position in the Canon had given rise to scruples or
perplexity. The reasons, however, which led to these
adverse criticisms are not such as would have any weight
in the present day. They reflect the subtlety of academical discussion more than the anxiety of a perplexed
conscience. As a rule, they illustrate only too well the
character of the Rabbinism from which they emanated.
At the most, they testify to the degree of tolerance
permitted in the range of controversy, and to the probability that, at an earlier date, the admission of certain
books into the Hebrew Canon had met with considerable opposition, or with only a moderate degree of
approbation.

Ezekiel. The difficulty raised concerning this book *Ezekiel.*
could never have seriously compromised its position in
the Canon. The objection was felt that, in several points,
it apparently contradicted the Pentateuch. According
to one tradition (*Menachoth*, 45 *a*), it was resolved that,
on account of its discrepancy with the law of Moses in
the matter of priestly regulations, it was necessary to
exclude the book from public reading. 'Elias, when he
comes, it was said, will explain the difficulty.' At this
crisis, Hananiah, the son of Hezekiah, the son of Garon,
a younger contemporary of Hillel, is said to have arisen
and to have succeeded in showing by 'Haggadic'[1] inter-

---

[1] 'Haggada' was the Rabbinic term given to *doctrinal* exposition ;
Halaka to *practical* exposition. Parable, legend, and allegory entered
largely into Haggada. The 'Mercaba' or 'Chariot' vision of Ezekiel was
the nucleus of the *Kabbala* or esoteric teaching of the Jews.

CHAP. X. pretation that the apparent discrepancies could be reconciled (cf. *Sabbath*, 13 *b*, *Chagigah*, 13 *a, b*). 'But as for
Hananiah, the son of Hezekiah, blessed be his memory,
—if it had not been for him, the Book of Ezekiel would
have been hidden (i.e. made apocryphal, withdrawn from,
public reading, placed among the *Genuzim*), because its
words contradict the words of the Torah.   What did
he do?   They brought him 300 measures of oil; and
he sate down and explained it.'   The manner in which
Hananiah disposed of the difficulty was so satisfactory,
that the Book of Ezekiel was afterwards quoted as pos-
sessing the full authority of the Torah itself, on matters
of ceremonial and cleanliness (cf. *Moed Qatan*, 5 *a*).

It is very possible that the real objection felt to the
public reading of Ezekiel was due to the great obscurity
of certain passages, especially the visions of the Chariot
and the Temple (ch. i. and xl–xlviii).   The contradictions
to the law of Moses, in matters of detail, added to
the general perplexity, and afforded an intelligible
pretext for those who advocated its withdrawal from
public reading in the Synagogues.   The introduction of
the Haggadic method of interpretation was the means
both of reconciling contradictions and of importing
mystic explanations for that which had hitherto been
obscure.   Jerome (*Ep. ad Paul.*, Ep. liii) records the
existence of such difficulties experienced by the Jews
in the interpretation of these passages, and reports the
custom that these portions were not to be read until
thirty years of age were reached.   'Tertius principia et
finem tantis habet obscuritatibus involuta, ut apud
Hebraeos istae partes cum exordio Geneseos ante annos
triginta non legantur.'

Jonah.   *Jonah.*   The adverse testimony is here very slight,

The idea that the book contained only a legendary story may possibly have induced some Jewish scholars to exclude it from the Canon, and may account for the language of the Midrash Bammidbar (c. 18), 'Lord of fifty, that is, of fifty books, that is, the twenty-four books of Holy Scripture, with eleven of the Twelve (Minor Prophets), excluding the Book of Jonah, which is a book by itself, and with the six Seders (of the Mishnah), and the nine Midrash books on the law of the Priests: behold the fifty.' Without pausing except to point out that, as, in the canonical twenty-four books, the Twelve Minor Prophets were already represented as one book, there was no need for them to be counted over again, we may suppose the passage to indicate a doubt whether Jonah was of equal historical value with the other prophets. Kimchi (A.D. 1240), in the introduction to his commentary on 'Jonah,' hints at the same suspicion. But there is no evidence to show that the recognition of Jonah as a book of Canonical Scripture was ever seriously imperilled.

Proverbs. Any doubts that may have arisen as to the canonicity of this book probably arose from its being generally classed with the two other so-called Solomonic works. The suspicions in which Ecclesiastes was involved seem to have spread to the earlier representative of the Khokmah, or Sapiential, literature. The objections to Proverbs were based, partly upon verbal contradictions in the book itself, partly upon the ground that it was supposed to favour heretical (query: Sadducean) proclivities. But the authority of the book was never in reality seriously compromised. There is a well-known passage in the *Bab. Sabbath* 30 *b*: 'Some desired also to withdraw (lit. to hide, *ganaz*) the book of Proverbs from

CHAP. X.   use, because it contained internal contradictions[1], but the
attempt was abandoned because the wise men declared,
"We have examined more deeply into the Book of
Ecclesiastes and have discovered the solution of the
difficulty ; here also we wish to enquire more deeply." '
A similar account is given in *Aboth R. Nathan* (cap. i),
'At first, they withdrew Proverbs, and the Song of
Songs, and Ecclesiastes from public use (i.e. placed them
among the *Genuzim*), because they spoke in parables.
And so they continued, until the Men of the Great
Synagogue came and expounded them.'   The passages
referred to in Proverbs are ch. vii. 7–20, xi. 9. From
this it is evident that, if ever its canonicity was impeached,
it was upon the same internal grounds as the Book of
Ecclesiastes, and that it was never at any moment in
danger of being absolutely rejected.   The removal of
doubts about Ecclesiastes sufficed to allay any appre-
hensions about Proverbs.

Ecclesiastes   *Ecclesiastes, or Koheleth.*   In the case of this book,
there is a much clearer and stronger tradition, recording
the hesitation as to its admission into the Canon.   The
grounds of this hesitation are stated by Jewish tradition
to have been, (1) that the book contained contradictory
statements, (2) that it was opposed to other Canonical
Scripture, (3) that it favoured the views of the heretics
(i.e. Sadducees).

alleged to be   The first of these charges is stated in *Sab.* 30 *b*:
'The wise men desired to "hide" the Book Koheleth
(i.e. withdraw it from public use), because its language
(1) *self-*   was often self-contradictory.'   As instances were given,
contradic-
tory,   'sorrow is better than laughter' (vii. 3), which was

[1] e.g. xxvi. 4 and 5, ' Answer not a fool according to his folly .   .   .   .
Answer a fool according to his folly.'

considered to contradict 'I said of laughter, it is to be
praised' (R.V. 'mad'; ii. 2); 'Then I commended mirth'
(viii. 15), which was considered to contradict '(I said of
mirth, what doeth it?' (ii. 2); 'Wherefore I praised the
dead which are already dead more than the living which
are yet alive' (iv. 2), which was considered to contradict
'For a living dog is better than a dead lion' (ix. 4).

A second charge is found in the same context, *Sabbath* (2) *opposed*
30 *a*, where the Preacher is asserted to contradict the *to Psalter;*
words of the Psalter: 'O Solomon, where is thy wisdom?
where thy discernment? Doth it not suffice thee that
many of thy words contradict the utterances of David,
that thou contradictest even thyself.'

A third charge is found, in combination with the (3) *unortho-*
second, in a passage of the *Midrash Vayyikra Rabba*, c. *dox.*
28 : 'They sought to withdraw (lit. to hide) the book
"Koheleth" because they found in it words which
favoured heresy, and because Solomon said, "Rejoice, O
young man, in thy youth," &c., &c. (Ecc. xi. 9), whereas
Moses said, "And that ye go not about after your own
heart and your own eyes" (Num. xv. 39).' The same
charge of heresy is brought on account of the words, 'What
profit hath a man of all his labour,' &c. (Ecc. i. 3), which
were considered to favour the 'heretics,' a phrase that
seems to have been intended for the Sadducees, or
generally those who denied the doctrine of the resurrection. Other passages illustrating the doubts raised by
this book are *Eduyoth*[1], v. 3; *Yadaim*, iii. 5; *Midrash
Koheleth* i. 3, xi. 9. *Aboth. R. Nathan* (*ut supra*).

---

[1] *Eduy.* 5, 3, R. Simon says, 'In three cases the School of Shammai makes
easy, and the School of Hillel makes difficult. According to the School of
Shammai, Koheleth defileth not the hands; the School of Hillel says, It
defileth the hands.'

These charges against the canonicity of Ecclesiastes were apparently more gravely considered than those against any other book (see below, *Meg.* 7 *a*). The 'Wise,' however—by whom we should probably understand the scribes and principal Rabbins of the first and second centuries A.D.—seem to have investigated the question carefully. They found that the difficulties were all capable of explanation. Perhaps, recourse to the methods of 'Haggadic' interpretation facilitated this favourable judgment. Perhaps, the concluding verses (xii. 13, 14), which, according to some scholars, were added at a date subsequent to its actual composition, were able, by the utterance of their simple faith, to redress the balance that seemed to be so cruelly disturbed by the expressions of despair occurring earlier in the book. There is, however, no probability in the conjecture of Krochmal, adopted by Fürst[1], that these concluding verses were added by Hananiah and his colleagues, in order to justify their opinion as to the canonicity of the book, and to declare by their means that the contents of the Canon were now finally completed.

The Talmudic passage quoted above (*Sabbath* 30 *b*) records the conclusion of the Wise Men: 'Why did they not "hide" it? Because the beginning and the end of it consist of words of Torah.' With this we should compare Jerome's statement respecting the Jewish doubts as to this book. He says in his comment on chap. xii. 13, *Jerome on Eccles.* xii. 13, 14: 'Aiunt Hebraei quum inter cetera scripta Salomonis quae antiquata sunt nec in memoria duraverunt et hic liber obliterandus videretur eo quod vanas Dei assereret creaturas et totum putaret esse pro nihilo, et cibum, et

---

[1] Fürst, *Kan. d. A. T.* pp. 90-96.

potum, et delitias transeuntes praeferret omnibus; ex
hoc uno capitulo meruisse authoritatem ut in divinorum
voluminum numero poneretur, quod totam disputationem
suam, et omnem catalogum, hac quasi ἀνακεφαλαιώσει
coarctaverit et dixerit finem sermonum auditu esse
promtissimum, nec aliquid in se habere difficile : ut scilicet
Deum timeamus et ejus praecepta faciamus.'

The Song of Songs. The acceptance of this book into
the Canon possibly implies a date at which allegorical interpretation—in other words, the influence of Haggadic
teaching—had come into use. The Canonicity of the
Song of Songs could thus be defended on other grounds
besides that of its being a writing of Solomon, and in
spite of the objections that were felt on account of the
primarily secular character of its contents. But its
reception did not pass without opposition. At least, this
is the natural explanation of the vehement anxiety with
which Jewish tradition has insisted upon its sanctity.
Thus, after saying that 'all the Holy Scriptures defile
the hands,' it is expressly added, as if to meet an obvious
criticism, that 'the Song of Songs and Koheleth defile the
hands' (*Yad.* iii. 5). In another passage (*Meg.* 7 *a*), we
find an interesting allusion to the variety of opinion held
upon this book, and to the way in which it was expressed :
' Rabbi Meir saith, " The book Koheleth defileth not the
hands, and with respect to the Song of Songs there is
difference of opinion." Rabbi Joshua saith on the other
hand, " The Song of Songs defileth the hands, and with
respect to Koheleth there is dispute." Rabbi Simeon
saith, " Koheleth belongeth to the things which the
school of Shammai maketh easy and the school of Hillel
maketh difficult ; but the Books of Ruth, the Song of
Songs, and Esther defile the hands." That is what Rabbi

CHAP. X. Joshua said. We are taught that Rabbi Simeon ben Menasiah saith, " Koheleth defileth not the hands, because it containeth the Wisdom of Solomon." '

Most noticeable of all is the passage in which the sentence, 'All Holy Scriptures defile the hands, even the Song of Songs and Koheleth,' is discussed. 'R. Juda saith : "The Song of Songs defileth the hands, but Koheleth is disputed." R. Jose saith : "Koheleth defileth not the hands, and the Song of Songs is disputed." R. Simeon saith : "Koheleth belongeth to the things which the school of Shammai maketh easy and the school of Hillel maketh difficult." R. Simeon ben Azai said : "1 received it from the seventy-two Elders, that on the day when R. Eleazar ben Azariah was made President (i.e. in the school at Jamnia), it was determined that the Song of Songs and Koheleth defile the hands." R. Akiba said, " God forbid that any man of Israel should deny that the Song of Songs defileth the hands ; for the whole world is not equal to the day on which the Song of Songs was given to Israel. For all the Scriptures are holy, but the Song of Songs is the holiest of the holy ; and if there is dispute, it is groundless except in the case of Koheleth "' *(Yad.* iii. 5). Rabbi Akiba's encomium upon such a book suggests an allusion to some serious objection. It is as if at the weakest link of the chain it was deemed politic to make the loudest assertion of confidence in its strength.

Esther.

Esther. The Book of Esther gave rise to disputes among the Rabbins of a similar nature. Like the Book of Ecclesiastes, it was probably among the last to be received as canonical. This fact alone would probably account for some of the opposition which it encountered. But a more serious ground for questioning its right to be

regarded as Scripture was found in its apparently inten-
tional omission of any reference to the Divine Name.
It is this peculiarity which no doubt occasioned the
questionings implied in the following extracts from
Jewish tradition (*Meg.* 7a). (*a*) 'Esther (i. e. the book)
sent to the Wise the following entreaty, "Write me
in the Book (? the Canon) for all ages." They sent
to her in answer, "(It is written), Have not I written
three things?"' i.e. three and not four. The quotation is
from Prov. xxii. 20, where the Hebrew text is doubtful
and the meaning obscure. The doubtful word (translated
in the R.V. 'excellent things[1],' marg. 'heretofore,' according to a variant reading) is accepted by the Jewish
tradition to mean 'three,' and to contain an allusion to
the 'Law, Prophets, and Writings.' The three classes of
Scripture are complete, say the Wise men ; there is no
warrant for making a fourth class in order to receive the
Book of Esther : it is written, 'I have written three.'

(*b*) 'Rabbi Jehuda said in the name of Samuel, "The
book of Esther defileth not the hands." Is then the Book
of Esther not inspired ? Could Samuel have thought
this ? He said however, Is it inspired ?" Answer. "He
understood, it is given for reading, and is not for
writing."'

(*c*) 'We are taught: Rabbi Eleazer saith, "The Book
of Esther is inspired, for it is said (Esth. vi. 6), 'Now
Haman said in his heart' (i.e. which could be known to
none but the Holy Spirit)." Rabbi Akiba saith, "The
Book of Esther is inspired ; for it is said (Esth. ii. 22),
'And the thing was known to Mordecai.'" Rabbi Josse
ben Durmascit said, "The Book of Esther is inspired ;
for it is said (Esth. ix. 10), 'But on the spoil they laid not

[1] Kethib, שׁלושׁים; Qeri, שָׁלִישִׁים.

CHAP. X. their hand.'"   Samuel said, "Had I been there, I would
have said one word, which surpasses all ; it is said (Esth:
ix. 27), '(the Jews) ordained and took upon them' (that
is, that was ordained above in heaven, which they took
upon them on earth)".'

Such sayings imply, that there had been some hesitation in accepting the canonicity of the book.   But
the difficulties that had been felt, vanished before the
application of these strange methods of interpretation.
According to the tradition, 'The Wise men ceased not
discussing the matter backwards and forwards until
God enlightened their eyes, and they found it written in
the Law, the Prophets, and the Writings.' (See also the
next chapter.)

Such are some of the chief objections that Jewish
scholars are reported to have raised against the canonicity
of certain canonical books. The reader will form his own
judgment as to the amount of weight to be attached to
their evidence. It cannot, however, in any way qualify
the results of our enquiry into the history of the Canon.
The earliest Jewish traditions that have been quoted were
probably not committed to writing until the close of the
second cent. A.D. We have no means of verifying the
facts preserved by such oral tradition, or, in case of interpolation, of discriminating between the original tradition
and the glosses which it may have acquired in the process
of transmission. It is impossible, therefore, to say for
certain, how far these strange academical discussions,
turning wholly on subjective criticism, accurately reproduce the actual controversies which closed the Canon, or
resulted from its conclusion. They, at least, reflect the
spirit in which the Jewish doctors met the real and
imaginary difficulties which they and their disciples

delighted to multiply, and gloried in either surmounting CHAP. X.
or evading.

Perhaps the most important thing for us to observe *Canonicity presupposed.*
is that the discussions of the Jewish doctors, whether
serious controversies or only academic displays of verbal
adroitness, presuppose the existing canonicity of the disputed books.

CHAPTER XI.

THE HEBREW CANON IN THE CHRISTIAN CHURCH.

CHAP. XI. ONLY in one instance do the objections, which had been felt against the inclusion of a book within the Canon, appear to have survived for long, or to have resulted, in some quarters, in its actual withdrawal from the list of Holy Scripture.

Esther excluded from public use, locally. Opposition to the Book of Esther appears to have taken this open form. Its withdrawal may, of course, have only expressed a local prejudice due to the teaching of some influential Rabbi. But the fact of the book having been actually excluded from a Jewish list of Canonical Scripture merits attention. For, although we learn of it from a Christian source, the position of the Book of Esther in certain other Christian lists, which profess to give the contents of the Hebrew Canon, indicates the suspicion with which it was apt to be regarded.

Melito, circ. 170 A.D. His list. Melito, the Bishop of Sardis (circ. 170 A.D.), sent to a friend a list of the Old Testament Scriptures, which he professed to have obtained from 'accurate enquiry,' when travelling in the East, in Syria (*ap.* Euseb. *H. E.* iv. 26[1]). Its contents agree with those of the Hebrew

---

[1] On Melito's list, see Chap. xii and the Table in Excursus C. The words with which he prefaces it are, ἀνελθὼν οὖν εἰς τὴν ἀνατολὴν, καὶ ἕως τοῦ τόπου γενόμενος ἔνθα ἐκηρύχθη καὶ ἐπράχθη καὶ ἀκριβῶς μαθὼν τὰ τῆς παλαιᾶς διαθήκης βιβλία, ὑποτάξας ἔπεμψά σοι. (*Ap.* Eus. *H. E.* iv. 26.)

Canon, save in the omission of 'Esther.' For 'Lamentations' is doubtless to be reckoned with Jeremiah, and Nehemiah with Ezra. Was the omission of Esther accidental? Or was it that the book had either been absolutely set aside as uncanonical, or been temporarily withdrawn from 'reading' as a doubtful work?

(1) The supposition that the name has only accidentally dropped out from the list, may fairly be claimed to be not altogether improbable. In Origen's list of the Old Testament Scriptures, the Minor Prophets are thus accidentally omitted; and it is certainly very possible that in Melito's list the name of 'Esther' may similarly have been passed over, either by the inadvertence of a scribe, or by the careless confusion of the name 'Esther' with that of 'Esdras,' after which book it appears in several other lists, e. g. Cyril of Jerusalem († 386) and Epiphanius († 403). But accident, though very possible, cannot be accepted as the most probable reason for the omission.

Omits Esther (1) by accident,

(2) That it was intentionally left out by Melito's Jewish informants, offers the more natural explanation. For the same unfavourable opinion, which the omission would denote, is not only expressed in the Rabbinical discussions mentioned in the previous chapter, but is also implied in the position allotted to the book in other Christian writings, which claim to reproduce the contents of the Hebrew Canon. In the list of the Hebrew books of the Old Testament, given by Origen († 253), the Book of Esther stands last. In the list of Athanasius († 373) in his Festal Epistle (xxxix), written in 367 A.D., the book 'Esther' is not classed among the canonical writings, but is found in the group of the other books that were to be read for instruction, i. e. the Wisdom of Solomon, the Wisdom of Sirach,

(2) purposely: compare later Christian lists.

CHAP. XI.　Esther, Judith, Tobit, 'the Didache,' and 'the Shepherd.'
In the so-called list of Amphilochius, Bishop of Iconium
(circ. 380 A.D.), the Book of 'Esther' is not included
among the Old Testament writings; but, at the end of
the list of the Old Testament Canon, it is stated that
'some add the Book of Esther[1].' In the list of Gregory
of Nazianzus († 391) it is omitted from the Old Testament writings; in the list of Leontius (circ. 590) it is not
mentioned among the 'twenty-two' of the Canon, while
in that of Nicephorus (814) it is not mentioned among
'the twenty-two books of the Old Testament,' but among
the 'Antilegomena' of the Old Testament along with
the Maccabees, Wisdom, Sirach, Proverbs of Solomon,
Judith, Susanna, and Tobit.

Cause of omission.　. It is difficult to feel certain whether the unfavourable
verdict of these Christian fathers was based upon Jew-
ish objections or Christian prejudices. In Melito's days,
the Hebrew Canon had evidently been decided by the
Jews. The position of the Book of Esther in it was
fully assured. How then can we account for its omission
in Melito's list? Possibly, on the ground that, objections
being felt to the Fast and Feast of Purim, it was thought
advisable, at least in the locality where Melito prosecuted
his enquiry, to discontinue the public use of the Book,
upon the authority of which those anniversaries were
observed. Thus, it may have been objected that the
day of Haman's murderous project (Esth. iii. 13), which
seems to have been commemorated by a fast (Esth. ix. 31[2]),
coincided with the Day of Nicanor (2 Macc. xv. 36), the
13th day of Adar, a Feast-day, on which fasting was

---

[1] Τούτοις προσεγκρίνουσι τὴν 'Εσθήρ τινες (*Iambi ad Seleuc. ap. Greg. Naz. Carm. Sect.* ii. vii.).

[2] The reference to fasting in Esther ix. 31 is omitted in the LXX

prohibited (cf. *Megillath Taanith*, xii. 30: *Texte de la M.T.*, CHAP. XI.
Derenbourg, *Hist. de la Pal.* pp. 442–444). Or, it may
have been objected, that the Feast of Purim was not of
ancient origin; and that its celebration, having certain
resemblances to the usages of a Persian Feast (*Fûrdigan*),
gave occasion to misunderstanding, and was apt to be
confounded with heathen practices[1]. For some such *Esther's place among 'Genuzim.'*
reason, or for the simpler reason that the book had locally
fallen into disrepute on account of its omission of the
Sacred Name, Esther was not included in the list that the
Bishop of Sardis obtained from his enquiries in the East.

In all probability, the Book had, temporarily and only
locally, been placed among the *Genuzim*. For reasons
which have not transpired, it was withdrawn from public
use. But it was not placed amongst the *Khîtzônîm*. It
was 'disputed,' not 'rejected.' This distinction, on the
part of Syrian Jewish converts, a Greek Bishop would
scarcely be able to appreciate.

To Christian readers the character of the book may
very naturally have given rise to difficulties. Its spirit
and teaching seemed to have little in common with the
New Testament. The knowledge that its canonicity *Not under-stood : pre-judice na-turally per-petuated by tradition.*
was not universally accepted by the Jews, would be
enough for those who were prejudiced against it. Some,
too, who appear to advocate its exclusion from the list of
the Old Testament Scriptures, merely repeat the opinion
of previous writers without attempting to investigate the
question afresh. Jerome, in his *Preface to Esther*, records
no adverse Jewish opinion. Aphraates, circ. 350 A.D., who
was well instructed in Hebrew tradition, omits no book
from the Hebrew Canon (Buhl). We may fairly assume

---

[1] See Lagarde (*Gesam. Abhandl.*, quoted by Robertson Smith, O.T.J.C.,
p. 161 sq., ed. 1; p. 184, ed. 2).

CHAP. XI. from what we know of Patristic methods, that the list of Melito, in the History of Eusebius, will account, in great measure, for the exclusion of Esther from late Christian lists of the Hebrew Canon. On such a question, the Fathers, who knew no Hebrew, were wont to rely on earlier tradition, and seek no fresh testimony [1].

But the adverse evidence of the Fathers quoted above, although it illustrates the independence of local Jewish opinion upon the Canon, is not sufficient to shake our confidence in the claim of Esther to its place in the Hebrew Scriptures.

Origen († 253) omits Min. Proph. adds 'Epistle.' The only other important variations in the contents [2], as distinct from the variations in the order, of the Hebrew Canon, as reported by a Christian Father, occur in the list of Origen (*ap.* Euseb. *H. E.* vi. 25), in which are to be noticed the omission of the Twelve Minor Prophets and the inclusion of a work entitled 'The Epistle' along with Jeremiah. The omission of the Twelve Prophets is undoubtedly due to an inadvertency, either on the part of Origen himself, or of Eusebius, or of some copyist. The addition of 'The Epistle,' by which we must probably understand the Book of Baruch, indicates that Origen gives the contents of the Hebrew Canon as they were represented in the LXX version.

[1] On the influence of Eusebius upon the lists of Gregory of Nazianzus and Amphilochius, see Westcott, *Bible in the Church*, pp. 167.

[2] We ought, perhaps, to mention the omission of Chronicles in the earliest Syrian Version. The books of Chronicles are not commented on by Ephrem Syrus; while Theodore of Mopsuestia seems to have excluded Job, Esther, and Ezra and Nehemiah. It does not appear probable that such omissions were based on any tradition of a shorter Hebrew Canon. Rather, they reflect the working of somewhat arbitrary subjective principles. (Cf. Buhl, pp. 52, 53). Is not the omission also of Esther, in Melito's list, to be attributed to the influence of similar doubts, entertained with as little historical reason, in the Syrian Church !

There is no sign of the Book of Baruch having ever CHAP. XI. found general acceptance in the Jewish Synagogue. The possibility may be conceded, that Origen is reporting a local practice. But it is more probable that, when he mentions Jeremiah among the Hebrew books, he has in his mind the expanded form in which it appeared in his Greek Bible; and, as we shall see in the next chapter, this explanation is confirmed by the order in which he enumerates the books. The subject of the order of the books in the Hebrew Canon belongs to a distinct enquiry; but, as it is not without interest for our subject, we shall touch upon it briefly in the following chapter.

The history of the admission of the books of the *'Apocrypha'* 'Apocrypha' into the Greek and Latin copies of the Old *belong to history of* Testament lies outside the scope of the present work. *LXX, not of Hebrew* The Christian Church of the Apostolic age accepted the *Scriptures.* Palestinian Canon of the Hebrew Scriptures in its entirety. The Palestinian Canon is that whose growth and formation we have endeavoured to trace. It is that which our Lord and the Apostles, by their usage, sealed for the blessing and divine instruction of all ages to come. It is that of whose compass and integrity we have assurance from the unalterable character of Hebrew tradition, as well as from the combined testimony of Melito, of Origen, of Ruffinus, of Jerome, and of others, who contended for the purity of the Hebrew Scriptures as the only true Canon of the Old Covenant.

The intermixture of the so-called Apocryphal books, and their quasi-recognition in the Christian Church, constitute the theme of a separate study[1]. The Apocryphal Books never had a place (see Chap. x.) in the Palesti-

---

[1] See Westcott's *Bible in the Church*, and my article 'Apocrypha,' in Smith's *Dictionary of the Bible*, ed. 2.

CHAP. XI. nian Canon.   The position which they obtained among Christians after the 2nd century, was due to the prevalent ignorance of Hebrew, and, as a consequence, to the ignorance of the true limits of that Jewish Bible, which the Apostles had sanctioned.   Defective acquaintance with the Hebrew tradition and with the Palestinian Canon is answerable, in the main, for the additions which were made in the Greek Bible and in the versions derived from it.   When once additional books were accepted in the list of the LXX, the enormous influence of that Version caused them to be regarded with a veneration, which only the more learned men in the Church could keep distinct from that which was due to the inspired and holy writings of the Hebrew Canon of Scripture, and to them alone, as the Bible of the Jewish Church on which our Saviour set the seal of His authority.

CHAPTER XII.

THE ARRANGEMENT OF THE BOOKS.

HITHERTO I have designedly abstained from touching upon the subject of the arrangement of the books, except so far as 'the tripartite division' of the Canon, and the position of the books, Ruth and Lamentations, have necessarily claimed attention in connexion with the historical argument.

If that historical argument has been as fully supported by evidence, as I think it has, it will long ago have become plain to the reader, that 'the tripartite division' gives no arbitrary grouping, but is a trustworthy witness and an invaluable memorial of the historical growth and gradual development of the Canon.

The arrangement of the Nebiim and Kethubim is not chronological, nor is it according to subject-matter. If they had been grouped upon either the one principle or the other, we should not have found Ruth, Chronicles, Ezra and Nehemiah, and Esther placed in a separate group from Judges, Samuel, and Kings, nor the Books of Lamentations and Daniel separated from those of Jeremiah and Ezekiel.

The Tri-partite Division:

The usual explanations which have been given, have gone, as a rule, very wide of the mark. They have partaken rather of the nature of comment, drawn from the fact of the triple division, than of explanation based upon actual evidence. Thus, the Jewish tradition that the three

Jewish explanations inadequate.

CHAP. XII. groups correspond to three descending stages of inspiration [1], 'the gradus Mosaicus,' 'the spirit of prophecy,' and 'the Holy Spirit' in its simplest form (or *Ruakh Haqqodesh*), offered no real explanation of the phenomena; but simply repeated the opinion which Jewish teachers pronounced upon the relative religious value of the three groups (see Maimonides, *Moreh Nebochim*, ii. 45).[2]

Modern teaching deduced from, not explaining formation of, tripartite division.

Modern explanations, which have not been based upon a recognition of the gradual expansion of the Canon, are liable to the same censure. Thus, it may, in a great measure, be perfectly true, that the three divisions of the Hebrew Canon correspond to the course of development to be traced in the history of Old Testament Theology, in (1) the nucleus of Mosaic Revelation, (2) the objective expansion of it through the Prophets, (3) its subjective expression through the poetry and 'Wisdom' of the Hagiographa (cf. Oehler, *Theology of the Old Testament*, i. 70 Eng. trans.). There may be a truth in the assertion that the three divisions reflect in a special manner the attitude of religious thought in Israel towards the Almighty, towards the Theocracy, and towards Revelation, respectively (cf. Keil, *Einleit*. p. 501). Still, these and similar explanations are pious reflexions, evoked by the existence of a tripartite division, rather than scientific arguments based on the literary or historical criticism of the groups. They are not without use as suggestive generalisations.

[1] See on this subject John Smith's *Discourse of Prophecy*, chap. ii. pp. 178 seq. (ed. Camb. Univ. Press, 1859).

[2] Some of the attempts to account for the position of Daniel among the Hagiographa, instead of among the Prophets, are almost absurd in their variety and obvious inadequacy, e.g. 'Daniel was a prophet in gift, not in office,' 'he prophesied in a foreign land, not in Palestine,' 'he received manifestations of angels' (Nachmanides), 'he was a politician, and lived at a royal court.'

But, as a rule, they are put forward on the assumption that the formation of the whole Canon was undertaken by one man, or by a single generation, endowed with special supernatural gifts for the work (cf. Keil, *Einleit.* p. 501). That assumption breaks down utterly, when confronted with the better knowledge of the books obtained by modern study, by a more careful analysis of the language, and by a stricter scrutiny of the contents of the individual writings. The generation to which Ezra belonged may have assisted at the first, they had nothing to do with the final, stage in the formation of the Canon. The books of Chronicles and Ecclesiastes alone would disprove the correctness of the traditional view.

Even apart from the results of recent criticism, the generalisations alluded to above equally break down, when tested by application to specific cases, to the peculiar anomalies of the tripartite division. Thus, the explanation that Daniel, being an apocalyptic work, could not take rank among the 'Prophets,' will hardly commend itself to the ordinary reader in the face of our Lord's words (Matt. xxiv. 15)[1]. Similarly, the contention that the narrative books of the Hagiographa, e. g. Ruth, Ezra, and Nehemiah, relate the sacred history from a different

---

[1] John Smith (page 243, *ut sup.*), in whose days the idea of a gradual formation of the O. T. Canon was unknown, attributes the position of Daniel in the Hagiographa to the error of the Jews. 'And, therefore, whatever the latter Jews here urge, for thus ranking Daniel's books with the other כתובים, yet, seeing they give us no traditional reason which their ancestors had for so doing, I should rather think it to have been, first of all, some fortuitous thing which gave an occasion to this after-mistake, as I think it is' (1650). So also Leusden, *Philolog. Hebrae. Dissert.* viii. p. 91 (ed. 2, 1672), 'Continet ergo (Daniel) prophetiam; et propterea Judaei eum immerito e choro Prophetarum extrudunt, et ad Hagiographa ablegant.' This appears to be a more candid explanation for the position of Daniel in the Hebrew Canon than the attempts to show that Daniel was not really a Prophet.

standpoint from the Books of Judges, Samuel, and Kings, may or may not be true ; but it conveys no sufficient reason for their non-admission into the group of the 'Prophets.' If the 'Prophets' included Haggai, Zechariah, and Malachi, the parallel narratives in Ezra, Nehemiah and Esther had just as much claim to admission among the narrative books of the same group.

The truth is, that explanations of the difficulties of the triple grouping are little better than guess-work, so long as the historical sequence in the formation of the Canon is not recognised. It is not, therefore, worth while here to discuss their inadequacy at any length. For as fast as one explanation is disposed of, another can always be discovered. On the other hand, so soon as the gradual growth of the Canon is admitted, the phenomena of the triple grouping are seen not to constitute difficulties, but to illustrate the history of the literary process at successive epochs.

The chief variations in the arrangement of the books fall into two main groups ; the one, representing the influence of the Alexandrine version ; the other, the changes that have, at different times, occurred within the second and third divisions of the Hebrew Canon.

I. Influence of LXX *on arrangement of books.* I. The Alexandrine version disregarded the Hebrew tripartite division, and generally endeavoured to group the books, according to their subject-matter, into the divisions of narrative, poetical, and prophetical books. But no uniformity of order seems to have been maintained.

Melito. The list of Melito (Euseb. *H. E.* iv. 26), though purporting to give the order and contents of the Hebrew

Canon of Scripture, probably enumerates the Hebrew books in the order of the Greek Bible. 'Five books of Moses, Joshua the son of Nun, Judges, Ruth, four books of the Kingdoms, two of Chronicles (= Paralipomena),the Psalms of David, the Proverbs of Solomon, Ecclesiastes, Song of Songs, Job, the prophets Isaiah, Jeremiah, the Twelve in one Book, Daniel, Ezekiel, Esdras.' We here notice (1) the general arrangement into narrative, poetical, and prophetical groups, the book Esdras (= Ezra, Nehemiah) being attached, as an appendix, to the prophets of the Captivity; (2) the use of the Septuagint titles, 'Joshua the son of Nun,' 'Kingdoms' (for 'Kings'), 'Paralipomena'; (3) the place of Ruth next after Judges, of Chronicles after Kings, of Lamentations, presumably, after Jeremiah, of Daniel before Ezekiel; (4) the subdivision of Samuel, Kings, and Chronicles.

The list of Origen is very similar:—'the five books *Origen.* of Moses; Joshua, the son of Nun; Judges, Ruth along with them, in one book; Kingdoms first, second, third, fourth; Chronicles, first, second; Esdras first, second; Book of Psalms; Proverbs of Solomon; Ecclesiastes; Song of Songs; Isaiah; Jeremiah, with Lamentations and the Epistle, in one book; Daniel; Ezekiel; Job; Esther (Euseb. *H. E.* vi. 25) [1]. Here, again, we notice (1) the same general arrangement into narrative, poetry, and prophecy; (2) the titles of 'Joshua, the son of Nun,' 'Kingdoms,' 'Paralipomena,' 'Proverbs of Solomon'; (3) the place of Ruth, Chronicles, Lamentations, Daniel; (4) the sub-division of Samuel, Kings, Chronicles, Ezra and Nehemiah; (5) the insertion of 'The Epistle' (= Baruch or Baruch vi, the so-called Epistle of Jeremy).

[1] The Twelve Minor Prophets have fallen out by accident (p. 218); probably they came after Jeremiah.

CHAP. XII.   Origen gives the Hebrew names of the books as well as the Greek, and expressly mentions that Samuel, Kings, Chronicles, Ezra and Nehemiah, are each but one book in the Hebrew Scriptures. His object is to give the names and the number of the Hebrew books; and he enumerates them, following the Alexandrine order, omitting all books not contained in the Palestinian Canon; 'the Epistle,' which was united with Jeremiah, being the only exception.

Cod. Vat. 4th Cent.   In the Codex Vaticanus, the books are arranged upon the same principle, the chief differences being (1) the introduction of 'Apocrypha,' (2) the place of 'Job' after the canonical writings of Solomon, due perhaps to the uncertainty about authorship; and (3) the place of the Twelve Minor Prophets before Isaiah, due probably to an attempt at chronological arrangement. The order in which the books follow one another is, 'Genesis—Chronicles, 1 *Esdras*, 2 Esdras (=Ezra, Nehemiah), Psalms, Proverbs, Ecclesiastes, Song of Songs, Job, *Wisdom of Solomon, Wisdom of the Son of Sirach*, Esther, *Judith, Tobit*, Twelve Minor Prophets, Isaiah, Jeremiah, *Baruch*, Lamentations, *Epistle of Jeremiah*, Ezekiel, Daniel.

Cod. Alex. 5th Cent.   The Codex Alexandrinus contains the books of the Old Testament in three volumes, in the following order: —vol. i. Genesis to Chronicles; vol. ii. Twelve Minor Prophets, Isaiah, Jeremiah with *Baruch*, Lamentations, and *Epistle of Jeremiah*, Ezekiel, Daniel (Theodotion's version), Esther with *Additions, Tobit, Judith*, 1 *Esdras*, 2 Esdras (=Ezra, Nehemiah), 1, 2, 3, 4 *Maccabees*; vol. iii. Psalms with *Canticles*, Job, Proverbs, Ecclesiastes, Song of Songs, *Wisdom of Solomon, Wisdom of the Son of Sirach*.

    In the Codex Sinaiticus, the books of the Old Testa-

ment *probably* followed one another in a somewhat similar Chap. XII.
order, Genesis to Chronicles, 1 *Esdras*, 2 Esdras (= Ezra, Cod. Sinai.
Nehemiah), Esther, *Tobit*, *Judith*, 1 *Maccabees*, 4 *Mac-* 4th Cent.
cabees, Isaiah, Jeremiah with *Baruch*, Lamentations,
and *Epistle*, [Ezek. Dan.], Minor Prophets, Psalms,
Proverbs, Ecclesiastes, Song of Songs, *Wisdom of
Solomon*, *Wisdom of the Son of Sirach*, Job. But the
fragmentary condition in which the Old Testament in
this MS. has survived, precludes any absolute certainty
as to the place of Ezekiel and Daniel.

Cyril of Jerusalem (†386) who gives the contents of Cyril, Bp. of Jerusalem.
Holy Scripture in his 4th Catechesis (*sec.* 33) shows
acquaintance with Hebrew usage, and expressly mentions
that the 1st and 2nd Books of ' Kingdoms ' were regarded
as one book by the Jews, as also the 3rd and 4th Books
of ' Kingdoms,' the 1st and 2nd of Chronicles, and the
1st and 2nd of Esdras. He mentions the books in the
following order :—the historical books, Genesis to Deuteronomy, Joshua, Judges with Ruth, 1–4 Kingdoms
(Samuel and Kings), 1, 2 Chronicles, 1, 2 Esdras, Esther ;
the poetical books, Job, Psalms, Proverbs, Ecclesiastes,
Song of Songs ; the prophetical books, the Twelve
Minor Prophets, Isaiah, Jeremiah with *Baruch*, Lamentations, and *Epistle*, Ezekiel, Daniel.

In the list of Athanasius (365), the books are given in Athanasius.
the following order :—Genesis to Deuteronomy, Joshua,
Judges, Ruth, 1, 2, 3, 4 ' Kingdoms,' 1, 2 Chronicles, 1, 2
Esdras, Psalms, Proverbs, Ecclesiastes, Song of Songs,
Job, Twelve Minor Prophets, Isaiah, Jeremiah with
Baruch, Lamentations, and *Epistle*, Ezekiel, and Daniel.
(*Ep. Fest.* xxxix.)

Gregory of Nazianzus (†390) gives an arrangement Gregory Naz. (Carm. Sect. i. xii.)
in three groups, of twelve, five, and five books respec-

CHAP. XII. tively; historical, Genesis to Deuteronomy, Joshua, Judges, Ruth 'the eighth book,' Kings, Chronicles, Ezra (Esther is omitted); poetical, Job, David (= Psalms), and three of Solomon (Eccles., Song, Prov.); prophetical, the Twelve Minor Prophets (*in the LXX order*), Isaiah, Jeremiah, Ezekiel, Daniel (Lamentations probably reckoned with Jeremiah).

Council of Laodicea 363 *spurious Canon* LIX, *later.*   The Spurious Canon (LIX) of the Council of Laodicea (363) composed probably about 400 A.D., thus enumerates the books of the Old Testament : (1) Genesis of the world, (2) Exodus from Egypt, (3) Leviticus, (4) Numbers, (5) Deuteronomy, (6) Joshua, *son* of Nun, (7) Judges, Ruth, (8) Esther, (9) 1, 2 'Kingdoms,' (10) 3, 4 'Kingdoms,' (11) 1, 2 Paralipomena, (12) 1, 2 Esdras, (13) Book of Psalms, (14) Proverbs of Solomon, (15) Ecclesiastes, (16) Song of Songs, (17) Job, (18) Twelve Prophets, (19) Isaiah, (20) Jeremiah and Baruch, Lamentations and Epistles, (21) Ezekiel, (22) Daniel.

Epiphanius.   In one list of Epiphanius (†403) the contents of the Hebrew Scriptures are given in the following order :— Genesis to Deuteronomy, Joshua, Judges, Ruth, Job, Psalms, Proverbs, Ecclesiastes, Song of Songs, 1–4 'Kingdoms,' 1, 2 Chronicles, Twelve Minor Prophets, Isaiah, Jeremiah with Lamentations, *Epistle*, and *Baruch*, Ezekiel, Daniel, 1 *Esdras*, 2 *Esdras*, Esther (*Haeresis* viii. 6). In another list, the order given is slightly different, the books are arranged in five 'pentateuchs' with two over :—(i) The legal, Genesis to Deuteronomy; (ii) The poetical, Job, Psalms, Proverbs, Ecclesiastes, Song of Songs; (iii) Records, or Hagiographa (*sic*), Joshua, Judges with Ruth, Chronicles 1 and 2, 'Kingdoms' 1 and 2, 'Kingdoms' 3 and 4; (iv) The prophetical, Twelve Minor Prophets, Isaiah, Jeremiah, Eze-

kiel, Daniel; and two others, 1, 2 Esdras and Esther CHAP. XII.
(*De Mens. et Pond.* 4). In another list the Hebrew books are
given in the following order :—Genesis to Deuteronomy,
Joshua the son of Nun, Job, Judges, Ruth, Psalms, 1, 2
Chronicles, 1, 2 'Kingdoms,' Proverbs, Ecclesiastes, Song of
Songs, Twelve Minor Prophets, Isaiah, Jeremiah, Ezekiel,
Daniel, 1, 2 Esdras, Esther (*De Mens. et Pond.* 22, 23).

Ruffinus (†410) gives the following order :—Genesis to *Ruffinus.*
Deuteronomy, Joshua, Judges with Ruth, four Books of
Kingdoms, Chronicles, 1, 2 Esdras, Esther, Isaiah,
Jeremiah, Ezekiel and Daniel, Twelve Minor Prophets,
Job, Psalms, Proverbs, Ecclesiastes, Song of Songs
(*Comm. in Symb. Apost.* § 36).

From an examination of these lists it appears that
even where it was intended to give the contents of the
Hebrew Canon, as distinguished from the longer Canon
of the Greek Bible, the Christian Fathers followed the
order of the books in the Greek Bible. Where no
acquaintance is shown with the Hebrew tripartite
division, there we may be sure the list of the Hebrew
Canon is taken from a Greek source. Its limitation, not
its arrangement, is reproduced : its contents, not their
order, have been preserved. Proof of this is to be
found in (1) the Greek titles, e. g. Joshua the son of Nun,
'Kingdoms,' 'Paralipomena' ; (2) the insertion of Greek
books, e. g. Baruch, Epistle of Jeremiah, and 1 Esdras ;
(3) the sub-division of Samuel, Kings, Chronicles, Ezra-
Nehemiah ; (4) the prevailing arrangement by subject-
matter, e. g. of Chronicles, Daniel, Esther, and the effort
to group chronologically, as in the position of the Minor
Prophets before Isaiah ; (5) the complete absence of any
uniformity in the arrangement. The tripartite division
of the Hebrew Canon was recognised universally by the

CHAP. XII. Jews when the Mishnah was committed to writing (circ. 200 A.D.). It was well known to Jerome (*vid. infr.*) in the fourth century. The fact that it is not adopted in the Christian lists, cited above, which claimed to give the Hebrew Scriptures, must be attributed either to general ignorance of the Hebrew tradition, or to disregard of what seemed to be a trifling divergence from the Bible in use among Christians.

II. Hebrew Canon: Variations in order.

II. We turn now to the variations in the arrangement of the books of the Hebrew Canon, where the tripartite division was known and recognised. The variations are confined to the second and third divisions. They may be discussed under the heads of (*a*) the position of Ruth and Lamentations ; (*b*) the order of 'the Prophets' ; (*c*) the order of 'the Hagiographa.'

(a) Ruth and Lam.

(*a*) We have already noticed that, in the earliest arrangement of the Hebrew Canon, Ruth and Lamentations were included among the Hagiographa. Some of the grounds for this belief have been mentioned in a former chapter. The lists in which they appear among the 'Prophets' are all, I believe, those which have been influenced by the usage of the Greek Bible. Even the list of Jerome, in his *Prologus Galeatus*[1], which claims to give the Hebrew books in the Hebrew order, offers no exception to this rule.

Evidence of Jerome in Prol. Gal.

The enumeration of twenty-two books in the Hebrew Scriptures requires the conjunction of Ruth with Judges, and of Lamentations with Jeremiah. Jerome gives one enumeration of twenty-two books, another of twenty-seven ; the former, he points out, corresponds to the letters of the Hebrew alphabet,

[1] See Excursus D.

the latter to the Hebrew alphabet with the letters, Caph, Mêm, Nûn, Pê, Tsade (which have a different shape at the close of a word) reckoned over a second time. The additional five letters correspond, according to Jerome, to the double books 1, 2 Samuel, 1, 2 Kings, 1, 2 Chronicles, Ezra-Nehemiah, Jeremiah-Lamentations. This assertion, however, illustrates how little we can rely upon Jerome's testimony for an accurate statement of Hebrew tradition. Nothing can be more certain than that, in the Jewish Church, the Hebrew books, Samuel, Kings, Chronicles, Ezra-Nehemiah were not subdivided till many centuries later[1]. Jerome's reference, therefore, to the 'double books' is proof that he is influenced by, and is alluding to, the usage of the Greek and Latin Bibles, and is not accurately reproducing the state of the case as to the Hebrew Canon. Once more, the imperfection of even his own artificial enumeration of twenty-seven books is exemplified by his omission of Judges-Ruth, which he regarded as two books in one, from the category of 'double books.' Had he included Judges-Ruth, his list of 'double books' would have exceeded the number of 'final' Hebrew letters, and would have spoiled the symmetry of his calculations[2].

Inaccurate as to Hebrew tradition.

The testimony, therefore, of Jerome to the view that Ruth and Lamentations belonged, in Hebrew copies, to 'the Prophets,' fails altogether to command our confidence. It is based on the assumption that the number of the books in the Canon was twenty-two. This was a

---

[1] Not till the beginning of the sixteenth century.

[2] John of Damascus (†750) avoids this difficulty by not including Jeremiah and Lamentations among the double books, typified by the five 'final' Hebrew letters. He boldly makes the assertion: Συνάπτεται γὰρ 'Ροὺθ τοῖς Κριταῖς καὶ ἀριθμεῖται παρ' 'Εβραίοις μία βίβλος. (*De fid. Orthod.* iv. 17.)

CHAP. XII.

Patristic idea, 22 Hebrew letters = 22 Hebrew Books, fallacious.

number which tallied with the Septuagintal arrangement, and also possessed, in Jerome's mind, especial virtue and significance, because it corresponded to the number of the Hebrew letters. The number 'twenty-two' is first given to the contents of the Hebrew Canon by Josephus (*Contr. Ap.* i. 8), who, as we have seen, used the Septuagint version. Origen was the first who pointed out that this number was also that of the letters in the Hebrew alphabet (Euseb. *H. E.* vi. 25), and the coincidence is emphatically repeated by Athanasius, Gregory of Nazianzus, Hilary of Poitiers, and Epiphanius, as well as by Jerome [1]. The coincidence, it was thought, could hardly be accidental. The 'twenty-two' books of the Greek Bible must, it was supposed, represent 'twenty-two' books of the Hebrew Bible; hence, it was concluded, the number of the books in the Hebrew Canon was providentially ordained to agree with the number of the Hebrew letters. On such a wholly shadowy hypothesis, the number 'twenty-two' received support from the Christian Fathers; and, in consequence, it was

---

[1] Orig. *ap.* Euseb. H. E. vi. 25.—οὐκ ἀγνοητέον δ' εἶναι τὰς ἐνδιαθήκους βίβλους, ὡς Ἑβραῖοι παραδιδόασιν, δύο καὶ εἴκοσι, ὅσος ὁ ἀριθμὸς τῶν παρ' αὐτοῖς στοιχείων ἐστίν.

Athan. *Ep. Fest.* xxxix.—ἔστι τοίνυν τῆς μὲν παλαιᾶς διαθήκης βιβλία τῷ ἀριθμῷ τὰ πάντα εἰκοσιδύο· τοσαῦτα γὰρ ὡς ἤκουσα καὶ τὰ στοιχεῖα τὰ παρ' Ἑβραίοις εἶναι παραδέδοται (observe the significance of ἤκουσα).

Greg. Naz. *Carm. Sect.* i. 12—

Ἀρχαίας μὲν ἔθηκα δύω καὶ εἴκοσι βίβλους
τοῖς τῶν Ἑβραίων γράμμασιν ἀντιθέτους.

Hil. *Prol. Comm. in Ps.*—Et ea causa est, ut in viginti duos libros lex Testamenti Veteris deputetur, ut cum literarum numero convenirent.

Epiphan. *Haer.* viii. 6.—αἱ εἴκοσι ἑπτὰ βίβλοι αἱ ἐκ θεοῦ δοθεῖσαι τοῖς Ἰουδαίοις, εἴκοσι δύο δέ εἰσιν ὡς τὰ παρ' αὐτοῖς στοιχεῖα τῶν Ἑβραϊκῶν γραμμάτων ἀριθμούμεναι, διὰ τὸ διπλοῦσθαι δέκα βίβλους εἰς πέντε λεγομέας.

not doubted that the books, Ruth and Lamentations, had, from the first, been united with Judges and Jeremiah. It is noteworthy that the supposed agreement in the number of the Hebrew letters with the number of the Hebrew sacred books seems to be of Greek origin, and does not appear in Hebrew tradition. This would hardly have been the case, if 'twenty-two' had been the original number of the books in the Hebrew Bible.

On the other hand, the number 'twenty-four' is uni- *Twenty-* formly given by genuinely Hebrew tradition as the number *four Hebrew books.* of the Hebrew books of Scripture. As has already been pointed out, this number most probably receives support from a testimony dating from the close of the first century A.D. (4 Esdras). It is the number found assigned to the contents of the Canon both in the Talmud and in Rabbinic literature generally. This number, 'twenty-four,' requires the enumeration of Ruth and Lamentations as separate works.

In the earliest Rabbinic list of Scripture, Ruth and *Talmud.* Lamentations are placed among the Hagiographa (*Baba Bathra* 14 *b*, see below); and in the Targums[1] of 'the Prophets,' even in the most ancient, that of Jonathan, Ruth and Lamentations do not appear. According to the legend, Jonathan-ben-Uziel was forbidden, by a

---

[1] Targum is the name given to the oral interpretation, or paraphrase, of the Scripture read in the Synagogue. Only the learned knew Hebrew in our Lord's time. An officer, called the *Meturgeman* (= Dragoman), gave the sense of the Lesson in the Aramaic tongue, which the people used. Gradually the oral interpretation assumed a fixed form, and was committed to writing. Hence the Torah Targum of Onkelos, i. e. the rendering according to the school of Aquila, and the Nebiim Targum of Jonathan, which some identify with the school of Theodotion. The Targums of the Kethubim were clearly not intended for use in the Synagogue.

CHAP. XII.

Targum.

Divine Message, to undertake the translation of the Kethubim (*Megilla 3 a*); and there can be no sort of doubt that the Targums of Ruth and Lamentations are of very much later date than those of 'the Prophets.' The Targum of Jonathan is probably a homogeneous work, dating possibly from the second century A.D.; and it never embraced either Ruth or Lamentations.

Jerome, Præfat. in Dan.

One single passage, taken from Jerome's own writings, is sufficient to demonstrate, that his inclusion of Ruth and Lamentations among the ' Prophets,' and his support of the number 'twenty-two' for the books of the Old Testament, have no critical value, and contradict the genuine Hebrew tradition. He himself, when he is not distracted from the simple narration of facts by imaginary symbolism, is able to reproduce the Hebrew Canon in accordance with the Hebrew tradition as to the number of the books. In his ' Preface to Daniel,' he states the Hebrew usage, assigning five books to the Law, eight to the Prophets, eleven to the Hagiographa:

'I call attention to this, that, among the Hebrews, Daniel is not reckoned with the Prophets, but with those who wrote the Ἁγιόγραφα. For all Scripture is by them divided into three portions, the Law, the Prophets, and the Ἁγιόγραφα, that is into five, and eight, and eleven books.'

Writing on Rolls.

(*b*) The order of the books of ' the Prophets' and the Hagiographa varies very much in the extant lists of the Hebrew Scriptures and in the Hebrew MSS.[1] For this,

---

[1] The reader will bear in mind, that no known (1891) Hebrew MS. of the Bible is earlier than the tenth century. The date, 856, claimed for the Cambridge MS. No. 12, is undoubtedly very considerably too early; cf. Schiller Szinnessy's Catalogue Hebrew MSS. in Cambridge University Library, and Neubauer's Essay in vol. iii. of *Studia Biblica.*

at first sight, startling phenomenon, a simple explana- CHAP. XII.
tion is forthcoming. For a long time each book was
written on a separate roll; and the question of the order
of the books was not mooted. In early times, to possess
more than one book in a single roll was an exception,
and called for remark. This may be illustrated from
the Talmud, ' Our Rabbis taught : it is not forbidden to
write the Law, the Prophets, and the Hagiographa in
a single volume. The words of Rabbi Meir[1] were, that
Rabbi Jehudah[2] used to say " The Law should be
written separately, and the Prophets separately, and the
Hagiographa separately." The Wise Men also used to
say, each book should be written separately. And
Rabbi Jehudah said, that Boethus, the son of Zonin, had
eight prophets united in one (book), with the approval
of Eleazar ben-Azariah[3]. But some say, they were not
united, but each one written separately. Rabbi[4] said in
reply, they brought before us the Law, the Prophets, and
the Hagiographa united together and we approved
them.' (*Baba Bathra*, fol. 13*b*[5].)

Similarly, questions are recorded as having been asked
by the Rabbins, whether it was lawful to combine the
Prophets with the Law in one volume, whether the Prophets and the Hagiographa might be included in the
same volume with the Law; and there seems to be no
doubt that, in those questions, the Prophets and Hagio-

---

[1] A pupil of Rabbi Akiba; eminent Jewish teacher in second century A.D.
[2] Rabbi Jehuda, ben-Ilai, lived in first century A.D.
[3] Eleazar, successor of Gamaliel, end of first century A.D.
[4] i.e. Rabbi Jehuda, the Holy, compiler of the Mishnah, *circ.* 200 A.D.
[5] '*Sopherim*, iii. 6, allows all the books to be united in inferior copies
written on the material called diphthera, but not in synagogue rolls; a
compromise pointing to the gradual introduction in post-Talmudic times of
the plan of treating the Bible as one volume.' Robertson Smith, O. T. J. C.
p. 410, ed. 1; p. 173, ed. 2.

CHAP. XII. grapha denote, not the whole groups, but only individual books belonging to those groups [1].

The unwieldy size and shape of the rolls made it almost impossible to combine many books in a single volume. The Rabbins also clearly viewed with suspicion the attempt to include more than one book in a single roll. Perhaps they foresaw difficulties from the combination of various books, if it should happen that one was to be removed from public reading. Perhaps too, they disliked the necessary variety in size both of the rolls and of the characters in which they were written, as likely to multiply errors in transcription.

The three groups were rigorously kept apart. But, within the Prophets and the Hagiographa, the order of sequence of the books was either not authoritatively laid down, or was not generally known. The rolls were preserved in their case (תיקא), and treasured in the Ark of the Synagogue. They were brought out as they were needed from time to time. The manner of their preservation did not help to determine their relative priority. This question only arose when the Codex began to supplant the Roll for the purpose of private study, and when more books than one were written in a single roll.

Nebiim rishonim,

The Prophets. As might be expected, no variation is found in the order of the four narrative books, 'the former prophets.' They follow the order of chronological sequence—Joshua, Judges, Samuel, Kings.

akharonim.

In the case of 'the latter prophets,' an interesting variation is found, which raises the question, whether the

[1] Cf. *Meg.* 27 a, and *Jer. Meg.* iii. 74 a quoted by Marx (*Tradit. Jud. Vet.* pp. 28-30).

order of 'the great prophets'—Isaiah, Jeremiah, Ezekiel
—really agrees with the earliest arrangement of the books
in the Hebrew Canon.   It is the obvious chronological
order; and it is found in the lists of Origen and Jerome,
who, however, are probably influenced by the LXX.

The Hebrew tradition preserved in *Baba bathra* 14 *b*, *Talmudic*
a passage which has already been referred to, mentions *order: Jer.,*
them in the order of Jeremiah, Ezekiel, Isaiah; and *Es., Is.*
they are found in that order in a large number of MSS.,
especially those of German and French origin.

Now Isaiah, we instinctively feel, is very naturally
placed at the head of the prophetical writings, as the
greatest and most majestic of all the prophets, and as
the earliest in date of 'the great prophets.' If its place
was originally at their head, it is certainly difficult to
account for its position in this fragment from Rabbinic
tradition.   If, on the other hand, its place was originally
between Ezekiel and the Minor Prophets, we can well
imagine, how, out of regard both for its chronological
position, for its commanding prestige, for its beauty, and
for its spiritual influence, it was transferred, at a later time,
to the post which it now holds in the Hebrew Bible,
at the head of the prophetical writings.   All we can say
is, that its Talmudic position, after Ezekiel and in front
of the Minor Prophets, is opposed to the idea of arrangement either in order of chronology or in order of dignity;
and that if this represents the earliest position assigned to
the prophet, it must have been owing to some very definite
purpose. What this purpose was, we can only determine
by conjecture.   And conjecture has not been idle.

(1) The Rabbins supplied a highly characteristic ex- *Explana-*
planation.   The order of the books was intended to *tions:*
(1) Rabbinic:
reproduce the continuity of the subject-matter.   The *subject-*
matter.

CHAP. XII.   Books of Kings closed with a picture of desolation, and
were therefore followed by Jeremiah, whose book was all
desolation.   Jeremiah was followed by Ezekiel, who
opens with words of desolation and closes with words of
comfort; Ezekiel is therefore followed by Isaiah, whose
book was all comfort (*Baba bathra*, 14).   See Excurs. B.

(2) *Geiger: size.*   (2) It was a simple, but ingenious, suggestion of Geiger[1] that the books are arranged in order of size.   If we
take a Hebrew Bible of Van der Hooght's edition, we find
that Jeremiah occupies 84 pages, Ezekiel 73, Isaiah 64,
the Minor Prophets 58.   But such an explanation seems
scarcely worthy of the subject.   The coincidence of the
size with the relative positions of the books is noteworthy.   But that it is anything more than a coincidence,
I cannot believe to be at all probable.   It is not supported by the analogy of the arrangement in the case
of other books.   For the group of Solomonic books,
Prov., Eccles., Song of Songs, being attributed to the
same author, obviously offers no real parallel.

(3) *Fürst: age of Is. xl-lxvi.*   (3) Another most improbable conjecture, that of
Krochmal, repeated by Julius Fürst in his book on the
Canon[2], deserves a passing notice in spite of its wildness.
He pointed out that the position of Isaiah after Ezekiel
agreed with the date of the latter portion of Isaiah
(xl-lxvi), and further that the consolatory tone of the
book, referred to by the Rabbins, is only characteristic
of Isaiah II.   He therefore suggested that originally

---

[1] Abr. Geiger (quoted by Strack, art. '*Kanon*') *Wissensch. Ztschr. f. Jüd. Theol.* ii. (1836), pp. 489-496.   The same view is put forward by Herzfeld *Gesch. Volks Jüd.* ii. p. 103 (1863), independently, or, at least, without re-ference to Geiger's having suggested it.

[2] *Kan. d. Alt. Test.* pp. 15-28.   Strack (Art. '*Kanon*' R.E.[2]) attributes the place of Isaiah in the Talmudic list to a recollection of the Exilic origin of the latter part of the book.

Isaiah I stood first, and Isaiah II fourth, but that after
the writings of Isaiah I had been united with those of
Isaiah II, the position of the exilic portion was retained, and for a long time determined the place of the
book in the Hebrew Canon. But to suppose that the
Rabbins from whom we receive the Mishnah and Gemara
would have assigned any portion of Isaiah to the period
of the exile, is a quite inadmissible assumption (cf. John
xii. 38–41). And the son of Sirach clearly shows that the
latter part of Isaiah was by the Jews of his time unquestionably assigned to the great prophet of Hezekiah's
reign (cf. Ecclus. xlviii. 24, 25).

(4) The explanation put forward by Marx (*Traditio* *(4) Marx:*
Iudaeorum Veterrima, p. 36) appears more probable. *Jer. and Ez.*
follow
The Book of Jeremiah followed naturally upon the Books *Kings.*
of Kings; it was similar in style; it dealt with the
closing scenes of the Jewish Monarchy. Jeremiah could
hardly be separated, in point of time, from Ezekiel.
Isaiah remained, and was naturally placed in front of
the Minor Prophets. In point of date Isaiah would pair
with Hosea as fittingly as Jeremiah with Ezekiel. At
first the books of the Great Prophets would have been
kept in separate rolls. The question of priority in order
hardly arose, until it began to be the custom to write
them in the same book. Thus, the Talmudic position of
Isaiah is a memorial of the time when no very sharp
distinction had yet been drawn between the narrative
and the prophetical books in the Second Group.

In mediaeval times the distinction between the historical and the prophetical books of 'the Prophets'
became more marked. They were divided into the
'former' and the 'latter' prophets. The Massoretes,
perhaps, first put Isaiah at the head of the 'latter'

CHAP. XII. prophets, in which place it stands in the earliest Hebrew MS., that of the *Prophetae Posteriores*, the Codex Babylonicus Petropolitanus, 916 A.D., edited by Strack (St. Petersburg, 1876), and in the many MSS. of Spanish origin. But there are traces of an intermediate stage. Some Jewish scribes, who united Jeremiah closely with the Books of Kings, placed Isaiah between Jeremiah and Ezekiel, so that Jeremiah might, as it were, close the historical, and Isaiah commence the prophetical books: this order is found in several MSS. (see Kennicott). A few MSS. (e. g. Kennicott, Cod. 330[1], 471, 587) give the strange order —Ezekiel, Isaiah, Jeremiah ('*Ezech.* praecedit *Isaiam*').

Min. Proph. The order of the Minor Prophets is doubtless intended as approximately chronological. The position of the Book of Jonah is probably due to the mention made of the prophet in 2 Kings xiv. 25, which helped to determine its reputed date. In the Septuagint Version an attempt, presumably made to secure greater accuracy in the chronological arrangement, led to the slightly different order—Hosea, Amos, Micah, Joel, Obadiah, Jonah, for Hosea, Joel, Amos, Obadiah, Jonah, Micah.

(c) Kethubim. (c) *The Hagiographa.* It is in the Hagiographa that we find the greatest amount of variation in the arrangement of the books. This is partly to be accounted for by the great variety of their subject-matter and style, partly also by the fact that the 'Kethubim' were not, at least after the completion of the Lectionary, read in the services of the Synagogue. The earliest arrangement of the books of the Hagiographa that has come down to us is given in the *Baba bathra* passage, quoted above,

---

[1] On the strange Paris Codex (330 Kennicott), see *Manuscrits Orientaux* (Tascheriau), No. 17, p. 2 (Paris, 1866).

which records that 'the order of the "Kethubim" is this: Ruth, the Book of Psalms, Job and Proverbs, Ecclesiastes, Song of Songs and Lamentations, Daniel and the Roll of Esther, Ezra and Chronicles.'

CHAP. XII.

In this Talmudic order of the books we should observe (1) that Ruth and Lamentations are reckoned among the Kethubim; (2) that Ruth is placed before Psalms, presumably on the ground that the record of David's ancestry should precede his writings; (3) that Job, a book which is considered in the *Baba bathra* to have been written by Moses, stands between Psalms and Proverbs, probably so as to leave the priority of place to the Psalter, and at the same time not to break the group of Solomonic books; (4) that the other books follow the order of their supposed date of composition, the Solomonic writings preceding the Lamentations of Jeremiah, while Daniel, Esther, and Ezra represent the beginning, the middle, and the close of the exile respectively. The Books of Chronicles, which were ascribed to Ezra, formed an appendix to the whole collection, the position of the books agreeing with the inference that has been drawn, as we saw in an earlier chapter, from our Lord's words in Matt. xxiii. 35, *viz.* that they were either the last book or, at least, the last narrative book in the Hebrew Canon.

Talmudic order.

The order of the Hagiographa, as given by Jerome in his *Prologus Galeatus,* is Job, Psalms, Proverbs, Ecclesiastes, Song of Songs, Daniel, Chronicles, Ezra, Esther, while Ruth and Lamentations are reckoned among 'the Prophets.' But it is not likely, as has already been shown, that he supplies us with the accurate order of the Hebrew books. It is more probable that he simply arranges the books in what seemed to be their natural

Order in Jerome's Prol. Gal.

CHAP. XII. chronological order.   We do not elsewhere find an instance in Hebrew literature in which the Book of Job is placed at the head of the Kethubim; again, the arrangement of Ezra and Esther after Chronicles suggests the influence of the Christian Bibles rather than the reproduction of the Hebrew order.   It is noticeable that Jerome concedes that, in the opinion of some (*nonnulli*), Ruth and Lamentations ought to be ranked among the Hagiographa, in which case, he says, the number of 'twenty-four' books of Scripture being obtained, a reference to them is found in the vision of St. John, where the four-and-twenty elders are around the Throne (cf. Rev. iv. 4–10, v. 8).   But reasoning of that kind is obviously not conclusive upon a question of fact. In his 'Preface to Daniel,' he says categorically[1], that 'all Scripture is divided by the Jews into three portions, the Law, the Prophets, and the Hagiographa, that is, into five, and eight, and eleven books.'   Here his testimony agrees exactly with that of the Hebrew tradition, and implies the inclusion of Ruth and Lamentations among the Hagiographa.   We do not, therefore, attach any importance to the variations from it into which he occasionally permits himself to fall.   He did not realise the necessity of accurately preserving the Hebrew tradition.   He could not foresee the confusion that might afterwards arise from carelessness, or want of thoroughness, in his use of it.   For to this, and nothing else, can we ascribe his mention of the tripartite division in the *Prologus Galeatus*, and his enumeration of the books, immediately afterwards, in an order which, claiming to be the Jewish order, fails to agree with that of genuine

---

[1] See above, p. 234.

Hebrew tradition, or even with his own explicit state- CHAP. XII.
ments elsewhere.

The order of the books of the Hagiographa in extant *In Hebrew MSS.*
Hebrew MSS. shows the utmost variety. The Massoretes
laid down no rule for their arrangement. For the most
part, these variations may be divided into three groups,
representing the Talmudic, the Spanish, and the German arrangement[1]. According to one tradition, the
Talmudic preserves the Babylonian, the Spanish the
Palestinian order.

(*a*) The Talmudic. This, which is probably the most (a) *Talmu-*
ancient order, is given in *Baba bathra*, quoted above. It *dic* (?) *Baby lonian.*
is followed in many of the best MSS.

It is the order in which the books are given in
Halakoth Gedoloth (sub fin.), a work composed in the
ninth century A. D., and in the *Anonymous Chronicle*,
edited by Neubauer (*Jewish Chronicles*, 1887, Oxford).

(*b*) Very many of the MSS., more especially Spanish, (b) *Spanish*
begin the Hagiographa with 'Chronicles,' either with (?) *Palesti- nian.*
the view of connecting the Hagiographa with the histori-
cal group that preceded it, or from the idea that a book
containing the primitive genealogies of the race was
entitled to a priority. The order commonly followed
in these MSS. is—Chronicles, Psalms, Job, Proverbs,
Ruth, Song of Songs, Ecclesiastes, Lamentations, Esther,
Daniel, Ezra[2]. But slight variations often occur: e. g.
Job is often placed after Proverbs, Ecclesiastes after
Lamentations.

It will be observed, that, according to this order, the

---

[1] For the distinction into Spanish and German MSS., see Elias Levita's
Massoreth Ha-Massoreth, ed. Ginsburg, p. 120.

[2] To this class belongs the MS. of the Firkowitzsch collection in the
Imperial Library at St. Petersburg (Cod. B. 19ᵃ), which contains the whole
O. T., and is dated 1009; the date, however, is not free from doubt.

CHAP. XII. Solomonic books are separated from one another, and that the Five Megilloth (Ruth, Song, Eccles., Lam., Esth.) are kept together, although not in the order of the sacred seasons, with which they were associated in the Synagogue services. The arrangement is, therefore, more artificial than the Talmudic, less so than that which we notice next [1].

(c) German, Printed Editions. (c) The commonest order of the books in the MSS. is that of the German MSS., which has been followed in the printed editions. The arrangement is in three groups: firstly, the Poetical books, Psalms, Proverbs, Job; secondly, the Five Rolls or Megilloth, Song of Songs, Ruth, Ecclesiastes, Lamentations, Esther; thirdly, the Narrative books, Daniel, Ezra-Nehemiah, Chronicles. The following points of interest, in connexion with this arrangement, may here be recorded.

Poetical Books. (1) The group of poetical books was sometimes referred to in Jewish literature by the name *'Emeth* (='Truth') (אמ״ת), a Hebrew word consisting of the initial letters of Job, Proverbs, and Psalms. But, in the MSS., the Psalter as the most important book of the Kethubim stands first, while Proverbs and Job are constantly interchanged, Job, as the reputed work of Moses, being placed before that of Solomon.

5 Megilloth. (2) The second group consists of five books, which are used for public reading in the Synagogue on certain sacred seasons. The Song of Songs is read at the Feast of Passover, Ruth at the Feast of Weeks or Pen-

---

[1] 'The Grammatico-Massoretic Treatise entitled *Adath Deborim* (A.D. 1207) describes this order, as far as the Hagiographa are concerned, as the correct one, exhibiting the Western or Palestinian practice; and the order which places Chronicles or Esther at the end of this division as the Eastern or Babylonian practice, which is to be deprecated.' Ginsburg's *Massoretic Introduction*, p. 4.

tecost, Lamentations on the day of the Destruction of Jerusalem (9th of Ab), Ecclesiastes at the Feast of Tabernacles, Esther at the Feast of Purim. The succession of the sacred days determined the order of the books in many MSS., and in the printed Bibles; and the name of the Five Rolls or Megilloth was given to the group because they were written on separate rolls to be read on these particular occasions, according to post-Talmudic liturgical usage.

But the MSS. give the Megilloth arranged with almost every possible variety of order. The most common variations are Ruth, Ecclesiastes, Song of Songs, Lamentations, Esther; and Ruth, Song of Songs, Ecclesiastes, Lamentations, Esther, in both of which the chronology of the books determines the order.

In such variations, as Ecclesiastes, Song of Songs, Lamentations, Ruth, Esther, or Ruth, Esther, Ecclesiastes, Song of Songs, Lamentations, the grouping is probably modified according to subject-matter.

In some MSS. and early editions of the Hebrew Bible, the Megilloth follow after the Pentateuch. For examples of these and other variations in the order of the Hagiographa, the reader is referred to Excursus C.

(3) In the last group of the Hagiographa, the commonest variation in the order in the MSS. is caused by the placing of Chronicles before the Psalms; and there are also numerous cases in which Daniel stands before Esther, doubtless for chronological reasons.

Another arrangement of the books is referred to in *Another Talmudic order.* the Babylonian Talmud, according to which three subdivisions were recognised, (1) the Former Kethubim, Ruth, and the Triad called 'the Greater Kethubim,'

CHAP. XII. Psalms, Proverbs, Job ; (2) the Lesser Kethubim, or the Triad, Song of Songs, Ecclesiastes, Lamentations ; (3) the Latter Kethubim, Esther, Daniel, Ezra-Nehemiah, Chronicles. (See Fürst, who quotes Berakoth 57 *a* and *b*, *Kanon des Alten Testaments*, pp. 60 and 82.) But it does not appear to have been ever in general use.

Division of Books. The sub-division of the Pentateuch into five books belongs possibly to its original formation. The division of the Psalter into five books was doubtless made in imitation of it.

The division of Samuel, Kings, Chronicles, Ezra[1], into two books each originated in Alexandria ; and was not introduced into Hebrew Bibles until the sixteenth century (Bomberg Bible, 1521).

Sections 'closed' and 'open.' In connexion with the arrangement of the books, we may here mention the system by which the books of the Hebrew Scriptures were divided into sections. A passage or section, 'Parashah,' was marked off by spaces or gaps in the writing. Small sections denote slight change of thought, and correspond to our paragraph. Large sections denote change of subject, and are more akin to our chapter. (1) A small section, or 'Parashah,' was denoted by a small gap in the writing, the space of three letters being left open. This was called a 'closed section,' or 'Parashah sethumah,' and in the space the letter 'S' (ס) was inserted, representing the word 'Sethumah.' The section was called 'closed,' because the line in the official copies was not left open ; the writing was resumed, after the space, in the same line. (2) A large section was denoted by a complete break in

---

[1] In some MSS., Nehemiah was separated by one blank line from Ezra. But it was always regarded as part of the same book, and was referred to under the same title, that of Ezra.

the line ; in the old copies the rest of the line was left completely open, and in later copies the space of nine letters was left open. In consequence of the line having been left completely open, the long section was called 'open,' 'Parashah pethukhah'; and where it occurred, the letter 'P' (פ), representing 'Pethukhah,' was inserted.

Both these sections appear in the Torah, and in Baer's edition of the Massoretic text they are given also in the other books of the Hebrew Canon[1].

The number of the sections given is not the same in all MSS. But the number of 'closed sections' in the Torah is between 370 and 380, the number of 'open sections' between 280 and 290.

Quite distinct from these sections is the Liturgical *Synagogue Lessons.* Division into sections for the Synagogue service. The lesson from the Torah was called the Parashah, that from the Nebiim the Haphtarah. The Babylonian *Babylonian use.* Lectionary was arranged so that the whole Torah could be read through in the year (*Megilla*, 31 b). There were fifty-four 'Parshiyyoth[2].' They begin as a rule with the commencement of one of the sections just described, and are indicated by the sign of a 'closed' or 'open' section, 'sethumah' or 'pethukhah.' In the former case the lesson is marked by a thrice repeated 'S' (ססס), in the latter by a thrice repeated 'P' (פפפ). Only in Gen. xlvii. 28 does a lection begin at a passage which does not happen to introduce either a 'closed' or an 'open' section.

The lessons from the Prophets were passages selected

---

[1] Evidence of a pre-Talmudic system of sections is to be found in Mark xii. 26 ἐπὶ τοῦ βάτου, Rom. xi. 2 ἐν Ἠλίᾳ.

[2] On the names 'Parashah' and 'Haphtarah,' see p. 126 n.

CHAP. XII. so as to correspond with the lessons from the Law. Thus, the 'Haphtarah,' Isaiah xlii. 5–xliii. 11, corresponded to and was read on the same day with the 'Parashah,' Gen. i. 1–vi. 9. The 'Haphtaroth,' however, are not indicated in the Massoretic text; but attention is called to them in the Massoretic notes.

Palestinian. Among the Palestinian Jews a different lectionary was used, according to which the Law was divided into 154 lessons and was read through every three years. The Palestinian lectionary was undoubtedly of greater antiquity than the Babylonian. Both systems are referred to in the Talmud (*Meg.* 29 *b*, 31 *b*). But the practical convenience of having the lectionary conterminous with the calendar probably led to the general adoption of the Babylonian system[1]. (See the articles by Dr. J. Theodor in M. G. W. J., 1885.)

It has often been too hastily assumed that the books of the Hagiographa were never, in the pre-Talmudic period, used for any purpose in the Synagogue services. But we know from the Treatise *B. Shabbath* (f. 116 *b*), that at Nehardea, in Babylonia, lessons from the Hagiographa were read at the Sabbath afternoon services in the Synagogues. Moreover the fact that books of the Hagiographa were liable, from one cause or another, to be removed from public reading (*genuzim*) leads us to suspect that, at the time when this could take place, extracts were wont to be read from the third group as well as from the Prophets. Perhaps this was the case before the Lectionary Cycle had been finally

---

[1] Perhaps as late as the 14th cent. The reader is referred to the learned discussion on 'The Reading of the Law and Prophets in a Triennial Cycle,' by Dr. Adolph Büchler, in the April and October numbers of *The Jewish Quarterly Review* for 1893.

reduced to a system. In connexion with this conjecture Mr. Schechter has called attention to the Mussaph Prayer in *Rosh Hashanah*, containing extracts from all three groups of Scripture, which formed the basis of religious exhortations at the Synagogue services. The Kethubim may thus have been used, along with the Torah and Nebiim, for homiletic purposes, although never, as the evidence of the Targums indicates, included in the Lectionary.

'The Samaritan text of the Law is divided into *Samaritan*. sections (קצין), which are carefully marked in all MSS., and their total number given at the end of each book[1].'

Lastly, we may notice the division into chapters and *Chapters and Verses*. verses that has been adopted in the printed editions of the Hebrew Scriptures. The Vulgate division into chapters, made in the 13th cent., was first employed upon the Hebrew Bible in the Hebrew Concordance of Isaac Nathan (1437–1448), but was not introduced into regular use until the following century. It first appears ' in the first two Bomberg editions [of the Hebrew Bible], the folio and the quarto of 1518. The numeration of the verses was introduced in Bomberg's Great Bible of 1547–1548, in which every fifth verse (1, 5, 10, &c.) is designated by the Hebrew numeral; the use of Arabic numerals for the intervening verses (2, 3, 4; 6, 7, 8, 9; &c.) was introduced by Leusden-Athias in 1661, though there were older editions (in Polyglotts or with inter-linear Latin version) in which *every* verse was indicated by an Arabic numeral[2].'

[1] A. Cowley on 'The Samaritan Liturgy and Reading of the Law' (*Jewish Quarterly Review*, Oct. 1894).

[2] Professor G. F. Moore (*Journal of Bibl. Lit.* xii. 1. 77), to whom my thanks are due.

EXCURSUS A.

THE ORIGIN OF THE CANON OF THE HEBREW SCRIPTURES,
ACCORDING TO TRADITION.

THE legendary accounts of the formation of the Hebrew Canon require separate treatment. They may be classed under two main heads according as they ascribe the work to Ezra or to the men of the Great Synagogue.

1. *The Legend of Ezra and the Books of Scripture.*

Ezra and Books of Scripture 4 Esdr. xiv.   The first we hear of the tradition that Ezra was inspired to recall to memory and to restore to the Jews in writing their Scriptures that had been destroyed by the Chaldeans, is the account given in the Jewish Apocalyptic work, 2 (4) Esdras, which was probably composed not long after the destruction of Jerusalem.

In chap. xiv it is related that Ezra, having been warned of God that his end was near at hand, bewailed the spiritual destitution of the people, 'for the law is burnt, therefore no man knoweth the things that are done of Thee, or the works that shall begin. But if I have found grace before Thee, send the Holy Ghost into me, and I shall write all that hath been done in the world since the beginning which were written in Thy law,' &c. (vv. 21, 22). Ezra's prayer is heard, and he is commanded to retire for forty days in company with five chosen men, Sarea (Seraiah), Dabria (?=Dibri), Selemia (Shelemiah), Ecanus (?=Elkanah), and Asiel (Asael), taking with them numerous tablets for writing (ver. 24). Ezra obeys, and the revelation vouchsafed to him is described as follows:—'So I took the five men, as he commanded me, and we went into the field, and remained there. And the next day, behold, a voice called me, saying, Esdras, open thy mouth, and drink that I give thee to drink. Then opened I my mouth, and, behold, he reached me a full cup, which was full as it were with water, but the colour of it was like fire. And I took it, and drank; and when I had drunk of it, my heart uttered understanding, and wisdom grew in my breast, for my spirit preserved (*conservabat*) memory: and my mouth was opened, and shut no more. The Highest gave understanding unto the five men, and they wrote the wonderful visions (?) of the night that were told, which they knew not (*or*, 'in letters which they understood not,' cf. *Aeth.* and *Ar.*); and they sat forty days, and they wrote in the day, and at night they ate bread. As for me, I spake in the day, and I held not my tongue by night. In forty days they wrote ninety-four (*other readings*, 'two hundred and four,' 'nine hundred and four') books. And it came to pass, when the forty days were fulfilled, that the Highest spake, saying, The first that thou hast written publish openly, that the worthy and unworthy may read it; but keep the seventy last, that thou mayest deliver them only to such as be wise among the people: for in them is the spring of understanding, the fountain of wisdom, and the stream of knowledge.' (2 (4) Esdr. xiv. 37–48.)[1]

Whether the legend which is thus described originated with the composer of the Fourth Book of Esdras, or whether he has merely incorporated an existing legend into his book, we have no means of deciding.

He wrote at a time (circ. 90 A.D.) when more than 500 years had elapsed since the death of Ezra. Josephus, his contemporary, did not apparently know the legend. He only agrees with it so far as to express his belief, that no Jewish works com-

---

[1] See Excursus D.

posed since the reign of Ahasuerus were to be reckoned in the sacred Canon [1] (*Cont. Ap.* i. 8).

Devoid of historical value though the Fourth Book of Esdras may be, the passage we have quoted above either originates or repeats a legend, which reflected one aspect of the popular Jewish opinion respecting the service rendered by Ezra towards the preservation of the Hebrew Scriptures. That opinion rested on the account in Neh. viii–x, where Ezra promulgates the Book of the Law, and finally establishes its authority.

Ezra and Jewish Tradition.

Later Jewish tradition, while it almost disregarded Nehemiah, exaggerated freely the Scriptural record of Ezra's share in that transaction. It has thus however, probably, borne true witness to the deep impression produced upon the imagination of the people by Ezra's work in connexion with the Torah. Ezra in Talmudic tradition was a second Moses: e. g. 'The Torah was forgotten by Israel until Ezra went up from Babylon and reestablished it' (*Succa.* 20 *a*). 'And Moses went up unto God (Ex. xix. 3); of Ezra it is said, "And Ezra went up from Babylon" (Ezr. vii. 6). What is the meaning of this expression "Go up"? It has the same meaning in the one passage as in the other, and refers to the Torah' (*Jer. Meg.* cap. i). No mention is made in Rabbinic literature of the legend contained in 4 Esdras, that Ezra was super-naturally empowered to recall to memory the Jewish Scriptures; but the tradition is recorded, that he was said to have committed to writing a pure copy of them, and to have deposited it in the Temple courts (*Moed Qatan* 18 *b*).

[1] Cf. 'Up to that time (Alexander the Great) the prophets prophesied through the Holy Spirit, from thenceforth the wise men only wrought,' *Seder Olam.*, p. 70, ed. Meyer, 1706. Only thirty-four years were supposed to have elapsed between Ezra and Alexander. That Josephus meant Ahasuerus, when he speaks of Artaxerxes in *Cont. Ap.* i. 8, is shown by a comparison of *Ant.* xi. cap. 6 with *Ant.* xi. cap. 5. In the latter chapter, speaking of the Persian King, who favoured Ezra and Nehemiah, Josephus calls him Xerxes, son of Darius. In the former chapter, speaking of the Persian King, who married Esther, he calls him Artaxerxes.

The Fourth Book of Esdras does not appear to have exerted
much influence upon later Jewish literature. The particular
legend contained in chap. xiv, seems, so far as we know, to have
passed unnoticed by the Midrashim. A reason for this is,
perhaps, to be found in the popularity which the book acquired
among the Christians, partly also in the fact that its original
language was, in all probability, Greek. From the Greek the
Fourth Book of Esdras was translated, apparently by Christians,
into Latin, Syriac, Arabic, Aethiopic, Armenian. In all of those
versions it is still extant. It has been transmitted to us by
Christian, not by Jewish, hands.

It can hardly be questioned, that it was from this source that
the Christian fathers derived their legend, that Ezra miraculously
restored the Hebrew books and formed the Canon of Scripture.
Just as they took their history of the origin of the Septuagint
version from a spurious Alexandrine work, the so-called Letter
of Aristeas, so they seem, with the same unquestioning confidence, to have derived their view of the origin of the Hebrew
Canon from a pseudepigraphic Greek Apocalypse of the close of
the first century A.D. It is, of course, *possible* that the legend
may have reached them through some other more trustworthy
channel. But the language in which they record it makes the
inference most probable, that the Fourth Book of Esdras is the
source from which the stream of an almost unbroken ecclesiastical tradition directly flows.

The following passages will illustrate the Patristic treatment
of the story as well as the way in which the same tradition was
repeated from generation to generation.

Circ. 170 †. Irenaeus (*Contr. Haer.*, lib. iii. p. 216, ed. Migne, *Irenaeus.*
p. 948) : ' And it is surely not a thing to be marvelled at, that
God should have brought this to pass (i. e. the miraculous
preparation of the LXX version). For, when the people
were carried away captive in the days of Nebuchadnezzar,
the Scriptures were utterly destroyed; but, after the space of
seventy years the Jews returned to their own land; and

EXCURS. A.   then in the times of Artaxerxes, king of the Persians, God did inspire Esdras, the priest, who was of the tribe of Levi, to set forth in order all the words of the prophets that had gone before, and to restore to the people the law that had been given by Moses.'

Tertullian. *Circ.* 200 A. D.   Tertullian (*De Cultu Feminarum*, i. 3): 'Assuredly, if it had been destroyed by the violence of the flood, he, in the power of the Spirit, could have reconstructed it again, just as is well known, when Jerusalem had been taken and destroyed by the Babylonians, the whole Canon (*omne instrumentum*) of Jewish literature was restored by means of Esdras.'

Clement of Alexandria.   *Circ.* 200 A. D.   Clement of Alexandria (*Strom.* i. 22, ed. Potter, i. p. 410): 'It was not strange that by the inspiration of God, Who hath given the gift of prophecy, should also be produced the translation, which was a kind of Greek prophecy, seeing also that, when the Scriptures had been destroyed in the captivity of Nebuchadnezzar, Ezra, the Levite, the Priest, in the times of Artaxerxes, King of the Persians, being inspired, prophesied and renovated (ἀνανεούμενος προεφήτευσε) all the ancient Scriptures' (cf. Irenaeus, l. c. above). Id. (i. 21, ed. Potter, p. 392: 'Ezra— through whom (instead of δι' ὅν, read δι' οὗ) comes to pass the redemption of the people and the recollection (ἀναγνωρισμός) of the inspired (writings), and the renovation of the oracles' (ἀνακαινισμὸς λογίων), &c.

Origen.   253†.   Origen (*Selecta in Psalmos*, ed. Lommatzsch, tom. xi. p. 371): 'Either Ezra recalled these (psalms) also to memory along with the rest of the Scriptures, or the wise men of old among the Hebrews collected those that were current as each man's memory happened to serve him.'

Eusebius.   *Circ.* 340†.   Eusebius (*Hist. Eccles.* v. 8. 15) quotes the passage from Irenaeus cited above. He says elsewhere, *Chronic. Lib.* i. § 5, ed. Migne, i. p. 177, 'He (Ezra) is moreover said to have recollected all the Scriptures spoken by God (*cunctas a Deo dictas Scripturas*), and to have committed them to the EXCURS. A. charge of the Jews written out in new characters of the Hebrew alphabet.'

Circ. 379†. Basil the Great, in his Epistle to Chilo (*Epistolarum* *Basil.* *Classis* I, Epist. xlii. p. 129, ed. Migne, iv. p. 357), uses the words: 'There is the field to which Ezra withdrew and in which, by the command of God, he indited all the inspired books,' in which he evidently refers to 4 Esd. xiv. 37, &c.

397 †. Ambrose (*Epistolarum Classis* I, Epist. lxii. 30, ed. *Ambrose.* Migne, iii. p. 1198): 'Ezra forgetful of the Scriptures, who restored the Scriptures by a feat of memory!'

407 †. John Chrysostom (*Hom. in Ep. ad Hebraeos*, cap. v. *Chrysostom.* Hom. viii. 4, ed. Migne, tom. xii. p. 74): 'War came upon them; they slew them all, they cut them down, the books were burned in flames. Again God inspired another wonderful man, I mean Ezra, to publish them (the books), and He caused them to be constructed from out of the remnants' (ἀπὸ τῶν λειψάνων).

Circ. 426†. Jerome (*Adversus Helvidium. De perpetuâ vir-* *Jerome.* *ginitate beatae Mariae*, p. 212, tom. 2, p. 190, ed. Migne): 'Whether you choose to speak of Moses as the author of the Pentateuch, or of Ezra as the restorer of the same work.'

Circ. 458†. Theodoret (*In Psal.* i. p. 606, ed. Migne, i. p. 864): *Theodoret.* 'One hundred and twenty years before their translation (i. e. the LXX), the wondrous Ezra, filled with divine grace, committed to writing the holy books (that) owing to the negligence of the Jews and the enmity of the Babylonians had long been destroyed' (*or*, corrupted, διαφθαρείσας).

(?) 500–600†. *Synopsis Scripturae Sacrae* (Pseudo-Athanas.), cap. *Synops.*
Script.
Sacr. 20 (*Athanasii Opera*, ed. Migne, tom. iv. p. 352): 'This too is related of Ezra, that, when the Scriptures had been lost in consequence of the negligence of the people and on account of the long period of the captivity, Ezra himself being a noble man, and of good ability, and a diligent student,

Excurs. A. preserved all their contents in his memory (καθ᾽ ἑαυτὸν), and
finally produced them and published them to all, and to this
is due the preservation of the Scriptures.'

Leontius. 590†. Leontius (*De Sectis*, Act. 2, § 8, p. 632, ap. Gallandi *Bibl.
Venet.* 1788): 'When Ezra came to Jerusalem and found
that all the books had been burned at the time when the
people were carried away captive, he is said to have written
down from memory the two and twenty books which we
enumerated above.'

Isidore. 636†. Isidore (*De Ortu et Obitu Patrum*, cap. lx, ed. Migne, v.
p. 146): 'He (Ezra) was a writer of sacred history, and
was the second giver of the Law after Moses; for, after
the captivity, he restored the Law which by the Gentiles had
been burned.'

*De Mirab.
Sacr. Script.* (?) 700–800 †. *De Mirabilibus Sacrae Scripturae*, cap. xxxiii
(Pseudo-Augustine, tom. iii. p. 2191): 'At which time Ezra
the priest of God restored the Law which had been burned,
among the archives of the Temple, by the Chaldeans; for
he was filled with the same Spirit whereby it had afore-
time been written.'

Bede. 737†. Bede (*In Esdr. et Neh. Prophetas Allegor. Expos.*, lib.
ii. cap. ix, ed. Migne, i. p. 859): 'Ezra was moreover a
ready scribe in the Law of Moses; for he restored the Law
that had been destroyed. He rewrote not the Law only,
but also, as is reported currently by the men of old time,
the whole Canon (*seriem*) of Holy Scripture, which had all
alike perished in the flames, according as he thought the
needs of readers required.'

*Rabanus
Maurus.* 856†. Rabanus Maurus (*De Instit. Cleric.* lib. ii., c. 54,
ed. Migne, i. p. 366): 'After the Jews had entered Jerusalem, he (Ezra) restored all the ancient sacred books
by means of the Divine Spirit of Inspiration, and purified
all the volumes of the prophets that had been defiled by
the Gentiles. And he arranged the whole Old Testament
into four and twenty books, so that there might be as many

books in the Law as letters in the Alphabet.' (N.B. The difference in the number of the letters between the Hebrew and the Greek Alphabet was presumably not known to Rabanus Maurus.)

(?) 800–850 †. Nicephorus Callistus (*Eccles. Hist.*, lib. iv. cap. 15) *Niceph. Callist.* quotes the passage from Irenaeus cited above.

891†. Photius (*Ad Amphilochium Quaestio*, ed. Migne, vol. i. *Photius.* p. 816): 'The books perished in the flames at the time of the captivity. Afterwards, when the Jews of Jerusalem and those of Babylon used to send to one another the oracles of God, the Gentiles laid in wait and destroyed their books. The Jews, on their side, took to writing in characters which the Gentiles could not understand, and from this cause also the uncertainty arose: until, at length, Ezra, being inspired, recalled to memory all (the books) and committed them to writing.'

1135 †. Rupert of Deutz (*De Victoria Verbi Dei*, lib. vii. *Rupert of Deutz.* c. xxxii. ed. Migne, iii. p. 1380): 'What ought not Ezra to be to us? For we ought not to forget that it was he who restored the Law, and that by him the Holy Scriptures which are the very voice of the Word of God that had been scattered far and wide and had scarcely escaped destruction in the flames, were collected and fashioned anew. . . . Verily, that imperishable work, the renewing of Holy Scripture, is and ever will be a performance of more enduring memory, greater renown and higher excellence,' &c.

1140 †. Hugo de St. Victor (*Allegor. in Vet. Test.*, lib. viii. c. x. *Hugo de St. Victor.* ed. Migne, i. p. 730): 'Ezra denotes Christ; for he fashioned anew (*reformavit*) Holy Scripture.'

1198 †. Petrus Comestor (*Liber Judith*, cap. v. ed. Migne, *Petrus Comestor.* p. 1483): 'At that time (i.e. in the reign of Artaxerxes) Ezra, of the house of Aaron, restored the Law which had been burned by the Chaldeans. . . . It does not behove us to marvel that he, through the Holy Spirit, should have

S

restored the books, seeing that many, even in our own days, have known how to restore (i. e. repeat by memory) the Psalter, the Book of Hymns, and numerous books of the same class.'

It will be observed that Rupert of Deutz lays emphasis on the work of collecting and editing the sacred books, and that Petrus Comestor endeavours, by introducing a comparison with feats of memory well known in his own day, to minimize the miraculous element in the legend. The improbability of the story could hardly fail to impress itself upon men's minds. But it was not until the era of the Reformation, that men found themselves at liberty to reject a form of legend which had been current for so many centuries in the Church. Among the Reformers it was natural enough that a legend which had no support in Scripture, and which contained so unlikely a narrative, should be discredited.

Reformers: Whitaker,

The English divine, Whitaker, may be taken as a representative of the opinion of the Reformed Churches. In his *Disputation on Scripture*, written in 1602 (pp. 114–116, ed. Parker Society), he mentions the legend. 'There are some, however, who imagine that the whole Old Testament perished in the captivity. This suspicion, perhaps, arose from considering that, when the temple was burnt, all that was in it must have been consumed in the same conflagration. Hence they believe that the sacred volumes of Scripture must have been destroyed in the flames; but, that, after the captivity, Ezra, instructed by the Holy Spirit, published these afresh, as it were again recovered.' He here quotes Clemens Alexandrinus, Irenaeus, Leontius, Isidore, and Rabanus Maurus, and then proceeds: 'They affirm, therefore, two things: one, that the whole sacred and canonical Scripture perished in the Babylonian captivity; the other, that it was restored to its integrity by Ezra, instructed and inspired in a wonderful manner by the direct agency of God. But the falsehood of this opinion is manifest. For the pious Jews had, no doubt, many copies of the Scripture

in their possession, and could easily save them from that
calamity.   What man in his senses will say that there was no
copy of the Scriptures beside that in the temple?   Besides, if
these books had been deposited in the temple, would not either
the priests or somebody else have been able to rescue them
from the flames?   It is incredible that the religious Jews should
have been so unmindful of piety and religion as to keep no
copies whatever of the Scriptures whilst they lived in Babylon,
especially while they had such men among them as Ezekiel and
Daniel.   But it is certain that they had many copies.   For even
Antiochus himself could not utterly destroy them all, though he
set himself to do so with the utmost zeal and sedulity.   Hence
it appears that there were everywhere a very great number of
copies; and now the Babylonians made no such fierce assault
upon the sacred books.   In accordance with what we might
expect from such premises, Ezra is simply said, Nehem. viii, to
have brought the book of Moses and read it.   The books of
Moses, therefore, and, in like manner, the other books of Scripture, were preserved safe in the captivity; and we have now no
other, but the very same books of Scripture of the Old Testament as those which were written by Moses and the rest of the
prophets.   However it is very possible that the books, which
may have been previously in some disorder, were corrected by
Ezra, restored to their proper places, and disposed according to
some fixed plan as Hilary in his prologue affirms particularly of
the Psalms, &c.'

We notice, therefore, with especial interest the position of *Bellarmine.*
Bellarmine (1542–1621), who, as the champion of the Roman
Catholics against the Reformed Churches, might be thought a very
unlikely man to acknowledge even the possibility of the ancient
traditional view, that a great miracle was wrought, being erroneous.
He, however, after relating the tradition, candidly mentions that
' there is another view according to which Ezra was indeed the
restorer of the sacred books, not however by dictating them all
afresh, but by collecting and arranging all the Scriptures, of

EXCURS. A. which he had found portions in different places, into a single volume, as well as by correcting them wherever they had suffered from the carelessness of copyists, seeing that during the whole period of the captivity, when the Jews were without temple or tabernacle, the law was carelessly preserved' (*Opp.* tom. i. lib. 2 ; *De Verbo Dei*, cap. i).

Cornelius Lapide.　1568–1637. We need quote only one other authority, the eminent Roman Catholic commentator, Cornelius a Lapide (van der Steen), whose words illustrate the change of view in reference to the legend (*Comment. in Esdr. et Neh.*, Prolog. p. 201). After quoting Patristic evidence in favour of the legend he goes on to say : ' Leo Castrius, in his preface to Isaiah iv, supports the same view, to wit, that Ezra restored the books of the law from memory. Nor is this wonderful. For that is even more wonderful which we read of St. Antonius of Padua, that he knew by heart (calluisse) the whole of Holy Scripture, insomuch that he was called by the Pope " The Ark of the Testament." " For he had the pages of both Testaments alike so clearly fixed in his memory, that, like Ezra, he had the power, if occasion had required it, of completely restoring from his memory the whole Canon of sacred literature, even though all the MSS. had been utterly destroyed "; so says the author of his life. Nevertheless, although this opinion appear probable on account of the weight of Patristic authority, the contrary opinion is yet far more probable and based on certain reasons, to wit, that the sacred books were neither all of them burned by the Chaldeans, nor restored from memory by Ezra.' He proceeds to give his reasons. The first is, that there is no record of the Chaldeans having burned the Scriptures ; and, considering the number of copies in use in Judea and elsewhere, if they had burned them, they could not possibly have completely destroyed them all. The second reason is, that Daniel (chap. ix. 2), in the first year of Darius, possessed the prophecy of Jeremiah and other prophets, and was in the habit of reading it. The third reason is, that Josephus (*Ant. Jud.*, lib. xi. 1) relates how Cyrus, having

been shown the prophecy of Isaiah (xlv) which he had fulfilled,
became kindly disposed to the Jews in consequence. Cornelius
a Lapide adds as yet another reason, that the Fourth Book of
Esdras was apocryphal, and that 'the two hundred and four
books' (the Vulgate reading) written by the five men at Ezra's
dictation had nothing in common with the books of Scripture.

We shall not perhaps attach the same value to all of the reasons
thus alleged. But it is clear that at the beginning of the 17th
century the legend that Ezra had alone, and by miraculous aid,
formed the Canon of the Hebrew Scriptures, had become
generally discredited and discarded. The story was inherently
improbable, and it rested on no historical evidence.

2. The Men of the Great Synagogue.

But the legend respecting Ezra and the books of Holy Scrip- *2. The Men of the Great Synagogue.*
ture could not be dethroned without some account of the forma-
tion of the sacred Canon being found to serve as its substitute.
Its place was filled by the tradition of ' The Men of the Great
Synagogue,' which had the twofold advantage of offering a more
probable explanation and of claiming to rest upon the authority
of trustworthy Hebrew tradition. For more than three centuries
this legend, or one or other of its modern modifications, has
held the field.

The reasons for its general acceptance may be recognised
without difficulty. The revival of learning in the fifteenth
and sixteenth centuries had given a new prominence to the
study of Hebrew and a fresh authority to the words of Jewish
writers. In the course of the controversy among Hebrew *Origin of the theory in Elias Levita's 'Massoreth Ha-Massoreth.'*
scholars respecting the origin and date of the Massoretic
system, an eminent Jewish writer, Elias Levita, maintained in
an important work, entitled *Massoreth Ha Massoreth* (1538),
that Ezra and his companions, the men of the Great Synagogue,
promulgated the correct consonantal text, and at the same
time collected the Holy Scriptures and formed the Canon.
Such a suggestion, put forward at a time when it seemed im-

possible to defend the historical character of the ecclesiastical tradition about Ezra, could hardly fail to command attention and to find a welcome. It quickly obtained great popularity. In the Hebrew controversy respecting the antiquity of the vowel-points, the subject of the Great Synagogue was frequently referred to; and, although very opposite opinions were freely expressed by able men, the preponderance of learning, among the scholars of the Reformed Churches, certainly leaned to the side of the new suggestion.   The most important work dealing

Buxtorf's 'Tiberias.' with it was the *Tiberias sive Commentarius Masorethicus* of John Buxtorf, published at Basle in 1620. This book, which admirably summarised all that was known, in the beginning of the sixteenth century, respecting the 'Massorah,' according to Jewish tradition, makes frequent allusions to 'the Great Synagogue' as its principal source. It contains all the principal evidence for 'the Great Synagogue' to be found in Rabbinic literature.

The weight of John Buxtorf's authority told enormously in support of the new theory upon the origin of the Old Testament Canon. It was reinforced by that of his son John Buxtorf (1599–1664) in his conflict with Morinus and Cappellus, who had dared to question the inviolable character of the Massoretic text, had impugned the antiquity of the square Hebrew characters, and even thrown doubts upon the accuracy of Rabbinic tradition generally, and respecting the Great Synagogue in particular. The 'Tiberias' appeared in a new edition in 1665, when it was issued by John James Buxtorf, the grandson of the author.

Acceptance of the theory. All subsequent writers have quarried from the *Tiberias*, and the influence of this treatise has had even more to do with the general acceptance of the tradition about 'The Men of the Great Synagogue' than the earlier work of Elias Levita.

The hold which the new view obtained over the best scholars of the seventeenth century may be exemplified by the following quotations :—

Bp. Walton. (1) Brian Walton, Bishop of Chester (1600–1661): 'The first and most famous edition of the books of the Old Testament

was that of Ezra (whom the Jews'call a second Moses), and the
Great Sanhedrim, or the men of the Great Synagogue, after the
return from Babylon. For as there no longer existed either
the Temple or the Tabernacle, where the authentic copies had
formerly been deposited, the sacred volumes were negligently
kept all through the period of the captivity. This being the case,
Ezra and his companions collected the MSS. from various quarters, arranged them in order, and reduced them to the compass of
a single volume. They removed the corruptions from which
the text had suffered, and restored it to its former pure state;
and thus they established the Canon. Their work of establishing the Canon possessed truly divine authority; for there
belonged to that Council not only Ezra but also the last of the
Prophets, Haggai, Zechariah, Malachi, and (as some think)
Daniel,' &c. (Walton's *Polyglott. Prolegg.* iv. 2, London 1657.)

(2) 'It has been an incontrovertible principle as well with *Hottinger.*
Christians—those indeed who have not a fungus for a brain—
as with Jews, that the Canon of the Old Testament was all, at
one and the same time, established, with an authority absolutely
divine, by Ezra and the men of the Great Synagogue.' (Hottinger, *Thesaurus Philologicus,* lib. i. c. 2. 1, p. 111, ed. 2, Zurich
1659.)

(3) Leusden (1629–1699): 'By the men of the Great Synagogue *Leusden.*
are understood not those who were members of ordinary
Councils, but those who were admitted to that extraordinary
Council of one hundred and twenty men. This Council reduced
the books of the Old Testament to the compass of a single
volume, separated Holy Scripture from the fictitious books of
Pseudo-Prophets, and rendered many other services in connexion
with the reformation of the Church, and in connexion with the
sacred books, by purifying (*emuscando*) them from the errors
that had become attached to them.' (*Philologicus Hebraeus,*
Dissertatio ix. c. 20, ed. 2, Utrecht, 1672.)

(4) Carpzovius (1767): 'Ezra's first and last thought being for *Carpzovius.*
the sacred volumes, he, in conjunction with the other members

EXCURS. A. of the Great Synagogue, among whom the Jews reckon Haggai, Zechariah, Malachi, and Nehemiah, collected from all sides the MSS. of the Scriptures, arranged them in order, separated them from the miscellaneous writings which had crept in among them; and he was the first of all to reduce the books to the compass of the single volume and 'System' which we call the Old Testament, from which time no other book has been admitted into the Canon of the Old Testament.' (*Introd. in libr. Canon. Bibl. V.T.,* P. i. 2. 1, Leipzig 1757.)

Opposition to the theory.   There were, however, many scholars who strongly objected to the new view. These were men who had no great confidence in the accuracy of Jewish tradition. Among them we may mention the names of Jacob Alting and Franciscus Burmann, both eminent scholars.

Alting.   Alting (1618–1697): 'For the Great Synagogue lived neither at one time nor in one place; that Synagogue had no existence, but is a fiction of the traditionalists who could nowhere else find any support for their παράδοσις.' (Jacobus Altingius, *Epist. ad Perigon.*, op. tom. v. p. 382, quoted by Rau, P. i. cap. iii. vii.)

Burmann.   Burmann (1632–1679): 'But that account of the Congress, I speak of the Great Synagogue, since there is no mention of it in Scripture, and it is open to various objections, is more disputable than certain.' (Franciscus Burmannus, *Synops. Theol.,* tom. i. lib. iv. 37. 7, Utrecht 1671.)

Rau's 'Diatribe de Syn. Mag.'   1727. The objections to the whole story of the Great Synagogue were put forward in a very complete and interesting form by Joh. Rau in his *Diatribe de Synagoga Magna,* published at Utrecht in 1727. This work is the most considerable monograph upon the subject. But it was doubtless written with a certain degree of animus; for, besides the passage just quoted from Franz Burmann, he placed on the title-page of his work the words of Hugo Grotius, 'The Jews are the worst teachers of history. For ever since they were driven from their country, all their history has been marred with crass errors and legends,

to which absolutely no credence is to be given unless other ExcurS. A.
witnesses be brought in their support.' (*Comm. in Matt.* xxiv.
24.) Still, his work must be regarded as a protest against the
blind veneration for the mere authority of the great Hebrew
scholars, and against the uncritical acceptance of Jewish tradition. It gives a full account of the tradition of the Great
Synagogue, shows how devoid it is of historical support, and
seeks to explain its origin.

Another shorter work by Aurivillius, published in his *Disser-* *Aurivillius.*
tationes which were edited by Michaelis in 1790 (Leipzig),
dealt with the same subject on very similar lines.

The objections that were levelled against the story of ' the Men *Modifica-*
of the Great Synagogue ' succeeded in causing certain modifica- *tions of the*
theory.
tions in it to be accepted. Jewish tradition which regarded the
whole interval of time between the Return and the age of Alexander
as included within thirty-four years, and which called Zechariah,
Haggai, Mordecai, and Simon the Just, members of the Great
Synagogue along with Ezra, Nehemiah, and Malachi, could
not be accepted in a literal sense. Accordingly, it became
necessary to introduce certain modifications into the story.
Variations were from time to time suggested. According to some,
the Great Synagogue was, as the tradition had asserted, an
assembly of Jewish Divines, who constituted a special court, dealing only with matters of religion, during the whole period between
Ezra and Simon the Just (445–290 or 196 B.C.). According to
others, e.g. Selden, *De Synagogis* (1679), it was the same as the
Sanhedrim of later times. According to John Lightfoot, ' the
date of its first institution is not certain, but under this title the
Jews include the whole administration of the nation from the
time of the return from Babylon down to the time of the presidency of Simon the Just' (*Opera posthuma, Memorabilia*, p. 86,
ed. 1699).

In modern times the story of 'the men of the Great Synagogue'
has found favour up to a very recent date. But there has been
a very considerable diversity shown, and not a little freedom

EXCURS. A. exercised, in the handling of the tradition. The following references will serve as illustrations :—

Herzfeld.

Herzfeld, in his *Geschichte des Volkes Israels* (1ᵗᵉ Band, 1863, Leipzig), devotes his Twelfth Excursus (pp. 380 ff.) to the careful discussion of the Great Synagogue, which he identifies with the Sanhedrim.

Ginsburg.

Ginsburg, in his edition of *Levita's Exposition of the Massorah* (London 1867, note on pp. 107, 108), says : 'The Great Synagogue . . . . denotes the Council, or Synod, first appointed by Nehemiah, after the return of the Jews from the Babylonish captivity, to reorganise the religious life of the people. It consisted originally of one hundred and twenty members, comprising the representatives of the following five classes, of the Jewish nation. (i) The Chiefs of the Priestly Divisions; (ii) the Chiefs of the Levitical Families; (iii) the Heads of the Israelite Families; (iv) Representatives of the Cities, or the Elders; and (v) the Doctors of the Law, or the Scribes. The number of one hundred and twenty was, however, not adhered to after the death of Nehemiah, and ultimately it was reduced to seventy. The period of its duration extended from the latter days of Nehemiah to the death of Simon the Just, B.C. 410–300; thus embracing about one hundred and ten years.'

Westcott.

Westcott (*Bible in the Church*, p. 300, Appendix A, 1863–1885) : 'This Great Assembly or Synagogue, whose existence has been called in question on insufficient grounds, was the great council of the nation during the Persian period, in which the last substantive changes were made in the constitution of Judaism. The last member of it is said to have been Simon the Just (c. B.C. 310–290). It was organised by Ezra, and, as commonly happens, the work of the whole body was transferred to its representative member. Ezra . . . probably formed a collection of the prophetic writings; and the Assembly gathered together afterwards such books as were still left without the Canon, though proved to bear the stamp of the Spirit of God.'

Fürst (*Kanon des Alt. Test.*, Leipz. 1868, pp. 22, 23): 'Dieses
grosse Kollegium oder der Staatsrath hatte seine erste Begrün-
dung im zwanzigsten Jahre des persischen Königs Artaxerxes
Langhand (Artachschasta) d. h. am 24. Tischri des Jahres
444 v. Chr. gefunden, als Nehemijah nach Jerusalem gekommen
war, um nachdem die Stadtmauern bereits im Monat Elul fertig
geworden, eine grosse religiös-constituirende, aus Priestern,
Leviten und Volksfürsten oder Stammhäuptern (Rasche ha-
Abot) bestehende Versammlung nach dem Laubenfeste abzu-
halten, welche die seit 515 v. Chr. (1. Jahr des Darius), nämlich
seit den 70 Jahren nach der Errichtung des Serubbabel'schen
Tempels, eingerissenen Missbräuche und Unordnungen be-
seitigen und überhaupt ein neues Nationalleben anregen
sollte. Durch Entwerfung und Unterzeichnung eines Statuts
und Vertrags wurde dieses Kollegium organisirt. Unter
persischer Oberhoheit leitete es Judäa religiös und politisch
128 (*sic*) Jahre (444–328), indem es sich stets bis zur von
Anfang an fixirten Zahl von 120 Mitgliedern ergänzte, dann
unter griechisch-seleukidischer Oberhoheit 132 Jahre (328–
196 v. Chr.), d. h. bis zum Tode des Hochpriesters Schimon b.
Chonaw II.'

Derenbourg (*Essai sur l'Histoire et la Géographie de la Palestine*,
Paris 1867, chap. ii. pp. 33, 34): 'Le nom spécial des docteurs
qui eurent alors la ferme volonté de propager la connaissance de
la parole divine, d'expliquer la loi à tous ceux qui voulurent
l'étudier, d'augmenter le nombre des disciples et de former de
nouveaux maîtres, de resserrer la chaîne des prescriptions afin
d'en assurer mieux l'observation et qui formèrent plutôt un
collége qu'un sénat, un corps de savants qu'une autorité con-
stituée, était, comme nous l'avons déjà dit, celui d'hommes de la
Grande Synagogue. . . . Nous considérons ce qui est raconté
de la Grande Synagogue comme historique. Un corps sem-
blable, nous croyons l'avoir démontré, répondait à la situation;
la transformation qui s'est opérée au sein du judaïsme est comme
l'effet incontestable d'une cause contestée mal à propos; le

Excurs. A. pontificat seul aurait amené encore une fois les conséquences funestes que nous avons vues se produire dans l'intervalle qui s'écoule entre le départ de Zérobbabel pour Babylon et l'arrivée d'Ezra à Jérusalem.   Nous ajouterons que le nom *d'Anschê Kenêset haggedôlah*, qui ne s'est jamais appliqué qu'aux hommes de ce temps, dont on ne comprend plus même tout à fait le sens, et qui, au iie siècle, céda la place à un nom nouveau et désignant une organisation plus artificielle, doit avoir été porté par un corps qui a existé, qui a vécu.   L'imagination aurait été chercher une dénomination ancienne, répondant à une institution généralement connue.'

Hoffman. C. H. H. Wright.   C. H. H. Wright (*Ecclesiastes*, London 1883, Excursus iii. p. 486): ' Hoffman further argues that even in the Books of Ezra and Nehemiah mention is made of a senate at Jerusalem under various names (Ezra x. 8, vi. 7, 14 ; Neh. x. 1, xi. 1, &c.).   The governing body was then composed of priests and Levites under the headship of the High Priest, and of Israelitish laymen under the headship of the Prince of the House of Judah.   "The Elders of the House of Israel" were all probably "scribes," skilled in the Law like Ezra himself (Ezra vii. 25).   Such a body would naturally be renewed from time to time, and the name of " the Great Synagogue" was given to it in later days not only on account of the important work it performed in the reconstruction and preservation of the Jewish Church and State in troublous times, but also because its members were originally more numerous than those of the Sanhedrin of a later period, or even of the council of elders which occupied its place in earlier and happier days.   Though we cannot narrate the history of the disruption of the Great Synagogue, it is highly probable that after the death of Simon the Just it was shattered by internal dissensions, &c. . . . " The Great Synagogue" was broken up some years previous to the heroic struggles of the Maccabees.'

See also Bloch's *Studien zur Geschichte der Sammlung der althebraischen Literatur*, Breslau 1870, pp. 99–132.

It is time now to turn from the modern, and often conflicting, representations of the old tradition to the actual evidence upon which it all rests.

For this purpose it will be convenient, firstly, to quote the description which Joh. Buxtorf gives of 'the Great Synagogue,' seeing that most of the subsequent descriptions have been drawn from his *Tiberias*; and, secondly, to sift and analyse the evidence which he and others cite in support of his account. For, as Buxtorf gives no dates in his citation of authorities, the reader is apt to carry away a very misleading impression from the array of Hebrew evidence advanced in support of his statements, unless he is able to check them by a knowledge of their age and literary value.

Joh. Buxtorfi Tiberias s. Comment. Masorethicus, recognitus *a Joh. Buxtorf. fil., ed. nov. accurante Joh. Jac. Buxtorf. nep.* (*Basileae*, 1665.)

p. 22 *b*, cap. x. ' " The men of the Great Synagogue." Such is the name given by the Jews to the Great Council assembled at Jerusalem by Ezra, the priest, its president, after the Babylonian exile. By its aid and support he restored the whole Church of Jerusalem and Judea, purged it of many corruptions, faults, and vices contracted in Babylon, and constructed it afresh. . . . Ezra and Nehemiah associated with themselves certain others of the more noble and learned of the people, so that the entire Council, or Ecclesiastical Senate, embraced the number of one hundred and twenty men. . . . It is said in the Book *Juchasin*, fol. 13, respecting this Council :—" Ezra's house of judgment is that which is called the Great Synagogue, which restored the Crown to its former state." Among the Jews there were three crowns, of the Law, of the Priesthood, and of the Kingdom. . . . The Crown of the Law, i. e. the study of wisdom and the knowledge of the Divine Law, was greater than all, as it is written, " By me kings reign " (Prov. viii: 15). This crown Ezra and his colleagues restored to its pristine condition, i. e. rid the ecclesiastical Republic of the pollutions and defilements of

EXCURS. A. Babylon, and restored it to its former purity, and purged Holy
Scripture of the fictitious books of the false prophets, and of
every sort of corruption. . . .'

p. 24 *a.* 'But in order that the Law of God itself and the
whole Scripture might continue among the people in their
purity, genuineness, and integrity, in order, too, that a distinction
might be drawn between the writings of numerous false prophets
and the books of the true prophets, and in order that any corruption might be removed which could appear to have been introduced into the sacred text through the stress of a long captivity,
there was the utmost need for mature deliberation, for the anxious
forethought of scholars and those best skilled in the study of Holy
Scripture and for the earnest efforts of many minds.   There
were present as Divinely appointed colleagues in the task
(*divini symmistae*) men endowed with the spirit of prophecy,
Haggai, Zechariah, Malachi, and Nehemiah, whose ardour and
glowing zeal are proclaimed in their own sacred words; there
was present Zerubbabel, that prince of utmost energy, whose
family and renown are ennobled by the genealogy of our Saviour
Christ; there was present the High Priest Jeschua, and other
leading priests and Levites that had accompanied Zerubbabel
from Babylon, and all as many as had been an example and a
support of true religion among the Jewish people.   These are
reinforced by Ezra with certain others of leading rank, mighty
in the Holy Scriptures, and excelling in influence, in number
one hundred and twenty, who were called "The Men of the
Great Synagogue," the Great Council, in order that they should
take pious and weighty counsel respecting the chief things of
their religion, not so much having regard to the advantage of
the moment or to any pressing need, but also so far as possible
with the view of providing for the salvation of posterity in all
future time, seeing that they knew the gift of prophecy would
soon be taken away from them.'

p. 24 *b*, cap. xi.   'On convening the Synod, Ezra first
gave attention to Holy Scripture as the undoubted Canon of

faith and true religion, and defined the limits of the Mosaic, the Excurs. A.
Prophetical, and the other books that were written by special
inspiration of the Holy Spirit, and rejected all the heterogeneous
writings that had crept in amongst them. . . . The canonical
books themselves were diligently searched, lest they should retain any foreign or mischievous interpolation.   Nor had it been
enough to have handed down to the Church the authentic sacred
books; but even the way of reading the same clearly, and of
expounding them, was given and laid down with the utmost
care.'

p. 25 *a.* 'First of all, they determined the number of the
canonical books, and then reduced them to the compass of
a single body of Scripture; they divided it into three principal portions, viz., the Law, the Prophets, and the sacred
writings.'

pp. 26 *b,* 27 *a.* 'The sum of it all amounts to this, that
Ezra, with the men of the Great Synagogue, in which were included the last of the Prophets, determined the limits of the
Canon of Holy Scripture within certain books, and distributed
them into those three portions, which from that time forward
have always been and are still even now recognised in the
Jewish Church; and this was the first beginning of the Massora
in connexion with Scripture.'

The following is the evidence upon which these statements *Evidence:*
are based, arranged in order of date: —

1572. Genebrardus (*Chronologia,* lib. 2) is quoted by Bux- *Genebrar-*
torf (p. 25 *a*): 'The prophets were succeeded by the Great *dus.*
Synagogue, whose leaders were Ezra, Nehemiah, Mordecai,
Zerubbabel, Jeshua.   These presided over the Council, into
which one hundred and twenty persons were admitted, some of
noble, some of humble origin, to provide for the correction of
the Holy Scriptures and the setting up of their Canon according
to the rule of the tradition.'

1538. Elias Levita (1472–1549). *Massoreth Ha-Massoreth.* *Elias*
(*a*) 'The men of the Great Synagogue, i. e. Haggai, *Levita.*

Excurs. A. Zechariah, Malachi, Daniel, Mishael, Azariah, Ezra, Nehemiah, Mordecai, Zerubbabel, with whom were associated other sages from the craftsmen and artizans to the number of one hundred and twenty persons' (ed. Ginsburg, pp. 110, 111).

(*b*) 'What shall we say to the various readings (Keri and Kethiv) which are found in the books written by the captives themselves, such as Haggai, Zechariah, Malachi, Daniel, Ezra, who wrote his own book and the Chronicles, and Mordecai, who wrote the Book of Esther? Were not these themselves among the men of the Great Synagogue? . . .' (*id.* p. 107).

(*c*) 'The whole period of the men of the Great Synagogue did not exceed about forty years, as is shown in *Seder Olam* and in Ibn Daud's *Seder Ha-Kabbalah*' (id. p. 108)[1].

(*d*) 'But when they failed to find the autograph copy itself, which seems most likely to have happened, they undoubtedly followed the majority of the MSS., which they had collected from different places, one here and one there, as the twenty-four books were then not joined together into one volume. Now they (i.e. Ezra and his associates) have joined them together and divided them into three parts, the Law, the Prophets, and the Hagiographa, and arranged the Prophets and Hagiographa not in the order in which they have been put by our Rabbins of blessed memory in *Baba bathra* (14 *a*)' (id. p. 120).

Abr. ben Sam. Zacuto. 1502. The book quoted as *Juchasin*, fol. 13, by Buxtorf in the *Tiberias* (cap. x. p. 22 *b*) is the *Sepher Juchasin* or Book of Generations, a chronological treatise by Abraham ben Samuel Zacuto, who lived in Spain about 1490. The passage quoted is, 'Now Ezra's house of judgment is that which is called the Great Synagogue or the Great Council, which restored the crown to its former condition.'

Abarbanel. Don Isaac Abarbanel, the introduction[2] to whose book

---

[1] N.B. The last quotation is not accurate; see Ginsburg's note *in loc.*

[2] Morinus quotes from the same introduction an illustration of Jewish ignorance or carelessness about chronology, 'Of the same generation as Simon the Just was Dosa, the son of Harcines. For he was of the number

entitled *The Inheritance of the Fathers* (*Nachalath Avoth*) is quoted by Buxtorf (cap. x. p. 23 *a*), lived 1436–1509. The passage quoted is the following: 'The list of the Men of the Great Synagogue is Haggai, the prophet; Zechariah, the prophet; Malachi, the prophet; Zerubbabel, the son of Shealtiel; Mordecai, the son of Bilschan; Ezra, the priest and scribe; Jeshua, the son of Jehozedek the priest; Seraiah; Realiah; Mispar Bigvaeus (Bigvai); Rachum; Baana; Nehemiah, the son of Chachiliah. These are the twelve chiefs expressly named who went up from Babylon to Jerusalem at the beginning of the (age of the) second temple. With them were likewise joined others from the more leading men of the people of Israel, until the number of one hundred and twenty was completed, and they were called the Men of the Great Synagogue, and they were so styled, because they were called together to establish good laws for the right government of the people and to repair the breaches of the Law.'

1360–1412. The passage from *Ephodi*, the literary title of '*Ephodi.*' Profiat Duran or Rabbi Isaac ben Moses ha-Levi (1360–1412), quoted by Buxtorf (cap. xi. p. 29*a*) and Morinus (lib. ii. *Exercit.* xxv. cap. iv.), bears less directly upon the subject of the Great Synagogue: 'The perfect one, the chief of the scribes, Ezra, the priest and scribe, shook out his lap, and exerted all the strength of his might to restore what had been perverted; likewise did all the scribes who followed him, and corrected these books with all the care they could, until they left them most perfect, by numbering the sections, verses, words, and letters .... and composed out of them books, which are the books of the Massorah.'

c. 1250. [Tanchuma ben Josef, generally called Tanchuma Jerushalmi, according to Herzfeld, reckoned the Nethinim of Ezra ii. 53 with the Great Synagogue (Tanchuma 19, referred to, *Gesch. d. Volk Isr.* p. 382, 1863).]

of the men of the Great Synagogue, and prolonged his life until he saw Rabbi Akiba' (*Biblic. Exercitt.* II. v. cap. iii.).

† 1235. The great Jewish commentator, Rabbi David Kimchi, who died in 1235 A.D., refers, though in very general terms, to the work of the Great Synagogue:

(a) 'It appears that at the first captivity the Scriptures were lost and scattered; and the wise men that knew the Law had died. Then the Men of the Great Synagogue, who "restored the Law to its former condition," found the doubtful passages in the Scriptures and followed the majority (of the MSS.) according to their knowledge' (*Praefat. in Jos.*). This passage Kimchi repeats in his comment on a various reading in 2 Sam. XV. 21.

(b) 'And Ezra united the book (Chronicles) with the Sacred Writings by the hands of (at the direction of, עַל יְדֵי) Haggai, Zechariah, and Malachi, the last of the Prophets, and they joined it with the Kethubim and not with the Nebiim, because it was a Chronicle' (*Praefat. in Chron.*).

1135-1204. The great Jewish philosopher of the Middle Ages, Moses ben Maimon (Maimonides), writes: 'Ezra's House of Judgment (or Council) consisted of those who are called the Men of the Great Synagogue; and they are Haggai, Zechariah, Malachi, &c., and many wise ones with them, up to the number of one hundred and twenty. The last of them was Simon the Just; he belonged to the number of the one hundred and twenty.' (*Praefat. in Yad Hachazakah*, quoted by Buxtorf, cap. x. p. 23 b.)

c. 1160. Rabbi Abraham ben David of Toledo says: 'Joshua handed it (the Law) on to the elders, who lived after him; the elders handed it on to the prophets; the prophets handed it on, from the one to the other, through successive generations, down to Haggai, Zechariah, and Malachi; the prophets handed it on to the Men of the Great Synagogue, who were Zerubbabel the son of Shealtiel, the son of Jechoniah, the king of the Jews, and those who came with Zerubbabel, Jeshua, Nehemiah, Seraiah, Realiah, Mordecai, Ritschan, Mistpar, Bigvai, Rechum, Baana, who were the heads of the Great Council.' (*Sepher ha-Kabbala*

or *Book of Tradition*, fol. 23, col. 4, quoted by Buxtorf, cap. x.
p. 23 *a*.)

† 1105. Rashi, or Rabbi Solomon Isaac, the celebrated com- *Rashi, or*
mentator, composed a Commentary upon most of the Talmudic *Jarchi.*
Tractates. Commenting upon *Baba bathra*, fol. 15, he says:
'The Men of the Great Synagogue, Haggai, Zechariah, and
Malachi, and Zerubbabel, and Mordecai, and their colleagues,
wrote Ezekiel which was prophesied during the Captivity: and
I know not why Ezekiel did not write it himself, unless it was
that prophecy was not permitted to be written outside the (holy)
land; and they wrote it, after they returned to the (holy) land.
So too, with the book of Daniel, who was in the Captivity; and
so too, with the Roll of Esther; and so with the Twelve (Minor
Prophets). Because their prophecies were short, the prophets
did not write them themselves, each one his own book. But
Haggai, Zechariah, and Malachi, on their return, saw that the
Holy Spirit would be taken away, and that they were the last
prophets. And they arose, and wrote their prophecies, and
combined with them the little (or, short) prophecies, and made
them into a great book, so that they should not be lost.'

Commenting on *Megilla*, fol. 2, he says: 'The Men of the
Great Synagogue are those who, in the days of Mordecai and
Esther, instituted the joy of Purim, and the reading of the Roll
of Esther.'

1092–1167. Abraham Aben-Ezra, the commentator, says: *Aben Ezra.*
'A few years after the building of the second Holy Temple, the
Spirit of the LORD, the Spirit of wisdom and understanding,
rested upon the Men of the House, which are called the Men of
the Great Synagogue, that they might interpret all that was
sealed, by precepts and words transmitted, according to the
mind of the just ones, from the mouth of the earlier and latter
prophets.' (*Sepher Moznaim*, a Hebrew Grammar, quoted by
Morinus, lib. ii. *Exercit.* xii. 7.)

9th cent. (?) The Targum of 'Song of Songs' speaks of *Targum to*
'Ezra, the priest, and Zerubbabel, and Jeshua, and Nehemiah, *'Song of Songs.'*

and Mordecai, and Belsan, the Men of the Great Synagogue, who are likened unto roses, that they may have strength to labour in the Law by day and night.' (Chap. vii. 1, 2.)

The oldest Jewish tradition is comprised in the following extracts, the exact antiquity of which it is impossible to compute. The earliest reference is that which is contained in the *Pirqe Aboth*, a Mishnic treatise committed to writing about 200 A.D.

Talmud.   Talmud.

Tal. Jer. Berakoth, ii. 4 (cf. 33 *a*, *Megillah*, fol. 17 *b*). R Jeremiah says : 'The 120 members of the Great Synagogue, including more than 80 prophets, have arranged this prayer (i.e. the 18 blessings), and put it in order.'

(The number of 'the elders' is stated to be 85 in *Jer. Meg.* i. 7, and *Midrash Ruth*.)

Tal. Jer. Berakoth, vii. 4 (cf. *Megillah*, iii. 8). 'And when the Men of the Great Synagogue arose, they restored "the greatness" to its pristine state.'

Of this tradition another form appears in *Yoma*, fol. 69 *b*, *Sanhedrin*, fol. 64. 'Why were they called the Men of the Great Synagogue? because they restored "the Crown" to its pristine state.'

Tal. Jer. Berakoth, vii. 4. 'When the Men of the Great Synagogue arose . . .' the formula was used again 'God the great, the strong, the terrible.'

Pesachim, cap. 4, fol. 50, 2, as quoted by Buxtorf, ap. *Tib.* p. 23 *a.* 'On four and twenty fast-days the Men of the Great Synagogue sate (?) on account of the scribes that wrote the Scriptures, Tephillim and Mezuzoth[1], lest they should grow rich; for if they were to grow rich they would not write.'

Megillah, iii. 7. (See below *Pirqe Aboth*.)

Baba bathra, fol. 15, 1. 'The Men of the Great Synagogue wrote Ezekiel, and the Twelve (Minor Prophets), Daniel and

---

[1] I. e. Phylacteries and Texts to be attached to doorposts, &c.

the Roll of Esther[1].' As quoted in *Mishpete-ha-Teamim* (in the
MS. Moses b. Asher, 895 A. D., ed. Baer-Strack), the first
sentence runs ' The Men of the Great Synagogue and among
them Haggai and Zechariah,' &c.

Pirqe Aboth, c. 1 (quoted also in *Aboth d'Rabbi Nathan* and
Meg. iii. 7): 'Moses received the Torah from Sinai and delivered
it to Joshua, and Joshua to the elders, and the elders to the
prophets, and the prophets to the Men of the Great Synagogue.
They said three things: Be deliberate in judgment, and raise
up many disciples, and make a fence to the Torah. Simon the
Just was of the remnants of the Great Synagogue.' The 'Pairs'
of Jewish Scribes preceding the schools of Hillel and Shammai
are then enumerated.

The Tractate, *Aboth d'Rabbi Nathan*, 'Sayings of the Rabbi
Nathan,' commenting on the first of these precepts, 'At first they
said, Proverbs and the Song of Songs and Ecclesiastes were
not for public reading (i.e. Genuzim), because they spake parables. And they remained. And they removed them from public
reading until the Men of the Great Synagogue came and expounded them.' (P. 2, ed. Schechter, Vienna, 1887.)

The passage from *Pirqe Aboth* should be carefully compared
with a similar statement in *Peah.* ii. 6, ' Nahum, the scribe, said
it was received from Rabbi Maesa (Meir), who received it from
Rab (i. e. Rabbi Jehudah), who received it from "the Pairs,"
who received it from the Prophets.' The absence of any reference to the Great Synagogue between ' The Pairs of Scribes '
and ' the Prophets ' is very noteworthy.

We have thus recorded the principal evidence to be adduced
in support of the Great Synagogue. There is no mention
of any such body conveyed in the use of the word συναγωγή
in 1 Macc. vii. 12, xiv. 28. In the former passage, where

[1] According to *Maccoth*, 23, and *Jer. Meg.* i. (quoted in Hamburger,
Real Lex. Talmud, sub voce Gr. Syn.), the Men of the Great Synagogue
established the authority of the Book of Esther, and caused the Days of
Purim to be observed; cf. Rashi, *ut supr.*

it is stated that a company of scribes (συναγωγὴ γραμματέων) re-
sorted to Alcimus and Bacchides, it is obvious that no formal
community is intended.   In the latter passage, the words 'at a
great congregation (or gathering) of priests and of the people
and rulers of the nation and the elders of the country' could
not admit of such a reference.   The μεγάλη συναγωγή seems to
denote the gathering of a representative meeting, not the title of
a recognised official body.   Had the latter been intended, the
article would have been prefixed.

*No historical
evidence.*
There is no mention of 'the Great Synagogue' in the writings
of either Josephus or Philo.   There is no allusion to it in the
Apocrypha.   There is not a sentence in Nehemiah which,
according to any literal interpretation, would lead a reader to
suppose that Ezra founded an important deliberative assembly,
or even a religious Synod or College.

The earliest evidence therefore is that supplied in the Mishnic Treatise, *Pirqe Aboth*, which may have been committed to
writing in the 2nd or 3rd century A.D.   The remainder of the
Talmudic evidence is Gemara, and not Mishnah, and therefore,
probably, was not committed to writing earlier than the 6th or
7th century A.D.   There is no evidence from any literary
source whatever, nearer to the historical period, to which the
Great Synagogue is assigned, than *Pirqe Aboth*; and all the
testimony of *Pirqe Aboth* amounts to is this, that, in the chain
of tradition from Moses to the Scribes of the 2nd century B.C.,
the Great Synagogue intervened between the Prophets and 'the
Pairs' of Scribes, and that Simon the Just ranked as its last
surviving member.

The argument from the silence of the Old Testament, of the
Apocrypha, of the *Antiquities* of Josephus, of Philo, is significant
enough by itself.   But when taken in conjunction with the late-
ness and meagreness of the earliest testimony in favour of the tradition, it is seen to be almost fatal to the historicity of the story.

*Summary
of earliest
evidence.*
Let us then briefly sum up the results of the earliest Hebrew
testimony upon the subject of the Great Synagogue.

1. It belonged to the era of Ezra and included in its members Simon the Just. (This, according to traditional chronology, was well within the bounds of possibility. Simon the Just was believed to have been High Priest in the days of Alexander the Great; and Alexander the Great was supposed to have reigned in the generation after the Return from the Exile.)

2. It consisted of 85 or 120 members, and therefore differed from the later Jewish Sanhedrin, which consisted of 70.

It contained in its ranks many prophets. It seems to have been an assembly convened for special purposes at a particular epoch, immediately before the disappearance of the gift of prophecy.

3. It was credited with having discharged important duties in connexion with the religious life of the people: (*a*) it restored the ascendency of the law; (*b*) it wrote certain books of the Hebrew Scriptures; (*c*) it drew up certain prayers; (*d*) it allayed the doubts that had been felt about the books Ecclesiastes and Song of Songs; (*e*) it instituted the observance of the days of Purim.

4. It was regarded, especially, as the sacred body which received the holy tradition of the 'Law' from the Prophets, and handed it on to the Scribes of the 2nd century B. C.

It may be said at once that this picture does not correspond *No resemblance to Jewish Councils in history.* with any Jewish Assembly or Council recorded in the Persian, Greek, or Roman period of Jewish history.

After the time of Ezra, the chief power in the Jewish community fell into the hands of the High Priest, under whom was a purely political body of aristocratic 'elders' or Gerousia. The assumption of the High Priesthood by the Asmonean family made the Government still more autocratic. The title of King was taken by the last Asmonean princes. The Gerousia continued to exist (cf. 1 Macc. xii. 6, xiv. 20, Jos. *Ant. Jud.* xiii. 6, 5); and when the Jewish Monarchy was abolished by the Romans, it was this body which, under the successive constitutions laid down by Pompey, Gabinius, and Caesar, became the principal domestic power in Judea.

EXCURS. A.　The name of Sanhedrin (συνέδριον) is first certainly used of this reconstituted assembly in a passage of Josephus describing an early adventure of Herod the Great (*Ant.* xiv. 9, 3–5), cf. *Ps. Sol.* iv. 1.

There is no evidence to show that the Gerousia, under the presidency of the High Priest, in the interval between Nehemiah and the Roman supremacy, was ever designated 'the Great Synagogue,' or ever possessed the administrative supremacy in religious matters assigned to it by very late Jewish tradition. None of the historical authorities for that period support such an idea ; certainly they do not lead us to suppose that the formation of the Canon was due to such a body.

Jewish traditions, often unhistorical.　. We know that mediaeval Jews (e. g. Tanchuma 39 *a*) could place the scribes, Shemaiah and Abtalion, at the head of the Great Synagogue ; and there is no doubt that the Jewish tradition which the Talmud represents fancied that the Sanhedrin was a Council of Scribes, and that, from the days of the Maccabees, it was presided over by the most eminent Scribe, the President being called the Nasi, the Vice-President the Abbêth-din.

The slightest acquaintance with Jewish history will show the unhistorical character of such a view. The origin of this transformation of a political assembly into a gathering of Scribes was due to the attempt to read into earlier times the Synagogue system which prevailed in the Talmudic period, and which, to the Rabbinic imagination, must have prevailed in earlier days (cf. Wellhausen, *Pharisaer u. Sadducaer*, pp. 26–43 ; Schürer, *Gesch. Jud. Volk*, vol. ii. 25).

Have we not good reason to suspect that the Great Synagogue is a similarly unauthenticated Rabbinic fiction ? If the Great Synagogue were a gathering of Prophets and Scribes, it was neither the administrative Council of the nation, nor the Sanhedrin in its earlier form. What then could it have been ?

Modern explanations : a college, or　To this the reply is made, *either* that it was a *religious College* instituted to establish the lines of Jewish worship in the time of

Ezra and lasting for a single generation, *or* that it denotes a
succession of great religious teachers.

Fatal to the first alternative are the two objections, (*a*) that
Simon the Just is emphatically pronounced to have been a
member of the same college as Haggai and Zechariah, (*b*) that
no mention of this institution is recorded by any trustworthy
authority, and that the first mention of it occurs in a tradition
committed to writing six centuries after Ezra's days.

Fatal to the second alternative is the objection, that the
Talmudic testimony clearly contemplates a corporate body
acting collectively. According to Talmudic chronology, there
was nothing improbable in this; for as the interval between
Ezra and Alexander the Great could be regarded as only
thirty-four years (*Aboda zara*, 9 *a*, *Seder Olam*, p. 41), it was
perfectly possible for Ezra and Simon the Just to be members
of one assembly. But, for our purposes, such a chronological
confusion heightens suspicion, if it does not absolutely destroy
confidence.

On the one hand, if the Great Synagogue be regarded as a
definitely appointed religious assembly, we are, of course, obliged
to assume that, Haggai, Ezra and Simon the Just being members of it, its functions must have been continued for at least
two centuries. But this is a departure from the actual tradition,
which makes it all the more inexplicable, that no reference
to such an institution should appear in Josephus, or in Philo, or
in the Apocrypha.

If the Great Synagogue be a name for a succession of eminent
Jewish Scribes, the Jewish tradition is no longer treated seriously
as evidence; its whole character is altered and modified in
such a way as to become plausible. But are we justified in thus
handling the meagre, late, and doubtful testimony? Can we
accept it, and reserve to ourselves the right of altering it until we
have reduced it to proportions of historical probability?

I believe that the evidence is quite insufficient to justify us
in regarding 'the Great Synagogue' as an institution which ever

played a real part in the History of the Jews.   But the evidence, defective as it is, is sufficient to account for the rise of such a legend.

The period between Ezra and the Maccabean war was hidden in an obscurity, upon which the Jewish Annals completely failed to throw any satisfactory light.   Josephus contributes practically nothing; and, as the example above mentioned shows, the greatest ignorance, as to the chronology of that period, prevailed in the Talmudic age and among the Jews of the Middle Ages.

The Jewish Doctors, however, sought to fill the gap.   They felt compelled to account for the transmission of the true tradition of the Torah, after the spirit of prophecy had failed; and before the great Rabbinic schools arose.   Into the gap between the prophets and Antigonus[1], they inserted the fiction of ' the Great Synagogue.'   The Synagogue system was that which to them embodied the hope and strength of religious Judaism. The Synagogue system was supposed to have arisen in the period of Ezra.   What was more likely, then, than that it had been based on the model of a Great National Assembly? Such an assembly would have given the pattern of which all Jewish Synagogues were smaller copies.   Such an assembly determined finally the ascendency of the ' Torah,' restored ' the Greatness ' of it to Israel, supervised the composition of certain of the Sacred Books, and drew up liturgical devotions and prayers to accompany the reading of the ' Torah.'   Such an assembly would have been ' *the* Great Synagogue.'

It was, we believe, a dream of the Jewish Doctors.   But it was not destitute of a specious plausibility.   There was no real evidence to support it; but then, owing to the dearth of historical materials, there was no obvious evidence against it.   That the idea may have arisen from an Haggadic expansion of Neh. *Neh* viii-x. viii-x, and that the number of the 120 members may have been based on the combination of the lists of names contained in that

---

[1] Antigonus of Soko (*Pirqe Aboth,* i. 2).

passage, is not altogether improbable. In Neh. x. 1–28, as Krochmal pointed out (*Kerem-chemed*, 5, 68), we have the names of 84 or 85 (see ver. 10) Signatories: in Neh. viii. 4–7, the names of 26 who stood by Ezra at the promulgation of the Torah: in Neh. ix. 5, 6, the names of 8 Levites who sang and uttered prayer on the occasion (see Kuenen, *Over de mannen des Groote Synagoge*, 1876[1]).

But, while the correctness of this last ingenious conjecture must be left undetermined, we may safely infer from the legend, that it affords one further illustration of the deep impression which the action of Ezra and his colleagues, in the public promulgation of the Torah, produced upon the mind of succeeding generations.

In conclusion, the reader will be careful to observe that no early Jewish testimony associated with the Men of the Great Synagogue the work of completing the Hebrew Canon of Scripture. This was a late expansion of the legend, and one of which no trace is found in the earlier forms of the tradition.

[Cf. also article on 'Great Synagogue' in *Herzog-Plitt, R. E.*[2] and the references to it in Robertson Smith's *Old Test. in Jewish Ch.* (1881), Taylor's *Sayings of the Jewish Fathers* (1877), Streane's *Chagigah* (Introd. p. vii. 1891), Driver, *Introd. to Lit. of O. T.* (Introd. p. xxxv), 1891.]

---

[1] Translated into German by K. Budde in *Gesammelte Abhandlungen zur Biblischen Wissenschaft von Dr. Abraham Kuenen* (Leipzig, 1894).

EXCURSUS B.

THE Baraitha, or unauthorized Gloss, dealing with the Hebrew Scriptures in this portion of the Talmudic Tractate, *Baba Bathra*, has often been considered to have an important bearing upon the history of the Hebrew Canon. For this belief a glance at its contents will show that very little can be said. The passage contains strange and often impossible traditions respecting the composition of certain books of Scripture. But on the formation of the Canon it tells us nothing. It is however full of interest; and as a curious specimen of the uncritical character of Rabbinic speculation in Scriptural questions deserves attention.

We subjoin a translation from the critical text supplied by G. A. Marx in his *Traditio Rabbinorum Veterrima* (Leipzig, 1884):

'Our Rabbins teach, that the order of the Nebiim is Joshua, Judges, Samuel, Kings, Jeremiah, Ezekiel, Isaiah, the Twelve (Minor Prophets).

'But, was not Hosea first (i. e. chronologically)? As it is written (Hos. i. 2) "When the Lord spake at the first by Hosea." Well, how then spake He with (*or* by) Hosea "at the first?" For from Moses to Hosea, were there not many prophets? Rabbi Jochanan said, At the first, that is, first in respect of the four prophets who prophesied at the same time; and they were Hosea and Isaiah, Amos and Micah. Let, then, Hosea be placed at the head. Seeing that his prophecy was written along with Haggai, Zechariah and Malachi, and

that Haggai, Zechariah and Malachi were the last of the Nebiim,
it must be reckoned with them. And yet they wrote it separately,
and placed it in front! Because it is so small, it might easily
slip out of sight.

'But was not Isaiah before Jeremiah and Ezekiel? then Isaiah
should be placed at the head! The reason (i.e. for the Talmudic order) is that Kings ends with desolation, and Jeremiah
is all of it desolation, while Ezekiel opens with desolation, and
ends with consolation, and Isaiah is all of it consolation;
accordingly we join desolation to desolation and consolation to
consolation.

'The order of the Kethubim is Ruth, the Book of Psalms, Job
and Proverbs, Ecclesiastes, Song of Songs and Lamentations,
Daniel and the Roll of Esther, Ezra and Chronicles.

'Now if it be said, Job lived in the days of Moses; Job therefore should be placed at the head: *the answer is* verily, we do
not begin with calamity. And yet, is not Ruth calamity? It
is calamity with a good end to it: as said Rabbi Jochanan,
"Why was her name called Ruth?" because from her there
went forth David, who satiated (*rivvāthŏ*) the Almighty with
songs and hymns.

'And who wrote them (i. e. the books of Scripture)? Moses
wrote his own book, and the section about Balaam and Job.
Joshua wrote his own book, and eight verses in the Torah. *Deut. xxxiv.*
Samuel wrote his own book, and the Book of Judges and Ruth. *5-12.*
David wrote the Book of Psalms at the direction of (*or* for) the
ten elders, the first man, Melchizedek, and Abraham, and Moses,
and Heman, and Jeduthun, and Asaph, and the three sons of
Korah. Jeremiah wrote his own book, and the Book of Kings
and Lamentations. Hezekiah and his company wrote Isaiah,
Proverbs, Song of Songs, and Ecclesiastes. The Men of the
Great Synagogue wrote Ezekiel, and the Twelve (Minor
Prophets), Daniel, and the Roll of Esther. Ezra wrote his own
book and the genealogies in Chronicles down to his own time.

'With this agrees the saying of the Rabbi (Abba Aricha, third

EXCURS. B. cent.), whom Rabbi Jehudah[1] reports to have said, Ezra went not up from Babylon until he had written his genealogy: and then he went up. Who completed it? Nehemiah, the son of Hachaliah.

'Whereas it says, Joshua wrote his own book and eight verses in Torah, its teaching agrees with those who affirm, Eight verses which are in Torah, Joshua wrote: for the reading is, *Deut.* xxxiv. 5. "And Moses the servant of the Lord died there": is it possible that Moses should have in his lifetime written the words "And he died there?" Was it not that Moses wrote so far, and from that point and onward Joshua wrote? The words of Rabbi Jehuda[2], or, as others say, of Rabbi Nehemiah, when Rabbi Simeon said to him, "Was it possible that the book of Torah lacked a single letter, when it was written, Take this book of the *Deut.* xxxiv. 5. Law?" Verily, up to this point the Almighty dictated and Moses wrote; but from that point and onward the Almighty dictated, and Moses wrote with tears. Just as we read in the passage, *Jer.* xxxvi. 18. "And Baruch said unto them," "He pronounced with his mouth &c." With whom does that agree? Even with the Rabbi whom Rabbi Jehoshua, the son of Abba, reports, on the authority of Rabbi Giddel, to have said "Eight verses in Torah one pronounced alone." Is this as much as to say, that it is not as Rabbi Simeon said? well, even if you say, Rabbi Simeon, still, since it was once altered, it was altered for ever.

'Joshua wrote his own book: but as for that which is written *Jos.* xxiv. 29. "And Joshua the son of Nun the servant of the Lord died," *Id.* 33. Eleazar added it at the end. And whereas it is written, "And Eleazar, the son of Aaron, died," Phinehas and the elders added that.

'Whereas it is said Samuel wrote his own book, and it is *1 Sam.* xxviii. written, "And Samuel died," Gad, the seer, and Nathan, the prophet, added that.

'Whereas it is said, "David wrote the Book of the Psalms at

---

[1] This was probably R. Jehuda, ben Ezekiel, of the 3rd cent. A.D.

[2] R. Jehuda, the compiler of the Mishnah.

the direction of (*or* for) the ten elders," should not also Ethan Excurs. B.
the Ezrahite be reckoned among them? Rab said, Ethan the
Ezrahite is Abraham; for it is written in one place, "Ethan the *Ps.*
lxxxviii. 1.
Ezrahite," and in another, "Who hath raised up one from the *Isa.* xli. 2.
east (*mimmizrah*)?" If it be said, and Ethan may be Jacob, as *Gen.* xxxii.
31.
it is written, "And the sun rose upon him," that only means to
say, the sun that had gone down for his sake now rose for his
sake. Assuredly, Moses is reckoned in the number (of the
elders), and Heman is reckoned in their number: but Rab said,
Heman is Moses, as it is written in one place "Heman," and in *Ps.*
lxxxviii. 1.
another, "He is faithful (*ne'eman*) in all my house." There were *Num.*
xii. 7.
two of the name Heman.

'Whereas it is said, "Moses wrote his own book, and the
passage about Balaam and Job," that agrees with the words of
Rabbi Levi bar Lachma, who said, "Job lived in the days of
Moses," for it is written in one place, "O that (*épho*) my words *Job* xix. 23.
were now written," and it is written in another place, "For (*épho*) *Ex.* xxxiii.
16.
wherein now shall it be known?" But he might be said to have
lived in the days of Isaac, for it is written, "Who then (*épho*) is *Gen.* xxvii.
33.
he that hath taken venison?" Or, again, in the days of Jacob,
for it is written, "If it be so now (*épho*), do this." Or, again, in *Gen.* xliii.
11.
the days of Joseph, for it is written, "Where (*épho*) are they *Gen.*
xxxvii. 16.
feeding?" But you are not to think so, for it is written, "Oh
that they were inscribed (ויחקו) in a book," but Moses is
called "the Inscriber" (מחוקק), as it is written, "And he pro- *Deut.* xxxiii.
21.
vided the first part for himself, for there was the law-giver's
(Inscriber's, מחוקק) portion reserved."

'Rabba said, "Job lived in the days of the spies," for it is
written in one place, "There was a man in the land of Uz (עוץ), *Job* i. 1.
whose name was Job," and in another place, "Whether there be *Num.* xiii.
20.
wood (עץ) therein," in the one place "Uz," in the other "Êz."
Thus Moses spake to Israel, bidding them see, whether there
was there the man whose years were as a tree, and who defends
his generation like a tree.

'There sate one of our Rabbins before Rabbi Samuel bar-

Nachmani, and said, "Job was not, nor was created, but is a parable." He said unto him, "Against thee, pronounces the sentence, 'There was a man in the land of Uz whose name *2 Sam. xii. 3.* was Job.'" "Still, the words, 'But the poor man had nothing save one little ewe lamb, &c.,' what are they but a parable?" He replied: "Even if it be granted so, there is still his name and the name of his town; to what end do they serve?"

Rabbi Jochanan and Rabbi Eleazar believed that Job was one of those who went up out of the captivity (Golah), and that his School was in Tiberias. Others reply: The days of the years of Job began at the entering of Israel into Egypt and ended at their going forth. But it is not so; it is only said, His days were as many as from the entering in of Israel into Egypt unto their going forth from the same.

'Some object: Seven prophets prophesied to the Gentiles, and they are Balaam, and his father, and Job, Eliphaz the Temanite, and Bildad the Shuhite, and Zophar the Naamathite, and Elihu the son of Barachel the Buzite. But think you that Elihu the son of Barachel was not of Israel? Surely he was, and yet he prophesied unto the Gentiles. But thus, too, Job prophesied unto the Gentiles. Therefore, is it not the case that all the prophets prophesied unto the Gentiles? In some, the substance of their prophecies is directed towards Israel, in others towards the Gentiles.

'Some reply: There was one pious among the Gentiles, and his name was Job; and he was only born into the world that he might receive his reward. When the Almighty brought chastisement upon him, he began to revile and curse; and the Almighty doubled unto him his reward, to the intent that he might drive *Job xlii. 10.* him from the world (to come), as it is said, "And the Lord gave Job twice as much as he had before."

'This is the teaching of the Tannaim. Rabbi Eleazar saith, Job lived in the days of the judging of the Judges, as it is said, *Job xxvii. 12.* "Behold, all ye yourselves have seen it." What generation was it that was all vanity? he saith, it was the age of the judging of

the Judges. Rabbi Jehoshua, the son of Korkhah, used to say,
"Job lived in the days of Ahasuerus, as it is said, 'And there *Job* xlii. 15.
were no women found, &c.'" What was the generation in which
they sought for fair women? he saith, it was the generation of
Ahasuerus. But it might have been in the days of David, as it
is written, "So they sought for a fair damsel." There, however, 1 *Kings*
it was "throughout all the coasts of Israel," here it is "in all i. 3.
Esth. ii. 3.
the provinces of thy kingdom."

'Rabbi Nathan used to say, Job was in the days of the kingdom of Sheba, as it is said, "Sheba fell upon them and took *Job* i. 15.
them away." And the Wise Men used to say, "Job was in the
days of the Chaldeans, as it is said, 'The Chaldeans made three *Job* i. 17.
bands.'" And there are some who say "Job was in the days of
Jacob, and Dinah, Jacob's daughter, was his wife"; for it is
written in one place, "Thou speakest as one of the foolish *Job* ii. 10.
women speaketh," and in another place, "Because he wrought *Gen.*
xxxiv. 7.
folly in Israel."

'And thus all the Tannaim considered that Job was of Israel,
save those referred to under "There are some who say."

'If it should occur to you that he was of the Gentiles, ask
yourself, "From Moses onward, who is there among the Gentiles
to whom the Shechinah was revealed?" as it is said, "So that we *Ex.* xxxiii.
be separated, I and thy people, &c.," and it is written, "Before 17.
Ex. xxxiv.
all thy people I will do marvels."' 10.

Upon this strange document much might be said. But we
must confine our remarks to two points that deserve notice.

(1) The Men of the Great Synagogue are stated to have
'written' certain books: Ezekiel, Minor Prophets, Daniel,
Esther; and Hezekiah and his company are said to have
'written' Isaiah, Proverbs, Song of Songs, Ecclesiastes. We cannot interpret the word 'write' in a different sense from that in
which it is applied in the context, in the case of Moses, Joshua,
Samuel, &c. We cannot say that in the two former cases it
denotes 'committed to writing,' and in the other cases 'com-

U

posed.' Doubtless, the statements in this document are generally fanciful and wild, and not least so in respect of authorship. But we must bear in mind that the Men of the Great Synagogue were considered by ignorant tradition to belong to a generation which included Haggai, Zechariah, Daniel, and Esther.

In the other case, Isaiah may well have been included in the 'company' of Hezekiah; and, on the authority of Prov. xxv. 1, tradition may have assigned 'Proverbs' to this same band, and, if Proverbs, then the other Solomonic writings.

But no one, after reading the document translated above, will be surprised at finding any assertion, however improbable, respecting the origin of the books.

(2) The books stated to have been written by Hezekiah and his council were denoted by a 'memoria technica,' YiMSHaQ, giving the initial letters of Isaiah, Proverbs, Song of Songs, and Ecclesiastes (יִשְׁעְיָהוּ, מִשְׁלֵי, שִׁיר הַשִּׁירִים, קֹהֶלֶת).

The books stated to have been written by the 'Men of the Great Synagogue' were also denoted by a 'memoria technica,' QaNDaG, giving the fourth letter of Ezekiel, the second letter of 'The Twelve,' the initial letter of Daniel, and the second letter of 'Roll of Esther' (יְחֶזְקֵאל, שְׁנִים עָשָׂר, דָּנִיֵּאל, מְגִלַּת אֶסְתֵּר).

This selection of letters appears at first sight arbitrary. But it is not so in reality. The *first* letters of Ezekiel, Twelve, and Roll (מ, שׁ, י), had been used up in the previous 'memoria technica.' The only 'initial' in QaNDaG is D for Daniel, and D had not occurred in the previous 'memoria technica.' If the *initial* letters of the three other books could not be used without confusion with those of Isaiah, Song of Songs, and Proverbs, then the *second* letter would naturally be selected, which explains the N and the G. But the Q presents a difficulty; it is neither the first, nor the second, but the fourth letter of Ezekiel's name: and what is more, it has occurred in the previous 'memoria technica.' The last-mentioned fact possibly accounts for its selection. In order to facilitate the recollection of the

two groups of books, the second group was denoted by a
memorial word whose initial letter (Q) recalled the last letter of
that which denoted the first group. Thus each memorial word
supplied a key to the remembrance of the other: the one ending,
the other beginning with Q.

EXCURSUS C.

'THE order of the books' has been a special subject of investigation in Dr. Ginsburg's *Massoretico-critical edition of the Hebrew Scriptures*. I very gratefully acknowledge my indebtedness to the generosity with which he has forwarded for my use the first sheets of his valuable and laborious Introduction. The following useful tables are the result of his collation of the best MSS. and earliest editions of the Hebrew Bible.

i. *The order of the Megilloth after the Pentateuch.*

I.	II.	III.	IV.	V.
MSS. Nos. 1, 2, 3.	MSS. Nos. 4, 5, 6.	MSS. Nos. 7, 8.	MS. No. 9.	Early Editions.
Song of Songs	Esther	Ruth	Ruth	Song of Songs
Ruth	Song of Songs	Song of Songs	Song of Songs	Ruth
Lamentations	Ruth	Ecclesiastes	Lamentations	Lamentations
Ecclesiastes	Lamentations	Lamentations	Ecclesiastes	Ecclesiastes
Esther	Ecclesiastes	Esther	Esther	Esther

The *nine* MSS. collated for this Table are the following, in the British Museum :—(1) Add. 9400; (2) Add. 9403; (3) Add. 19776; (4) Harley 5706; (5) Add. 9404; (6) Orient. 2786; (7) Harley 5773; (8) Harley 15283; (9) Add. 15282.

The fifth column represents 'the order adopted in the first, second and third editions of the Hebrew Bible, viz., Soncino 1488, Naples 1491–93, and Brescia 1492–94; as well as that of the second and third editions of Bomberg's Quarto Bible (Venice 1521 and 1525), in all of which the five Megilloth follow immediately after the Pentateuch.'

ius	N	O Cod. B (Vati- canus).	
ns. *d.*	(*De Mens.* *et Pond.* *cc.* 22, 23).		
			12
	Pent.	Pent.	
cal			
ry *ol.* *s.* *t.*			
a, *Nun* *uth*	Joshua, son of Nun Job	Jos. Jud.	
lp.	Jud.	Ruth	
ms,	Ruth	Kingdoms, 1-4	
ms,	Pss.	Paralip. 1, 2	
h. *ph.*	Paralip. 1, 2	1 *Esdr.* 2 Esdr. (Ezr. Neh.)	5
	Kingdoms,	Ps.	
	„ 1		
	„ 2	Prov.	
	„ 3		
t.	„ 4		
	Prov.	Eccles.	
2	Eccles.	Cant.	
l.	Cant.	Job	
	xii Proph.	*Wisd.-Sol.*	5
	Is.	*Wisd.-Sir.*	
	Jer.	Esth.	
	Ezek.	*Jud.*	
	Dan.	*Tob.*	
	Ezr. 1	xii Proph.	
	„ 2	Is.	
	Esth.	Jer.*Bar.* } Lam.*Ep.* }	
		Ezek.	
		Dan.	
	27		

ssibly following arrangement

is mentioned in that of Am

Exc

'It will thus be seen that the early editions of the Hebrew Bible adopted unanimously the order exhibited in the first column. It is also to be remarked that the different sequences do not belong to different countries. The three MSS. which head the first column belong, respectively, to the German and Franco-German schools. The three MSS. in the second column are German, Franco-German, and Italian. The two in the third column are Italian and Spanish; whilst the one MS. at the head of the fourth column is of the German school.'

ii. *Table showing the order of the Latter Prophets.*

I.	II.	III.	IV.
Talmud and three MSS.	Two MSS. Paris & London.	Eleven MSS.	Five Early Editions.
Jeremiah	Jeremiah	Isaiah	Isaiah
Ezekiel	Isaiah	Jeremiah	Jeremiah
Isaiah	Ezekiel	Ezekiel	Ezekiel
Minor Prophets	Minor Prophets	Minor Prophets	Minor Prophets

Column I. (1) The Babylon Talmud; (2) MS. No. 1 National Library, Madrid, dated A.D. 1280; (3) Orient. 1474; (4) Orient. 4227; (5) Add. 1545. (The last *three* in the Brit. Mus.)

Column II. (1) MS. National Library, Paris, dated A.D. 1286; (2) Orient. 2091, Brit. Mus.

Column III. (1) St. Petersburg Codex, dated A.D. 916; (2) the St. Petersburg MS., dated 1009; (3) Orient., dated A.D. 1246, in Brit. Mus.; (4) Arund. Orient. 16, (5) Harley 1528, (6) Harley 5710-11, (7) Add. 1525, (8) Add. 15251, (9) Add. 15252, (10) Orient. 2348, (11) Orient. 2626-8, in the Brit. Mus.

Column IV. (1) The first edition of the entire Bible, Soncino A.D. 1488; (2) the second edition, Naples A.D. 1491-93; (3) the third edition, Brescia A.D. 1494; (4) the first edition of the Rabbinic Bible, edited by Felix Pratensis, Venice A.D. 1517; (5) the first edition of the Bible with the Massorah, edited by Jacob ben Chayim, Venice A.D. 1524-25.

iii. *Table showing the order of the Hagiographa.*

	I.	II.	III.	IV.	V.	VI.	VII.	VIII.
	Talmud and six MSS.	Two MSS. Paris & London	Add. 15252.	Adath Deborim and three MSS.	Ar. Or. 16.	Or. 2626-28.	Or. 2201.	Five Early Editions.
1	Ruth	Ruth	Ruth	Chronicles	Chronicles	Chronicles	Psalms	Psalms
2	Psalms	Psalms	Psalms	Psalms	Ruth	Psalms	Job	Proverbs
3	Job	Job	Job	Job	Psalms	Proverbs	Proverbs	Job
4	Proverbs	Proverbs	Proverbs	Proverbs	Job	Job	Ruth	Song of Songs
5	Ecclesiastes	Song of Songs	Song of Songs	Ruth	Proverbs	Daniel	Song of Songs	Ruth
6	Song of Songs	Ecclesiastes	Ecclesiastes	Song of Songs	Song of Songs	Ruth	Ecclesiastes	Lamentations
7	Lamentations	Lamentations	Lamentations	Ecclesiastes	Ecclesiastes	Song of Songs	Lamentations	Ecclesiastes
8	Daniel	Esther	Daniel	Lamentations	Lamentations	Lamentations	Esther	Esther
9	Esther	Daniel	Esther	Esther	Esther	Ecclesiastes	Daniel	Daniel
10	Ezra-Nehemiah	Ezra-Nehemiah	Ezra-Nehemiah	Daniel	Daniel	Esther	Ezra-Nehemiah	Ezra-Nehemiah
11	Chronicles	Chronicles	Chronicles	Ezra-Nehemiah	Ezra-Nehemiah	Ezra-Nehemiah	Chronicles	Chronicles

Column I. (1) The Talmud; (2) Codex No. 1 in the Madrid University Library, dated A.D. 1280; (3) Harley 1528, (4) Add. 1525, (5) Orient. 2212, (6) Orient. 2375, (7) Orient. 4227 (the last *five* in the Brit. Mus.).

Column II. (1) MS. Nos. 1-3, dated A.D. 1286, In the National Library, Paris; (2) Orient. 2091, Brit. Mus.

Column III. Add. 15252, Brit. Mus.

Column IV. (1) St. Petersburg MS, dated A.D. 1009; (2) *Adath Deborim*, A.D. 1207; (3) Harley 5710-11, (4) Add. 15451, in the Brit. Mus.

Column V. Arund. Orient. 16, Brit. Mus.

Column VI. Orient. 2626-28, Brit. Mus.

Column VII. Orient. 2201, dated A.D. 1246, Brit. Mus.

Column VIII. The five Early Editions, described above.

EXCURSUS D.

TEXT OF IMPORTANT QUOTATIONS.

I.

2 Kings xi. 12 (2 Chr. xxii. 11).

ויתן עליו את־הנזר ואת־העדות

LXX. καὶ ἔδωκεν ἐπ᾿ αὐτὸν ἱέζερ (A. τὸ ἔζερ) καὶ τὸ μαρτύριον.

II.

Dan. ix. 2.

בשנת אחת למלכו אני דניאל בינתי בספרים מספר השנים אשר
היה דבר־יהוה אל־ירמיה הנביא למלאות לחרבות ירושלם שבעים שנה:

III.

Ecclesiasticus xlix. 10 (12), circ. 180 B.C.

Καὶ τῶν ιβ΄ προφητῶν τὰ ὀστᾶ ἀναθάλοι ἐκ τοῦ τόπου αὐτῶν.

Prologue to Ecclesiasticus, circ. 132 B.C. Πολλῶν καὶ μεγάλων
ἡμῖν διὰ τοῦ νόμου καὶ τῶν προφητῶν καὶ τῶν ἄλλων τῶν κατ᾿ αὐτοὺς
ἠκολουθηκότων δεδομένων, ὑπὲρ ὧν δέον ἐστὶν ἐπαινεῖν τὸν Ἰσραὴλ παιδείας καὶ σοφίας· καὶ ὡς οὐ μόνον αὐτοὺς τοὺς ἀναγινώσκοντας δέον ἐστὶν
ἐπιστήμονας γίνεσθαι, ἀλλὰ καὶ τοῖς ἐκτὸς δύνασθαι τοὺς φιλομαθοῦντας
χρησίμους εἶναι καὶ λέγοντας καὶ γράφοντας· ὁ πάππος μου Ἰησοῦς ἐπὶ
πλεῖον ἑαυτὸν δοὺς εἴς τε τὴν τοῦ νόμου καὶ τῶν προφητῶν καὶ τῶν ἄλλων
πατρίων βιβλίων ἀνάγνωσιν, καὶ ἐν τούτοις ἱκανὴν ἕξιν περιποιησάμενος,
προήχθη καὶ αὐτὸς συγγράψαι τι τῶν εἰς παιδείαν καὶ σοφίαν ἀνηκόντων,
ὅπως οἱ φιλομαθεῖς καὶ τούτων ἔνοχοι γενόμενοι πολλῷ μᾶλλον ἐπιπροσ-
θῶσιν διὰ τῆς ἐννόμου βιώσεως. παρακέκλησθε οὖν μετ᾿ εὐνοίας καὶ
προσοχῆς τὴν ἀνάγνωσιν ποιεῖσθαι, καὶ συγγνώμην ἔχειν ἐφ᾿ οἷς ἂν δοκῶ-
μεν τῶν κατὰ τὴν ἑρμηνείαν πεφιλοπονημένων τισὶ τῶν λέξεων ἀδυναμεῖν·
οὐ γὰρ ἰσοδυναμεῖ αὐτὰ ἐν ἑαυτοῖς Ἑβραϊστὶ λεγόμενα καὶ ὅταν μεταχθῇ
εἰς ἑτέραν γλῶσσαν· οὐ μόνον δὲ ταῦτα, ἀλλὰ καὶ αὐτὸς ὁ νόμος καὶ αἱ
προφητεῖαι καὶ τὰ λοιπὰ τῶν βιβλίων οὐ μικρὰν ἔχει τὴν διαφορὰν ἐν

EXCURS. D. ἑαυτοῖς λεγόμενα.　ἐν γὰρ τῷ ὀγδόῳ καὶ τριακοστῷ ἔτει ἐπὶ τοῦ Εὐεργέτου βασιλέως παραγενηθεὶς εἰς Αἴγυπτον καὶ συγχρονίσας, εὗρον οὐ μικρᾶς παιδείας ἀφόμοιον. ἀναγκαιότατον ἐθέμην αὐτὸς προσενέγκασθαί τινα σπουδὴν καὶ φιλοπονίαν τοῦ μεθερμηνεῦσαι τήνδε τὴν βίβλον· πολλὴν γὰρ ἀγρυπνίαν καὶ ἐπιστήμην προσενεγκάμενος ἐν τῷ διαστήματι τοῦ χρόνου πρὸς τὸ ἐπὶ πέρας ἄγοντα τὸ βιβλίον ἐκδόσθαι καὶ τοῖς ἐν τῇ παροικίᾳ βουλομένοις φιλομαθεῖν, προκατασκευαζομένους τὰ ἤθη ἐν νόμῳ βιοτεύειν.

IV.

1 Maccabees vii. 16, 17 (quot. from Ps. lxxix. 2, 3), circ. 100 B.C. Cod. Alexandrinus (A), _ed._ Swete.

Καὶ ἀπέκτεινεν αὐτοὺς ἐν ἡμέρᾳ μιᾷ κατὰ τοὺς λόγους οὓς (v. l. τὸν λόγον ὃν) ἔγραψεν· Σάρκας ὁσίων σου καὶ αἵματα αὐτῶν ἐξέχεαν κύκλῳ Ἰερουσαλήμ, καὶ οὐκ ἦν αὐτοῖς ὁ θάπτων.

V.

2 Maccabees ii. 13, 14 (extract from spurious Epistle, of uncertain date, perhaps 1st cent. B.C.).　Cod. Alexandrinus (A), _ed._ Swete.

Ἐξηγοῦντο δὲ καὶ ἐν ταῖς ἀναγραφαῖς καὶ ἐν τοῖς ὑπομνηματισμοῖς τοῖς κατὰ τὸν Νεεμίαν τὰ αὐτὰ (v. l. ταῦτα), καὶ ὡς καταβαλλόμενος βιβλιοθήκην ἐπισυνήγαγεν τὰ περὶ τῶν βασιλέων καὶ προφητῶν βιβλία, καὶ τὰ τοῦ Δαυεὶδ καὶ ἐπιστολὰς βασιλέων περὶ ἀναθεμάτων.

Ὡσαύτως δὲ καὶ Ἰούδας τὰ διαπεπτωκότα διὰ τὸν γεγονότα πόλεμον ἡμῖν ἐπισυνήγαγεν ταῦτα (v. l. πάντα), καὶ ἔστι παρ' ἡμῖν.

VI.

New Testament.

Ὅπως ἔλθῃ ἐφ' ὑμᾶς πᾶν αἷμα δίκαιον ἐκχυνόμενον ἐπὶ τῆς γῆς ἀπὸ τοῦ αἵματος Ἄβελ τοῦ δικαίου ἕως τοῦ αἵματος Ζαχαρίου υἱοῦ Βαραχίου, ὃν ἐφονεύσατε μεταξὺ τοῦ ναοῦ καὶ τοῦ θυσιαστηρίου (Matt. xxiii. 35).

Ὅταν οὖν ἴδητε τὸ βδέλυγμα τῆς ἐρημώσεως τὸ ῥηθὲν διὰ Δανιὴλ τοῦ προφήτου (Matt. xxiv. 15).

Ὅτι δεῖ πληρωθῆναι πάντα τὰ γεγραμμένα ἐν τῷ νόμῳ Μωυσέως καὶ τοῖς προφήταις καὶ ψαλμοῖς περὶ ἐμοῦ (Luke xxiv. 44)

VII.

2 (4) Esdras xiv. 44–46 (circ. 90 A.D.).

Scripti sunt autem per quadraginta dies libri *nonaginta*[1] quatuor. Et factum est, cum completi essent quadraginta dies, locutus est Altissimus dicens: priora quae scripsisti in palam pone, et legant digni et indigni, novissimos autem septuaginta conservabis, ut tradas eos sapientibus de populo tuo.

VIII.

Josephus: *Contra Apionem* i. 8 (i. 37–41, ed. Niese), circ. 100 A.D.

Εἰκότως οὖν, μᾶλλον δὲ ἀναγκαίως, ἅτε μήτε τὸ ὑπογράφειν αὐτεξουσίου πᾶσιν ὄντος μήτε τινὸς ἐν τοῖς γραφομένοις ἐνούσης διαφωνίας, ἀλλὰ μόνον τῶν προφητῶν τὰ μὲν ἀνωτάτω καὶ παλαιότατα κατὰ τὴν ἐπίπνοιαν τὴν ἀπὸ τοῦ θεοῦ μαθόντων τὰ δὲ καθ' αὑτοὺς ὡς ἐγένετο σαφῶς συγγραφόντων, οὐ μυριάδες βιβλίων εἰσὶ παρ' ἡμῖν ἀσυμφώνων καὶ μαχομένων, δύο δὲ μόνα πρὸς τοῖς εἴκοσι βιβλία τοῦ παντὸς ἔχοντα χρόνου τὴν ἀναγραφήν, τὰ δικαίως πεπιστευμένα.

Καὶ τούτων πέντε μέν ἐστι Μωυσέως ἃ τούς τε νόμους περιέχει καὶ τὴν ἀπ' ἀνθρωπογονίας παράδοσιν μεχρὶ τῆς αὐτοῦ τελευτῆς· οὗτος ὁ χρόνος ἀπολείπει τρισχιλίων ὀλίγῳ ἐτῶν. ἀπὸ δὲ τῆς Μωυσέως τελευτῆς μεχρὶ τῆς Ἀρταξέρξου τοῦ μετὰ Ξέρξην Περσῶν βασιλέως οἱ μετὰ Μωυσῆν προφῆται τὰ κατ' αὐτοὺς πραχθέντα συνέγραψαν ἐν τρισὶ καὶ δέκα βιβλίοις· αἱ δὲ λοιπαὶ τέσσαρες ὕμνους εἰς τὸν θεὸν καὶ τοῖς ἀνθρώποις ὑποθήκας τοῦ βίου περιέχουσιν. ἀπὸ δὲ Ἀρταξέρξου μεχρὶ τοῦ καθ' ἡμᾶς χρόνου γέγραπται μὲν ἕκαστα πίστεως· δ' οὐχ ὁμοίας ἠξίωται τοῖς πρὸ αὐτῶν διὰ τὸ μὴ γενέσθαι τὴν τῶν προφητῶν ἀκριβῆ διαδοχήν. δῆλον δ' ἐστὶν ἔργῳ, πῶς ἡμεῖς πρόσιμεν τοῖς ἰδίοις γράμμασι· τοσούτου γὰρ αἰῶνος ἤδη παρῳχηκότος οὔτε προσθεῖναί τις οὐδὲν οὔτε ἀφελεῖν αὐτῶν οὔτε μεταθεῖναι τετόλμηκεν. πᾶσι δὲ σύμφυτόν ἐστιν εὐθὺς ἐκ τῆς πρώτης γενέσεως Ἰουδαίοις τὸ νομίζειν αὐτὰ θεοῦ δόγματα καὶ τούτοις ἐμμένειν καὶ ὑπὲρ αὐτῶν, εἰ δέοι, θνήσκειν ἡδέως.

[1] The Oriental versions (Syr., Arm., Aeth., Ar.) read '94.' The Latin MSS. vary; the best supported Latin reading is DCCCCIIII, others are 204, 84, 974.

X.

[Philo: *De Vita Contemplativa* § 3 (Mangey, ii. 475).]
(Treatise of disputed genuineness.)

Ἐν ἑκάστῃ δὲ οἰκίᾳ ἐστὶν ἱερόν, ὃ καλεῖται σεμνεῖον καὶ μοναστήριον, ἐν ᾧ μονούμενοι τὰ τοῦ σεμνοῦ βίου μυστήρια τελοῦνται, μηδὲν εἰσκομίζοντες, μὴ πότον, μὴ σίτιον, μηδέ τι τῶν ἄλλων ὅσα πρὸς τὰς τοῦ σώματος χρείας ἀναγκαῖα, ἀλλὰ νόμους καὶ λογία θεσπισθέντα διὰ προφητῶν, καὶ ὕμνους, καὶ τὰ ἄλλα οἷς ἐπιστήμη καὶ εὐσέβεια συναύξονται καὶ τελειοῦνται.

XI.

Melito: ap. Euseb. *Hist. Eccles.* iv. 26 (circ. 170 A.D.).

Ἐν δὲ ταῖς γραφείσαις αὐτῷ ἐκλογαῖς ὁ αὐτὸς κατὰ τὸ προοίμιον αὐτὸ ἀρχόμενος τῶν ὁμολογουμένων τῆς παλαιᾶς διαθήκης γριφῶν ποιεῖται κατάλογον, ὃν καὶ ἀναγκαῖον ἐνταῦθα καταλέξαι. Γράφει δ' οὕτως· "Μελίτων Ὀνησίμῳ τῷ ἀδελφῷ χαίρειν. Ἐπειδὴ πολλάκις ἠξίωσας σπουδῇ τῇ πρὸς τὸν λόγον χρώμενος, γενέσθαι ἐκλογάς σοι ἔκ τε τοῦ νόμου καὶ τῶν προφητῶν περὶ τοῦ σωτῆρος καὶ πάσης τῆς πίστεως ἡμῶν, ἔτι δὲ καὶ μαθεῖν τὴν τῶν παλαιῶν βιβλίων ἐβουλήθης ἀκρίβειαν, πόσα τὸν ἀριθμὸν καὶ ὁποῖα τὴν τάξιν εἶεν, ἐσπούδασα τὸ τοιοῦτο πρᾶξαι, ἐπιστάμενός σου τὸ σπουδαῖον περὶ τὴν πίστιν καὶ φιλομαθὲς περὶ τὸν λόγον, ὅτι τε μάλιστα πάντων πόθῳ τῷ πρὸς θεὸν ταῦτα προκρίνεις, περὶ τῆς αἰωνίου σωτηρίας ἀγωνιζόμενος. Ἀνελθὼν οὖν εἰς τὴν ἀνατολὴν καὶ ἕως τοῦ τόπου γενόμενος ἔνθα ἐκηρύχθη καὶ ἐπράχθη, ἀκριβῶς μαθὼν τὰ τῆς παλαιᾶς διαθήκης βιβλία, ὑποτάξας ἔπεμψά σοι· ὧν ἐστι τὰ ὀνόματα· Μωϋσέως πέντε, Γένεσις, Ἔξοδος, Ἀριθμοί, Λευιτικόν, Δευτερονόμιον· Ἰησοῦς Ναυῆ, Κριταί, Ῥούθ· Βασιλειῶν τέσσαρα, Παραλειπομένων δύο. Ψαλμῶν Δαβίδ, Σολομῶνος Παροιμίαι, ἣ καὶ Σοφία, Ἐκκλησιαστής, Ἆσμα Ἀσμάτων, Ἰώβ. Προφητῶν, Ἡσαΐου, Ἰερεμίου, τῶν δώδεκα ἐν μονοβίβλῳ· Δανιήλ, Ἰεζεκιήλ, Ἔσδρας. Ἐξ ὧν καὶ τὰς ἐκλογὰς ἐποιησάμην, εἰς ἓξ βιβλία διελών."

XII.

Origen: ap. Euseb. *Hist. Eccles.* vi. 25 († 253).

"Οὐκ ἀγνοητέον δ' εἶναι τὰς ἐνδιαθήκους βίβλους, ὡς Ἑβραῖοι παραδιδόασιν, δύο καὶ εἴκοσι, ὅσος ἀριθμὸς τῶν παρ' αὐτοῖς στοιχείων ἐστίν"   Excurs. D.

. . . Εἰσὶ δὲ αἱ εἴκοσι δύο βίβλοι καθ' Ἑβραίους αἵδε· ἡ παρ' ἡμῖν Γένεσις κ.τ.λ. . . . Ἐσθήρ. Ἔξω δὲ τούτων ἐστὶ τὰ Μακκαβαϊκά, ἅπερ ἐπιγέγραπται Σαρβὴθ Σαβαναιὲλ (Sleph. Σαρβανὲ Ἐλ)."

XIII.

Jerome († 420).

Præfat. in Dan. Illud admoneo, non haberi Danielem apud Hebraeos inter prophetas, sed inter eos qui Ἁγιόγραφα conscripserunt. In tres siquidem partes omnis ab eis Scriptura dividitur: in Legem, in Prophetas, in Ἁγιόγραφα, id est, in quinque, et octo, et in undecim libros. . . . . .

Præfat. in libr. Samuel et Malachim. Viginti et duas litteras esse apud Hebraeos, Syrorum quoque et Chaldaeorum lingua testatur, quae Hebraeae magna ex parte confinis est: nam et ipsi viginti duo elementa habent eodem sono, sed diversis characteribus, Samaritani etiam Pentateuchum Mosi totidem litteris scriptitant, figuris tantum et apicibus discrepantes. Certumque est Esdram, scribam, legisque doctorem, post captam Ierosolymam, et instaurationem templi sub Zorobabel, alias litteras reperisse, quibus nunc utimur; cum ad illud usque tempus iidem Samaritanorum et Hebraeorum caracteres fuerint. In libro quoque Numerorum (cap. iii. 39) haec eadem supputatio, sub Levitarum ac sacerdotum censu, mystice ostenditur. Et nomen Domini tetragrammaton in quibusdam Graecis voluminibus, usque hodie antiquis expressum litteris invenimus. Sed et psalmi tricesimus sextus, et centesimus decimus, et centesimus undecimus, et centesimus octavus decimus, et centesimus quadragesimus quartus, quamquam diverso scribantur metro, tamen ejusdem numeri texuntur alphabeto. Et Jeremiae Lamentationes, et Oratio ejus: Solomonis quoque in fine Proverbia, ab eo loco in quo ait, *Mulierem fortem quis inveniet,* iisdem alphabetis vel incisionibus supputantur. Porro quinque litterae duplices apud Hebraeos sunt, CAPH, MEM, NUN, PHE, SADE : aliter enim per has scribunt principia medietatesque verborum, aliter fines. Unde et quinque a plerisque libri duplices aestimantur : Samuel, Malachim, Dabre-Jamim, Ezras, Jeremias cum Cinoth, id est, Lamentationibus suis. Quomodo igitur viginti duo elementa sunt, per quae scribimus Hebraice omne quod loquimur, et eorum initiis vox humana comprehenditur : ita viginti duo volumina supputantur, quibus, quasi litteris et exordiis, in Dei doctrina, tenera adhuc et lactens viri justi eruditur infantia.

Primus apud eos liber vocatur *Bresith* quem nos Genesim dicimus. Secundus *Elle smoth* qui Exodus appellatur. Tertius *Vajecra*, id est, Leviticus. Quartus *Vajedabber* quem Numeros vocamus. Quintus *Elleaddabarim* qui Deuteronomium praenotatur. Hi sunt quinque libri Mosi, quos proprie *Thorath*, id est, legem appellant.

Secundum Prophetarum ordinem faciunt ; et incipiunt ab Jesu filio Nave, qui apud eos *Josue ben Nun* dicitur. Deinde subtexunt *Sophtim*, id est, Judicum librum : et in eundem compingunt *Ruth*, quia in diebus judicum facta narratur historia. Tertius sequitur *Samuel*, quem nos Regnorum primum et secundum dicimus. Quartus *Malachim*, id est, Regum, qui tertio et quarto Regnorum volumine continetur. Meliusque multo est, *Malachim*, id est, Regum, quam *Malachoth*, id est, Regnorum dicere. Non enim multarum gentium regna describit ; sed unius Israelitici populi, qui tribubus duodecim continetur. Quintus *Isaias*. Sextus *Jeremias*. Septimus *Iezechiel*. Octavus liber duodecim Prophetarum, qui apud illos vocatur *Thare asar*.

Tertius ordo Ἁγιόγραφα possidet ; et primus liber incipit ab *Job*. Secundus a *David*, quem quinque incisionibus, et uno Psalmorum volumine comprehendunt. Tertius est *Salamon* tres libros habens : Proverbia, quae illi Parabolas, id est, *Masaloth*, appellant : Ecclesiasten, id est, *Coeleth* ; Canticum canticorum, quem titulo *Sir assirim* praenotant. Sextus est *Daniel*. Septimus *Dabre Ajamim*, id est, verba dierum, quod significantius

Χρονικόν totius divinae historiae possumus appellare. Qui liber apud nos Παραλειπομένων, primus et secundus inscribitur. Octavus *Ezras*, qui et ipse similiter apud Graecos et Latinos in duos libros divisus est. Nonus *Esther*.

Atque ita fiunt pariter veteris legis libri viginti duo; id est, Mosi quinque: Prophetarum octo: Hagiographorum novem. Quamquam nonnulli *Ruth* et Cinoth inter Ἁγιόγραφα scriptitent, et libros hos in suo putent numero supputandos: ac per hoc esse priscae legis libros viginti quatuor: quos sub numero viginti quatuor seniorum Apocalypsis Joannis inducit adorantes Agnum, et coronas suas prostratis vultibus offerentibus: stantibus coram quatuor animalibus oculatis et retro et ante, id est, et in praeteritum et in futurum respicientibus, et indefessa voce clamantibus, Sanctus, Sanctus, Sanctus, Dominus Deus omnipotens, qui erat, et qui est, et qui venturus est (Apoc. iv. 8).

Hic prologus Scripturarum, quasi galeatum principium omnibus libris, quos de Hebraeo vertimus in Latinum, convenire potest: ut scire valeamus quidquid extra hos est, inter ἀπόκρυφα esse ponendum. Igitur Sapientia, quae vulgo Salamonis inscribitur, et Jesu filii Syrach liber, et Judith, et Tobias, et Pastor, non sunt in Canone. Machabaeorum primum librum Hebraicum repperi. Secundus Graecus est: quod ex ipsa quoque φράσει probari potest. . . . . . .

EXCURSUS E.

TITLES OF HEBREW SCRIPTURES.

EXCURS. E. **1. Old Testament.**

(*a*) The Law.

'The book of the Law of Moses,' Neh. viii. **1.**

'The Law of Moses,' Ezr. vii. 6; Mal. iv. **4.**

(*b*) Prophets, or the Law and the Prophets.

'The books,' Dan. ix. **2.**

2. Apocrypha.

(*a*) The Law.

Ecclus. xxiv. **22** 'The Book of the Covenant (βίβλος διαθή-κης) of the Most High God.'

1 Macc. i. **56** 'The books of the law' (τὰ βιβλία τοῦ νόμου).

     „   **57** 'The Book of the Covenant' (βιβλίον διαθήκης).

2 (**4**) Esdr. xiv. **21** 'Thy law was burnt,' **22** 'Written in Thy law.'

(*b*) The Law and the Prophets.

Ecclus. Prolog. 'The Law and the Prophets and the rest of the books.'

2 Macc. xv. **9** 'And comforting them from the Law and the Prophets.'

3. New Testament.

(*a*) General titles.

αἱ γραφαί, 'the Scriptures,' frequently, e.g. Matt. xxii. **29**; John v. **39**; Acts xvii. **2, 11.** (γραφή in Sing., of a passage of Scripture, as is shown by the use of ἡ γραφή.

See Bp. Lightfoot's note on Gal. iii. 22, and on ἡ γραφή=
'the Scripture,' personified, in Gal. iii. 8.)

γραφαὶ ἅγιαι, 'the Holy Scriptures,' Rom. i. 2.

ἱερὰ γράμματα, 'the sacred writings,' 2 Tim. iii. 15.

ὁ νόμος, 'the law,' e.g. John x. 34 (Ps. lxxxii. 6), 1 Cor.
xiv. 21 (Is. xxviii. 11).

ὁ νόμος καὶ οἱ προφῆται, 'the Law and the Prophets,' e.g.
Matt. vii. 12 ; Luke xvi. 16.

'The law of Moses and the Prophets,' Acts xxviii. 23.

'Moses and the Prophets,' Luke xvi. 29, 31.

'The Oracles of God,' Rom. iii. 2 (Acts vii. 38).

(*b*) Contents of three groups.

'The law of Moses, the prophets, and the psalms,' Luke
xxiv. 44.

(*c*) The Law.

'Moses,' e.g. Acts xv. 21; 2 Cor. iii. 15.

'The Old Covenant,' 2 Cor. iii. 14.

4. Josephus.

τὰ ἱερὰ γράμματα, 'the sacred writings,' *Antiq. Jud.* Prooem. 3.

αἱ ἱεραὶ βίβλοι, 'the sacred books,' e.g. *Antiq. Jud.* xx. 261
(xii. 1). αἱ τῶν ἱερῶν γραφῶν βίβλοι. *Cont. Ap.* ii. 4.

τὰ ἱερὰ βιβλία, 'the sacred books,' e.g. *Cont. Ap.* i. 1.

Philo.

αἱ ἱεραὶ γραφαί, e.g. *Quis rerum div. heres*, § 32, i. 495;

ἱεραὶ βίβλοι, e.g. *Quod det. pot. insid.* § 44, i. 222; ἱεροὶ
χρησμοί, e.g. *De Somn.* ii. § 32, i. 687.

αἱ ἱεραὶ ἀναγραφαί, e.g. *Quis rerum div. heres*, § 4, i. 474;

ὁ ἱερὸς λόγος, e.g. *De Ebriet.* § 36, i. 380;

and ὁ χρησμός, οἱ χρησμοί, τὸ λόγιον, τὸ θεσπισθὲν λόγιον
occur frequently.

5. Patristic.

τὰ τῆς παλαιᾶς διαθήκης βιβλία, e.g. 'the books of the Old
Covenant,' e.g. Melito ap. Euseb. *H. E.* iv. 26, and
commonly.

αἱ ἐνδιάθηκοι βίβλοι, 'the Covenant-books,' e.g. Origen ap.
Euseb. *H. E.* vi. 25.   Cf. αἱ ἐνδιαθέτοι βίβλοι, Epiphanius
(*De Mens. et Pond.* 4).

ἡ παλαιὰ διαθήκη. 'the Old Covenant,' e.g. Cyril of Jer.
(*Catech.* iv. 33).

τὰ ἐκκλησιαστικὰ βιβλία τῆς παλαιᾶς γραφῆς, 'the ecclesiastical
books of the Ancient Scripture,' Leontius (*De Sectis,*
Act. ii).

'Vetus testamentum,' e.g. Tert. *Adv. Prax.* 15; Augustin *de
Civit. Dei,* xx. 4.

'Vetus instrumentum,' Tert. *Apol.* 47.

'Vetus Scriptura,' Rufinus, *Expos. in Symb. Apost.*

Law = ἡ πεντάτευχος (sc. βίβλος), 'Pentateuchus.'

XII Prophets = τὸ δωδεκαπρόφητον.

6. Rabbinic.

(*a*) General Titles.

כִּתְבֵי הַקֹּדֶשׁ, 'the holy writings.'

מִקְרָא, 'that which is read,' i.e. the text.   Miq'ra formed the
lowest stage in the ascending scale of Miq'ra, Mishnah,
and Gemara (cf. Weber, *Die Lehren des Talmuds,*
p. 83. 1880).

תורה, 'law' (*pars pro toto*); and sometimes its Aramaic
equivalent אֹורָיְיתָא.

הַסֵּפֶר, 'the book.'

סְפָרִים, 'books.'

כ״ד סְפָרִים, 'the twenty-four books.'

תורה נביאים וכתובים, 'the Law, the Prophets, and the
Writings'; in late Hebrew this title is abbreviated into
תֲּנַךְ (T.N.K. for Torah, Nebiim, Kethubim).

(*b*) Special Titles.

The Torah.

חמשה חומשי תורה, 'the five-fifths of the law,' e.g. Sanh. 44ᵃ.

The Prophets.

נביאים ראשונים, 'the former prophets,' Jos., Jud., Sam., Kings.

נביאים אחרונים, 'the latter prophets,' Is., Jer., Ezek., twelve Minor Prophets.

אשלמתא, 'tradition.' (Massoretic title).

Hagiographa.

כתובים, 'Writings.'

חכמה, 'Wisdom.'

חמש מגלות, 'the five rolls,' Ruth, Song, Lam., Eccles., Esth.

אמ״ת, 'Psalms, Proverbs, Job,' from the initial letters in the reverse order.

כתובים גדולים, 'Psalms, Proverbs, Job'': כתובים קטנים, 'Song of Songs, Ecclesiastes, Esther' (*Berakoth* 57ᵇ).

Prophets and Writings, as separate from Torah.

קבלה, 'tradition'; or הנביא, 'the prophet.'

TITLES OF HEBREW BOOKS.

English.	Hebrew (with English Translations).	Origen ap. Euseb. H. E. vi. 25; cf. Jer. Prol. Gal.	Other Hebrew titles (Mishnic).	
Genesis	בראשית (In the beginning)	Βρησίθ	ספר יצירה	Book of Creation
Exodus	ואלה שמות (Now these are the names)	Οὐελεσμώθ	ס' אלה שמות ויראן ס' ואלה	Book of Patriarchs; Book of Penalties (Ex. xxi.)
Leviticus	ויקרא (And ... called)	Οὐικρά	ס' כהנים	Book of Priests
Numbers	במדבר (In the wilderness)	Ἀμμεσφεκωδείμ[1]	ס' קרבנות ס' פקודים	Book of Offerings; Book of Precepts; Book of Numbers
Deuteronomy	אלההדברים (These are the words)	Ἐλεαδδεβαρείμ	ס' משנה ס' תוכחות	Book of Reiteration; Book of Reproofs
Joshua	יהושע (Joshua)	Ἰωσοῦε βὲν Νοῦν		
Judges	שפטים (Judges)	Σαφατείμ		
Samuel 1, 2	שמואל (Samuel)	Σαμουήλ		
Kings 1, 2	מלכים (Kings)	Οὐαμμέλχ Δαβίδ[2]		
Isaiah	ישעי (Isaiah)	Ἰεσσία		
Jeremiah	ירמי (Jeremiah)	Ἱερεμία		
Ezekiel	יחזקאל (Ezekiel)	Ἰεζεκιήλ		
12 Min. Proph.	עשר תרי (Twelve)	(Epiphan. δαθαρασαρά) Σφαρθελλείμ		
Psalms	תהלים (Psalms)	Μελῶθ	תהלים	Prayers
Proverbs	משלי (Proverbs of)		חכמה	Book of Wisdom
Job	איוב (Job)	Ἰώβ		
Cant.	השירים שיר (Song of Songs)	Σὶρ ἀσσιρίμ		
Ruth	רות (Ruth)	(Epiphan. Ῥούθ, Jer. Ruth)		
Lam.	איכה ('How')	(Epiphan. Κινώθ, Jer. Ruth)	קינות	Lamentations
Eccles.	קהלת (Koheleth)	Κωέλθ		
Esth.	אסתר (Esther)	Ἐσθήρ		
Dan.	דניאל (Daniel)	Δανιήλ		
Ezr. (Neh.)	עזרא (Ezra)	Ἐζρά		
Chronicles 1, 2	הימים דברי (Words of the days, i.e. Chronicles)	Δαβρηϊαμείν		

[1] ס' פקודים חמש = fifth part of Precepts; Jer. 'Vajedabber;' Epiphan. Ἰουδδββέρ.

[2] = 'Now the king David,' 1 Kings i. 1; Jer. 'Malachim,' Epiph. ὀμαλαχεί.   * Opening word.

INDEX TO SCRIPTURE REFERENCES.

OLD TESTAMENT.

GENESIS.

i. 1-vi. 9 . . . 248
ii. 1-3 . . . 28
viii. 10 . . . 28
ix. 4-7 . . . 28
xiv. 20 . . . 28
xv. 10 . . . 28
xvii. . . . 28
xxvii. 33 . . . 287
xxviii. 20, 22 . . 28
xxxi. 32 . . . 28
xxxii. 31 . . . 287
xxxiv. 7 . . . 289
xxxvii. 16 . . . 287
xxxviii. . . . 28
xliii. 11 . . . 287
xliv. 9 . . . 28
xlvi. 27 . . . 169 n
xlix. 4 . . . 28

EXODUS.

iv. 24-26 . . . 28
xv. 1 . . . 18
xv. 27 . . . 169 n
xvi. 23 . . . 28
xvi. 34 . . . 45
xvii. 14 . . . 18
xviii. . . . 68
xviii. 13-27 . . 32
xix. 3 . . . 252
xx.-xxiii. . 52, 57, 68
xx. 1-17 . . 23, 43
xx. 20-xxiii. 33 . 24
xxi. 2, 28-36 . . 25
xxii. 18-20 . . 25
xxiii. 15 . . . 52

xxiii. 19 . . . 25
xxiv. 4 . . . 18
xxiv. 7 . . 18, 51
xxv.-xxxi . . 87
xxv. 16, 21 . . 45
xxvii. 21 . . . 45
xxix. 38-42 . . 85
xxx. 11-16 . . 85
xxxiii. 16 . . 287
xxxiii. 17 . . 289
xxxiv. 10 . . 289
xxxiv. 10-26 . . 25
xxxiv. 27 . . 18, 25
xxxiv. 28 . . . 25
xxxv.-xl. . 84, 87
xl. 20 . . 41, 45

LEVITICUS.

i.-viii. . . . 30
iv. 13-21 . . . 78
vi. 8-13 . 84, 85, 88
xi.-xv. . . . 30
xvi. 13 . . . 45
xvii.-xxvi. . 25, 72
xxiv. 3 . . . 45
xxvi. . . . 50
xxvii. 30-33 . . 86

NUMBERS.

iii. 39 . . . 299
iv. 3 . . . 78, 87
v. . . . 30
vi. . . . 30
viii. 23-26 . . 78
viii. 24 . . . 87
ix. . . . 30
xi. 25 . . . 169 n

xii. 7 . . . 287
xiii. 20 . . . 287
xv. . . . 30
xv. 22-26 . . 78
xv. 39 . . . 207
xvii. 4, 10 . . 45
xviii. 21-32 . . 81
xix. . . . 30
xx. . . . 68
xxi. . . . 68
xxi. 14 . . . 19
xxi. 14-18 . . 18
xxi. 27 . . . 21
xxi. 27-30 . . 18
xxviii. 1-8 . . 85
xxix. 12-38 . . 81
xxxiii. 2 . . . 18

DEUTERONOMY.

i. 9-17 . . . 68
i.-iv. . . . 69
ii. 26-32 . . . 68
iv. 19 . . . 51
iv. 20 . . 53, 65
v.-xxvi. . . 26
v. 6-21 . . 23, 43
x. 5 . . . 53
x. 16 . . . 65
xii. 5 . . 51, 53
xii. 9, 10 . . 53
xiv. 2 . . . 75 n
xiv. 4-20 . . 30
xiv. 22-29 . . 81, 86
xvi. 1-8 . . . 51
xvi. 13-17 . . 76, 81
xvi. 22 . . . 56
xvii. 3 . . . 51

APOCRYPHA.

GENERAL INDEX.

OXFORD: HORACE HART, PRINTER TO THE UNIVERSITY

Lightning Source UK Ltd.
Milton Keynes UK
UKOW020155280612

195166UK00009B/150/P